SOLITARY CONSIGNMENT

SOLITARY CONSIGNMENT

*How Belief
Finds Conviction
in the
Great Commission*

Will You Be A Witness
as the Trial Unfolds?

BERT E. PARK, M.D.

VMI Publishers • Sisters, Oregon

My heartfelt thanks to Mary A. Hake, who edited this work and taught a less-than-gifted writer more than a thing or two about turning a good phrase.

∽

SOLITARY CONSIGNMENT

© 2009 Bert E. Park, MD

Published by
VMI Publishers
Sisters, Oregon
www.vmipublishers.com

Scripture quotations are taken from the *Holy Bible, New International Version* © 1973, 1978, 1984 by the International Bible Society.

ISBN: 1-935265-01-6
ISBN: 978-1-935265-01-6

Library of Congress: 2009942973

Printed in the USA

Cover design by Joe Bailen

CONTENTS

DEDICATIONS

To John, Tom, and Mark
You meant it for bad…but God intended it for good.

GENESIS 50:20

∞

For my dear wife, Vicki
You meant us for Him—through bad times and the good.

PROLOGUE

Kingdom work is a series of *solitary* encounters, by and for one person at a time. That's been God's way from the beginning. It remains so today for those Jesus entrusts with spreading the Good News. As a pearl of inestimable value, He committed the Gospel to those believers intent upon following the Way in grateful obedience—a sacred contract, if you will, divined to transfer its rights and privileges to another. Having received it ourselves on *consignment* as repentant "hired hands" (John 10:12–16), all the proceeds are then returned to the rightful Owner, who is Christ the Lord.

"Whom Shall I Send?"

"How, then, can they call on the one they have not believed in?
And how can they believe in the one of whom they have not heard?
And how can they hear without someone preaching to them?
And how can they preach unless they are sent?
'How [blessed] are the feet of those who bring [the] good news!'"

ROMANS 10:14–15

The widow's ninety-seventh birthday began with one thought in mind: preparing her only meal of the day before the sun went down on this all-but-empty village straddling the eastern border of Poland. Nine decades of subsistence living there had given ample time to grow accustomed to the routine: walking three blocks to draw water from the only well in the region; shuffling off to an unkempt orchard to pick what little fruit still lingered on the vine; hauling a rucksack of potatoes up fifteen mud-caked steps from a subterranean storage bin.

This day was like any other—the proverbial "day in a life." Uncluttered, unadorned, unrepentant. Nothing had changed in this ghost town of sorts, where Father Time had taken a holiday for nearly a century. There, this Mother Teresa look-alike eked out her solitary existence in the same clapboard cottage where she had been born, at the end of a dirt road she had never ventured down.

What set this particular day apart had nothing to do with birthdays; she'd seen enough of those come and go than could be recalled. Rather, this was but one of three or four days a year when her "extended" family came to visit, their arrival heralded by a trail of dust on the horizon like some primeval smoke signal. The only car she had ever seen belonged to her grandson, Mikola, a fiftyish doctor from somewhere east of there. "Ternople" they called it, corresponding with the return address on a letter that always preceded them. She would not have known of their coming otherwise; no phone lines had ever been installed in the village.

Yet the content of this particular letter piqued her interest. Apparently they were bringing a special visitor with them—an American who did the same kind of doctoring as her grandson—although she had never really understood what neurosurgery entailed, nor had she any idea of just what an American was. Preparing a meal, however, was something with which Grandmother was intimately familiar, and cooking for the first outsider to ever visit her home (other than family) was all the news she needed to know. That "distinguished" visitor coming to call was myself; the year 2001.

Through no fault of her own, such a monochrome, parochial "world" view had been mandated as far back as the 1930s by events far removed from this remote outpost of Mother Russia. It had something to do with power struggles in a distant land she knew nothing about and a policy of enforced isolation she never understood. Some people her father called "communists" (and a tyrant he scornfully referred to as "crazy Uncle Joe") had decreed that no one in their village was allowed to leave. That had been announced the day a wagon arrived with two uniformed thugs bearing rifles. They carted off all the village's able-bodied males at gunpoint, none of whom ever returned. Among them were her husband and her father.

Those who stayed behind fared even worse as time passed. Rotting crops went unattended that year, and for several thereafter—not because there was no one to harvest them, but that none were *allowed* to do so. This included their wheat, heretofore the sole staple of the village's barebones economy. Such a stark descriptive term applied in kind—and in short order—to this remnant of Stalin's wrath, who faced eventual starvation during one of history's lesser known holocausts, Soviet-style. Within five years, some three million inhabitants of the region died at the hand of this brutal dictator in an effort to starve these "recalcitrant Polacks" into submission. Consequently, an entire generation vanished during a single decade—leaving behind a

Potempkin village filled with memories, but little else, for its handful of survivors. No gravestones marked the others' disappearance; cannibalism rarely dignifies its actions with memorials to such "victims of necessity."

A valley of dried bones. The prophet Ezekiel might have understood, but Mikola's grandmother did not. Even less when the Nazis arrived a decade later and strip-mined the upper six feet of topsoil from their fields, revealing the horror hastily buried beneath. Not only had Hitler decreed this bountiful "harvest" of dirt to be transported by railcar back to Germany for its own use; he reveled in the exposure (literally!) of his Soviet adversary's depravity.

Grandmother was, in fact, the only member of the village to survive the 1940s. Yet once the bureaucratic restrictions on movement were loosened after the war, she never felt the need to go anywhere else. Her home had become a one-woman outpost warped in time, to be accommodated as best she could. She remained, despite all the other ramshackle farmhouses standing empty, no electricity, and but one passable dirt road bearing the tracks of the only car to ever use it—four times a year some six decades later. Such was her sole lifeline to a world she didn't know. Not that this engendered any sense of loss; she had never presumed to be a part of it to begin with.

The land was all Grandmother knew—and even that had once been stripped from under her. As for the Christ she *didn't* know, not one but two satanic imposters had turned His third beatitude inside out within a single decade: "Blessed are the meek, for they will inherit the earth." No mystery that she never derived any comfort from those words—only irony of the most iniquitous sort had she known them, which she did not. Rather, visions of what might have been had to suffice all those years. One in particular finally brought history full circle. Which brings me to that halcyon spring day in 2001 when His Story became her own. In retrospect, that's why I had been sent, "blessed feet" and all. Yet it was *her* vision, paradoxically, that finally gave the Good News the hearing it deserved.

As we were eating at her candlelit table, with the windows open and the sun beginning to set, we were startled to see a huge, white dove land on the windowsill across the room. There it sat, peering into the room as we sat in stunned silence! The spell was finally broken when Grandmother exclaimed she had never seen such a bird before—and most assuredly not a *white* one—at which point our visitor made its way over to a chair by the window and perched on the arm, now staring at her intently.

Suddenly, she became as animated as Mikola ever remembered his grandmother being. "There is a tradition in our country," she blurted out, "that when a dove comes to call, then a very important visitor will follow. And just last night I had a vision of a *white* dove, whose majesty I could not even fathom, that would bear a precious gift." Turning to look at me, she beamed a toothy grin and said: "An important visitor by our tradition, and a vision to match. Obviously you must be the one who was to come."

I gasped in astonishment. Those last words lit a fire in me that had been smoldering ever since I entered her two-room farmhouse and noticed a dusty Russian Orthodox icon in a cracked frame above the door. Pointing toward the pale portrait, long since yellowed through some seventy years of neglect, I asked her who she thought that was.

"Someone named Jesus," she replied offhandedly. "My mother always prized that picture. I don't know anything more about Him than that. Yet I do recall her once telling me something about a special man they used to worship before the communists came. Is there some connection? And if so, what does that have to do with this magnificent bird who chose to grace us with his presence here today?"

Drawing a deep breath, it was all I could do to compose myself. *How could they hear the Good News without someone sent there to teach them?* All of the necessary props to tell His Story had been arranged in perfect order: a musty icon dredging up the lost history of two generations in this remote part of eastern Europe who had never known Christ; a birthday vision concerning an "important visitor" and a "precious gift" that now cried out for fulfillment; a white dove presenting itself as the harbinger of both; not to mention her concluding surmise that I "must be the one who was to come."

Hastily I pulled out my pocket New Testament and turned to Luke chapter 7, reading to her while Mikola's son, Sasha, translated John the Baptist's sacred query to Jesus from his prison cell: "Are you the one who was to come, or should we expect someone else?"

Recalling her own words with some vague sense of déjà vu, Grandmother leaned forward in her chair to hear more of what this little book had to say. I quickly turned to Christ's baptism at John's hand in the Jordan River. "No, I'm not the 'special' visitor after all," I confided. "The bird is, and let me show you why." Whereupon the image of the dove descending on Jesus sprang from the pages—precisely at the time our feathered friend, with what seemed a bow of its head, spread its wings and flew out the window.

There could be no mistaking her vision of His message. Our esteemed visitor was none other than the Holy Spirit, who had chosen this particular birthday to honor the rebirth of an aging grandmother's soul with His presence. "You see," I explained, "like John, I'm just the messenger bearing a precious gift only the Lord Jesus can provide." As if to affirm that for herself, she pushed back her chair and rushed to the window where the bird had first appeared. There, on the broken-down picket fence outside, it still sat, staring intently at the house with its ninety-seven-year-old child of God within.

A year after having left Ukraine I received an e-mail from Mikola. He sadly informed me his grandmother had died some six months before, yet not without relating her passing in words that lit up the computer screen before me. "We had returned for another visit after you left, and found grandmother in peaceful repose with the Bible you read from now laying on her chest. It was open to the Gospel of John. A stump of a candle had long since burned out; yet the room seemed awash in the same type of glow we had witnessed on her last birthday we shared together. But the most amazing thing is this: silhouetted against the light of the open window was a large bird that seemed to acknowledge our presence and, as if satisfied we had returned, then took flight."

An exaggeration on my friend's behalf? Seeing more in a professed vision for my sake as a Christian than was really there? Perhaps we should let Grandmother answer that herself, if the "edited" version of John 1:32–34 she had underlined in the text is any indication: "I *saw* the Spirit come down from Heaven as a dove and *remain*…I would not have known him except that the one who was *sent*…told me…I have *seen* and *testify* that this is the Son of God." John the Baptist could not have witnessed to that sacred vision more powerfully.

Discovery and Opening Statements

Dying to Self

"Every man must die; some will never have lived."

HENRY WALLACE, "BRAVEHEART"

SAN SALVADOR, 1996

Five years earlier almost to the day, I had returned to my hotel room at 8:30 in the evening, exhausted after having seen well over one hundred patients in the primary-care clinic. Just that morning, halfway through my first medical missions experience abroad, the Lord had prevailed on me to remain for a second week with the Operation Blessing team in El Salvador. That had been a difficult and, in some ways, irreversible decision. In effect, I was closing the door on a part of my "first" life by canceling a speaking engagement in Washington, D.C., the coming weekend. Having carved a modest niche for myself in the academic community apart from neurosurgery, my about-face at the eleventh hour was certain to erase any credibility I had earned among my colleagues in history and political science. Yet the cost of answering His call as a newborn disciple would prove to be "pocket change" compared to what Jesus had already invested in me. Just as doors cannot be left half-open in God's Kingdom, a life lived for Him cannot be committed only in part.[1]

Those early morning hours had been a sleepless vigil, spent in unaccustomed prayer wrestling with God. Ultimately, He convinced me to fulfill the entire commitment I had made by going to Central America in the first place. My prayers centered upon the so-called Beatitudes from Jesus' Sermon on the Mount (Matthew 5:3–20). They had been the first verses I memorized following my conversion, and I sought some direction—no, affirmation—from them now. Still, I could not divorce my thinking entirely from the unfulfilled expectations of why I *thought* I had been called to El Salvador. The operations I envisioned doing on our L-1011 jumbo jet retrofitted with operating rooms had not materialized. Rather, I was mired in the clinic seeing all manner of diseases for which a neurosurgeon is ill-prepared to diagnose, much less treat effectively.

This only magnified my fatigue throughout the endless day in the one-hundred-five-degree heat, and I relished the thought of a shower before tumbling into bed. Ruefully glancing at the phone that would sound tomorrow's 5:00 AM wake-up call, I was startled to see the red message light blinking ominously. Was one of my patients doing poorly back home? Could the convener of the conference be calling to lambaste me (once again) for letting the participants down? Wearily, and with trepidation, I picked up the phone. A recorded message conveyed a sense of urgency: I was to meet our team leader in the hotel lobby the moment I returned. An unspecified neurosurgical emergency had arisen out at the "Flying Hospital," and I was needed there right away.

How could that be? I thought. *They were only doing eye surgery—cataracts and the like. What possible need could they have for a neurosurgeon?*

On the way to the military airport (some fifteen miles, since it was the only landing strip in El Salvador that could accommodate such a huge plane), we speculated as to what the emergency might be while listening to selections from *Fiddler on the Roof* on the radio. Yet my thoughts were elsewhere, still ruminating on the fateful decision I had made during the wee hours of the morning preceding. Were the Beatitudes a realistic life's view to have embraced, now that they had practical consequences?

The music on the car radio didn't help matters. "If I were a rich man," the disillusioned Russian peasant, Tevye, waxed philosophical as we drove through the night. Well, I already was, at least by the world's standards—and that was a big part of the problem. I faced the same predicament as the wealthy young man in Matthew 19:16–22, who had accosted Jesus with the question that goads us all: "Teacher, what good thing must I do to get eternal life?" This wannabe disciple had expected to hear some weighty pronouncement—not an *absolute claim* on his obedience! To his chagrin, and now my own, Jesus challenged us both to be done with academic arguments and get on with the task of simply obeying.

Sad irony, I remember thinking, *that the financial resources making this adventure possible were now being placed at risk.* For there was far more at stake than my reputation as an historian and political reformer. Those were mere diversions from a lucrative neurosurgical career, and ones that had recently taken a backseat to concerns about my practice. Relations with my two partners had become strained. Following my born-again commitment to Christ some eight months earlier, I had been branded as somewhat suspect.

Sure, I had changed—transformed may be the more appropriate term. My exuberance as a new child of God knew no bounds. Only in retrospect did I realize how naive I had been to present study Bibles to my two associates as Christmas presents. You could have heard a pin drop in the office that morning. "Where," the silence seemed to speak, "was the obligate case of California wine we had come to expect?" My subsequent decision thereafter to spend two weeks of vacation time ministering to the poor in El Salvador rather than golfing among the rich in Arizona sealed my fate: the partner they thought they had known for the past fifteen years had finally gone off the deep end.

And perhaps I had. The choice Jesus made on my behalf was now thrusting me into professional purgatory on a darkened airstrip in the bowels of Central America, when I could just as easily have been driving to the emergency room at home on a far more routine (and reimbursable) emergency there. Shuddering at the thought of what I might face upon returning to the States, remorsefully aware that my "backside" had been left uncovered, such thoughts were interrupted by the flashing red beacon of an ambulance that appeared at the airport gate just as we arrived.

I grabbed my knapsack, which seconded as a medical bag, while two soldiers with drawn AK-47s motioned for me to climb aboard. A fleeting thought crossed my mind: *Was this some ruse for a clandestine kidnapping of an American doctor that would appear in the newspaper headlines the next day? Or, like the infamous Nero, was I fiddling abroad while my "empire" of sorts burned back home?*

As the rear doors of the ambulance swung open, I sensed how Tevye's daughter must have felt the day she boarded the train and left her father to follow a teacher she barely knew and could only trust. For I was embarking upon my own faith-based venture into the unknown, with no other guidance but the hand of Jesus I had impulsively grasped up until now as a one-time-only, been there/done that "missionary." Should the journey prove longer than anticipated—or take me where I feared going—would His lead be strong enough to sustain me? Could I depend on Him to supplant the life I risked leaving behind? Was discipleship worth the cost?

It certainly hadn't seemed that way just after coming to Christ but a few months before. Jesus had "upped the ante" with His Beatitudes by giving me a new set of marching orders that superseded the Ten Commandments of His Father—laws I couldn't possibly fulfill, because they were written on the heart. And my heart had been the loneliest of hunters, betrayed by its own excesses. As the Good Book says, "…out of the overflow of the heart the mouth speaks."[2]

Spoken like a modern-day Tevye as the Old Order in Czarist Russia had crumbled about him: "On the other hand" (belying both of our tendencies to rationalize), how could either of us expect to have done any better than the Pharisees? Paying lip service to some Old Testament code of conduct was little more than an exercise in hypocrisy; I had been guilty on every count at one time or another. Sacred commandments certainly hadn't changed me. They highlighted my obvious shortcomings, but offered no solutions. Like many of my patients with brain tumors, I needed an operation—yet one that penetrated to the heart of the matter, and in more than just a metaphorical sense. After all, it's not so much the head as the *heart* that separates us from God.

If the Ten Commandments of the Old Testament were intended as inviolable absolutes, which have been "relativized" by contemporary values (or lack thereof, as Tevye had discerned in a different time and place), the Beatitudes of the New are diametrically opposed to what the secular world ascribes to today. I was among the latter—until viewing the wondrous cross through

Jesus' eyes. The manner in which He bore His own cross triggered a crisis in belief on my part that exacted a life-changing confession. I had simply been walking the wrong path and not bearing my share of His load. Awaiting me outside my comfort zone were encounters with God's Kingdom here on earth and the paradoxical blessings that bearing one's own cross affords—so long as my journey began at the foot of the only crucifix that mattered, the cross of Calvary.

The lamp that would light my way was Jesus' Sermon on the Mount, those troublesome Beatitudes notwithstanding. No denying the appeal of their promise. The very term "beatitude" means being "blessed" or "favored." And what favor could be more blessed than Christ's nine-fold prescription for living a life worthy of His calling? My own quest to abide by them was to follow thereafter what seemed a logical progression: from sight, through surrender, to faith. From "Are they true?" through "Am I willing to live by them?" to "Can they draw me closer to my Creator?" Reduced to their lowest common denominator—from belief, through confession, to affirmation.

What all of this might *cost* was another matter entirely! For one, I first had to undergo a painful operation of sorts—painful because granting permission to allow my heart to be tinkered with was intensely personal. Its dark recesses concealed fears and doubts that had never been exposed to the light of day, much less the Christ-light. Accepting that diagnosis and then having it treated triggered more spasms of remorse in the early going than any hunger for righteousness. I was experiencing a full-blown "heart attack," though not of the kind one usually associates with the term. From Jesus' perspective, dying to self is like undergoing open-heart surgery; at that critical moment when the patient "goes on the pump," the heart stops beating. A power outside the body takes over as the surgeon does his work. If all goes well, a bad heart is made good again, offering the initiate a new lease on life.

Despite Christ being my surgeon and the Beatitudes His operative manual, I vowed to become intimately acquainted with both before submitting my heart to His knife. That was akin to asking for some kind of informed consent where the physician offers a proposition, spells out the anticipated result, and warns the patient of any potential adverse consequences. Before consenting to the experience, of course, one has to believe in the surgeon Himself. Once convinced, you simply confess that you are at the end of your rope and can't make it as you are on your own. Only then do you feel comfortable (convicted?) enough to take such a leap of faith.

In anticipation of what lay ahead, I had turned to the first page of the manual that defined the context in which my "surgery" would be performed and its intended result, taking a compromised heart and making it whole again. And mine, quite frankly, was on its last leg. A solid reputation earned through years of exhaustive work and the financial rewards of a busy practice ultimately had their limitations. How far had I come, and for what purpose, when others were now conspiring to stigmatize me within the medical community to advance their own agendas? Hence, the compelling need for some new role models. Just as those "praise and worship" troubadours of my first life, Simon and Garfunkel, once rued the demise of the secular world's icons with that memorable line from "Mrs. Robinson," "Where have you gone Joe DiMaggio?," I now bid farewell to my own—the proverbial Renaissance Man.

Perhaps I should have read Ecclesiastes beforehand and seen the truth, rather than going deaf listening to my alter ego. Christ's reconstructive surgery consequently proved to be even more painful than it needed to be; for seeking God's Kingdom turns one's perceived table of plenty upside down. This is precisely what happened to me once I was called, with all the professional scraps (in both senses of the word) that implied.

Yet such a difficult convalescence was ultimately a small price to pay. It's simply what one has to go through to make life whole. I shouldn't have been surprised, because the Lord had included in His informed consent an age-old Christian caveat: anticipate facing reversals immediately after experiencing spiritual highs. As pertains to new believers reveling in their heady conversion experiences in the "recovery room," this inevitably entails being sent out into the *real* world to have those new hearts tested.

What makes all of this so perversely difficult for the "Braveheart" en route is that Jesus gave us a new set of laws from *His* heart, laws impossible for anyone to follow—and then He commands us to keep them! That compels us to confess we can't possibly go into battle alone. Yet once we surrender our self-absorption to a higher calling, we somehow manage to find our true selves—and sanctification—along the Way. Only through unconditional service to God's children do we come to *know* Him, which is what we were created for as His own from the beginning. Dying to that old self with whom we've been at war—going down into the valley—we are reborn in God's Kingdom as lilies of His field. This redefines the meaning of our existence: self-actualization in accord with the divine plan of our Creator; that spiritual reality within us; why we are here; the purpose for which we were made. That's what Christ meant when He said "the kingdom of God is within you" (Luke 17:21).

Acting upon this revelation is what makes Christians tick. What had I been searching for? Precisely the person He had created in His image to be! How could I have ignored the life God had planned for me—standing proudly and far removed from those distant shores where the Lord was working? Had He not given me a challenging profession and some unique surgical skills that simply could not be accessed in certain parts of the world? Sadly, for some twenty years the Siren's allure on this side of the pond had blinded me to that reality. That is why He declared war on my practice and, by extension, my professional relationships among those outside the Call. He had led me down into the valley.

That may be where the lilies grow, but some are adorned with thistles to mark the transition—what Paul once described as his "thorn in the flesh." My own thorn was a painful surgical scar: God's signature reminder that, despite head knowledge of (and heart feelings for) my newly professed Lord and Savior, I was still on the wrong path. Our descent into the valley together by way of El Salvador now turned me in a different direction. That's why just the evening before, He had placed the Beatitudes in my hand as a road map to follow.

Jesus also provided me with a warranty deed—what I was guaranteed to encounter as a consequence of my journey. Mind you, that wasn't buried somewhere in the fine print. It was spelled out in bold type: *suffering and rejection will be your cross to bear for becoming my disciple!* True, the beginning and end of the first eight Beatitudes offer the same redemptive promise in exchange: "for theirs is the kingdom of Heaven." Yet there's a costly cross to bear by reflecting the Christ-light in the here and now: "persecution because of righteousness." Not our own righteousness, to be sure; that's unearned. We are only made right in the eyes of God—"justified" is the precise term—by His Son's finished work on the only cross that counts. As such, the eighth beatitude would more properly read: "persecution because of [Jesus'] righteousness [reflected in me]."

To be truly justified, then, implies being changed from without—Christ "within" you yet "without" you as it were. Once that happens, even the casual observer now recognizes the born-again Christian to be somehow different. And this promises to have disturbing consequences. Change can be frightening, particularly for others when it threatens their own sense of self. A frequently exercised option is to "quarantine" the believer so as to avoid catching what C.S. Lewis termed the "good infection." For those who find themselves so isolated, Jesus added a ninth and very personal beatitude (Matthew 5:11) to remind us that our predecessors—and Christ Himself—had already suffered immeasurably more on our behalf. Hence the explicit change in the text from "blessed are those" found in every other beatitude to "blessed are *you*."

That comes, however, with yet another preemptive warning. Just as the apostle Paul had discerned, Jesus was personally alerting me in advance of the spiritual warfare to come, for which I needed to put on the "full armor of God." Providentially, Ephesians 6:10–18 had been the second portion of Scripture I had memorized—and, in fact, had recited many times before undertaking difficult operations or facing the slings and arrows of my associates. That was no coincidence. The Lord provides for our specific needs in preparation for what He knows we will face, whether in doing His work abroad or facing retribution at home. Such were the first lessons I had drawn from my study of the Beatitudes. There would be more to follow. Those began to unfold that fateful evening in El Salvador.

10:30 PM

Lying on the ambulance stretcher was a comatose child, intubated and supported by an ambu bag attached to his breathing tube. The faces of my colleagues in the ambulance reflected shock and disbelief. And with good reason. Eric, the poster child whom Operation Blessing had chosen in El Salvador as the symbolic beneficiary of the wonders of modern medicine, had undergone a brief anesthetic for a routine eye procedure to correct his crossed eyes. Inexplicably, he had suffered a cardio-respiratory arrest at induction, and now lay in a coma as a result of our team's best intentions.

As the ambulance sped through the gloom on its way to the national pediatric hospital in San Salvador, I was asked to shoulder the burden of monitoring Eric's progress (or lack of same) as his new doctor in an intensive care unit of Spanish-speaking medical personnel, with my patient attached to a primitive respirator and the reputation of our entire organization hanging by a thread. As a neurosurgeon, there was little if anything that could be done. Yet I was the only member of the team who had any experience with brain-injured patients—not to mention a working knowledge of respirators—once our distraught anesthesiologist "recused" himself, being so emotionally traumatized he could no longer function effectively. Perhaps our omniscient Lord had already anticipated the need; maybe that's why He convinced me to stay on for the second week of the trip.

Nothing would make this tragic tale more redemptive than to report Eric made a dramatic recovery. Such was not to be. Nor could his shell-shocked parents comprehend the magnitude of their loss in the early going. Unwittingly, our team chaplain contributed to their remorse in the long run by assuring them God would heal their broken son. Certainly that did not square with my own expectations; I'd seen far too many such patients through the years to believe otherwise. What made this particular situation all the more trying was that I was now their only medical link to the tragedy that had befallen them—a doctor whom they'd never met, but who, most assuredly, was a part of the team that had brought them such misery instead of the blessings the very name of our organization had led them to expect.

Day and night thereafter, they sat listlessly on the stone floor outside the ICU, awaiting a miracle that never materialized. At week's end, I was mercifully rescued from this lingering purgatory when the time came for our team to return home. But not without ruminating over the implications of Christ's first beatitude for everyone involved: "Blessed are the poor in spirit, for theirs is the kingdom of Heaven." An impetus for conversion? Not in the sense intended. To my way of thinking, little Eric's promised kingdom on high had been converted to hell on earth.

I found my only comfort—and some soul-searching edification—in recalling the travails of Joseph, who had been sold by his jealous brothers into slavery in Egypt. Despite a multitude of trials over the years, he ultimately found favor among the ruling hierarchy. As Pharaoh's prime minister, Joseph had earned his trust and, in time, was rewarded by being reconciled with his brothers absent any trace of revenge to despoil the reunion. "You meant it for bad," he informed his brothers, "but God meant it for good."[3] This was Joseph's way of telling them (and myself!), "Never judge God in the middle of your present circumstances."

I have no way of knowing whether Eric will ever improve enough to reconcile his own misfortune on this side of the Great Divide. But as a child of God on the other? By all means! That's what Jesus promised with His first beatitude. Still, I could not help but feel these children of God have every right to expect His blessing in the here and now. Isn't that also a part of the promise? By the end of the day, each is supposed to discover in his or her own way down in the darkest of valleys that theirs indeed is the kingdom of Heaven—His indescribable peace that passes all understanding. As for myself, both the discovery and the peace took some time in coming.

Divine Appointments

The first thing you discover as a Christian once you've been called down into the valley is that you're not alone. That's where servant and sufferer meet one another—and the Lord—on the road together. The servants might seem to be the more "favored" of the two only insofar as they have elected to be there, notwithstanding the apostle Paul's assertion that they've been *chosen*.[1] Lest there remain any confusion between "choosing" and "being chosen," perhaps my wife, Vicki, justified the use of the latter term more intuitively when she said, "God alone knows which hearts He can change." Yet another Paul [Azinger] intimated the same in his eulogy following the golfer Payne Stewart's untimely death and the transformation in his friend's life that preceded it: "Only God can cause a heart like that to change." From Jesus' perspective, however, His cause (and our choice) is not nearly so important as the intended effect, which is in the giving. And that, you see, is what Christians are *chosen* to do.

Though some might object to the pretentious ring of the word "chosen" (as did I before digesting Romans), of one thing there is no doubt: Christians have been favored by virtue of God's grace alone—and there's more than enough of that for those who gather in Jesus' name at the foot of the cross. What's left over, providentially, flows to everyone else around them. This enables us to be conduits of the Father's unconditional love to light their way; for the only Christ that others "see" is a reflection of the Christ-light from His servants.

Lacking the material advantages most of us possess, the impoverished turn by default to a higher power in times of need—which for them is *always*. God the Father intended that to be His Son, because He shares in their suffering and knows what it's like to be without. What's more, once the servant is privileged enough to meet one of Jesus' sufferers on the road, both lives will be changed immeasurably. That's the overriding theme of the Beatitudes: why the chosen are so blessed; and why the unlucky are so, well, *lucky!*[2] The servant receives affirmation; the downtrodden, a reason to believe.

There's an old saying among Christians that the only arms the Heavenly Father has to embrace His children are our own. As for the Son, He is disguised among the poor of whom the Beatitudes speak. Jesus surrendered His exalted position in order to walk among them and experience the trials of man through the prism of God—which is another way of saying both He and they are there to be served. Consider the proverbial bag lady: is she to be viewed as a burden on society or as an opportunity for God? How we respond to her defines the condition of our hearts. If our hearts are open, we discover that nothing can be quite so rewarding as *feeling* her greatest needs and then *fulfilling* them—because we're really serving Him! Therein lies the "double portion" that Christ's Kingdom affords: the Holy Spirit enriching our lives here on earth, and the Father's treasures thereafter in Heaven.

It all boils down in the end to what believers recognize as "divine appointments." Through those I began to appreciate the first of Jesus' Beatitudes: what it means to be "poor in spirit" when applied to medical mission's work. In the words of my favorite Christian writer, Philip Yancey, the term "desperate" covers all the bases. Having nowhere else to turn, the disadvantaged are providentially "advantaged" to turn to God. That brings with it His blessing, because the Lord has already served notice throughout the Beatitudes that He gives preferential treatment to the poor.

"So what makes *them* so deserving of His concern?" Their lack of pride is certainly high on His list. Pride is the root of all sin, and sin separates us from God. Having nothing to show for themselves, the poor don't carry the excess baggage you and I do. To paraphrase Yancey, that doesn't make them more virtuous—just less inclined to *pretend* to be virtuous.

Through no fault of their own, then, the poor in spirit are uniquely positioned to receive God grace—not to mention the "benefits" of dependency—simply because they have no choice in the matter. From the Father's perspective, that's also to their advantage; being interdependent, they expect (and receive) little from competition with others and much more from cooperation.[3] Yet their ultimate security rests with Him, not them. That's why they are so eager to embrace the Gospel as the Good News the Lord intended it to be.

Well acquainted with suffering, they're also used to waiting. Medical missionaries see both firsthand. Perhaps the most humbling aspect of what we do presents itself at the beginning of the workday. Whether in Latin America, Asia, or the Far East, the lines of sufferers patiently waiting to be seen are always huge. Cutting through this ocean of humanity as we make our way by bus to the clinic entrance inevitably evokes awe and fear.

Awe, because most of them have been standing in line for twenty-four hours or more, many after walking miles to get there, with babies (or even homes!) strapped to their backs. By Hebrew standards, they personify the term "poor in spirit," meaning literally "to crouch down" or "make oneself low." They have nothing to lose by coming, because they had so little before they came. What they invariably bring with them, however, is faith—blind (and in all too many instances, unwarranted) trust that we have something to offer them in the way of a medical cure.

Which leads to the fear. Not only does the crush of bodies always seem so close to our bus that we legitimately fear running over someone; each of us harbors the fear that we might not meet their expectations. No doubt we *do* have something to offer them: a gift that has eternal value far exceeding their physical needs. Yet at the beginning of the day, before seeing a doctor for ten minutes after waiting a seeming lifetime, by and large this is neither their perception nor desire. Invariably, I'm so humbled by their plight and what we can legitimately deliver that I find myself praying variations on the same theme: "Oh Lord, in your own way, please help us to meet every need so their waiting will not have been in vain—that they not be disappointed in us, which would only reflect unconscionably on who *You* are."

Throughout the course of every mission trip I've ever taken, I never quite manage to suppress these raw emotions of awe and fear at the beginning of the day. What diagnosis will I miss? Which medicine will the pharmacy be unable to provide? How many children with cerebral palsy will I cradle in my arms as the "neurologic consultant," knowing full well that I can do nothing for them as a doctor? Would the Divine Physician fill the voids I was sure to encounter that day? On a more personal (if perhaps self-serving) level, is the fire of His indwelling Spirit strong enough to refine me, warm enough to comfort me, bright enough to light my way?

It's precisely at such times of doubt that the Beatitudes come to my (and their) rescue. For the Lord promised that the poor in spirit will always have His undivided attention, His medicine, His blessing. The latter applies as much to the servant as the dispossessed. As befit my skeptical nature, of course, I had to be convinced of all three. After all, my experience with Eric in El Salvador had been a harsh introduction to the mission field. Yet, with that, came unforeseen guidance, healing, and grace that Jesus would reveal in His own time.

One such blessing stemmed from a divine appointment the Lord waited some four years to bestow. I suspect that delay had more to do with my own spiritual immaturity than His divine plan. God knows, I'm a slow learner…Despite my shortcomings as His messenger, however, the Lord's timing as a Revelator is always perfect.

During my third mission to China, Jesus saw to it that I revisit the tomb of the terra cotta warriors just outside the ancient imperial capital of Xi'an. In truth, I had little inclination to return, having already "reviewed the troops" the year before from the closest vantage point possible, an isolated platform reserved for visiting dignitaries such as President Clinton, who had been the last American to stand there some six months earlier (or so, at least, we were told).

Imagine, then, our astonishment on this occasion when we were ushered *into* the pit itself, where only restoration technicians tread, to view this eighth wonder of the world "up close and personal." That the heavily guarded, roped-off entry proved just wide enough for us to pass through single-file into this crypt of clay soldiers seemed oddly fitting. *Small is the gate and narrow is the road,* I remember thinking, *that leads to life after death.*[4] Not so the breadth of the Lord's revelations once we gained entry into the Qin Dynasty's reconstruction of what that afterlife entailed.

Why had a handful of Christian missionaries been granted this unique privilege to walk such "hallowed" ground? Though I still cannot fathom the motives of our hosts at the time, God took advantage of the opportunity to show us something of truly eternal value. Perhaps I should have anticipated that. Time and again, visits to others' holy shrines had provided me fresh new insights into my own faith. By way of example, just six months before while on mission in Ukraine, the Lord had accompanied me through yet another sacred, if even narrower, passage to reveal Himself so that others might come to know Him. To fully digest what God had to teach us in China requires a brief digression recounting that earlier lesson.

One Sunday my Ukrainian colleagues had accompanied me to the Pochaev Laura Monastery outside Ternople to view their own version of a sacred tomb. In continuous existence since 1240, the Assumption Cathedral is but one of three Eastern Orthodox shrines to have survived Adolf Hitler's wrath during World War II. It was there that Jesus had first drawn my attention to His metaphor of the narrow gate—if not the redeeming value of being stuffed through the eye of a needle more than once! For it seems that a seventeenth-century father superior of the monastery, one Saint Iov (Job), had spent the greater part of his life in communion with God by wedging himself through a tiny opening where he would pray for days on end, with no food or water, in a cave dimly lit by a single candle. What are purported to be his "imperishable" remains now lie in a silver shrine just outside the cave entrance, a hallowed relic of veneration for the faithful who visit daily by the thousands.

Just as would be the case in China, I had already been to Pochaev Laura the day before with the rest of our team. It was so crowded, however, that even getting close to the cave was out of the question. Yet the Lord had something He wanted to show my neurosurgical friend and his family, all of whom were professed agnostics. Was it any coincidence, then, that we would return the following weekend with special permission not only to visit the shrine but to crawl inside the Holiest of Holies of Ukraine's patron saint? For the claustrophobics among us that was no small feat, as we discovered while slithering through the shoulder-width tunnel one by one to the altar beyond. As ever, of course, God was directing our crawl. He had preceded us there so I might share the Gospel in an environment tailor-made to catch their attention.

Emerging from the grotto after our shared experience, the official guide sensed a "disturbing" change in my friends' demeanors and attempted to refocus their attention on the sacred relics. Yet the neurosurgeon and his son were now more interested in the depiction of Christ's Passion on the opposite wall, vividly portrayed in seven beautiful murals. Though my friends had been there many times, they confessed never to have noticed the murals before, nor had they ever heard the Good News. Oh, how God opens doors—though some may be smaller than man would like.

A few, to be sure, were never meant to be opened at all. That brings me back to China and its first emperor's morbid preoccupation with life after death. His take on what the future held was far different than our own. Whereas the believer's eternal peace of mind and salvation is assured by Christ's finished work on the cross, the Chinese of that era (and all but the most inveterate communists today) envisioned the afterlife as a continuation of things as they were before one's passing. From the Emperor Qin's paranoid perspective, this prompted him to make some unique preparations. The same life he had lived (infamously, it should be said) proved a vainglorious conceit in death—surrounded by thousands of clay soldiers standing guard as the emperor would continue to lust, scheme, and rule in a manner of his own choosing. Stated more familiarly for those who take God at His word: "… everyone did as he saw fit."[5]

Building a monument to that obsession had consumed four decades of the emperor's reign. In keeping with everything else man does apart from God, however, it wasn't enough to assure him the immortality he craved nor to protect him from the grave robbers he feared. The irony of that was not lost on those of us with eyes to see: here was an imperial guard of clay constructed to keep life *out*—much as the Roman guard around

Jesus' tomb would later be dispatched to keep death *within*. And neither, in the end, succeeded. Just as Pilate had lamely instructed his charges to "Go, make the tomb as secure as [best] you know how,"[6] the emperor had decreed his own tomb to be sealed forever. That meant burying countless artisans alive to keep the location and its contents secret.[7]

The inroads of time would nevertheless expose his treachery to the light of day, to which we believers were now bearing witnesses. I couldn't help but reflect on the emperor's motivations and their ultimate implications as they would have appeared 2,200 years later to the eminent Christian apologist C.S. Lewis. In his own words, "The natural life in each of us is something self-centered, something that wants to be petted and admired, to take advantage of other lives, to exploit the whole universe. And especially it wants to be left to itself; to keep well away from anything better or stronger or higher than it, anything that might make it feel small. For it knows that if the spiritual life gets hold of it, all its self-centeredness and self-will are going to be killed, and it is ready to fight tooth and nail to avoid that."[8]

Hence, I suppose, the need for an imperial guard; or so this overtly paranoid despot had perceived. John 3:20 spoke for the realists among us as we viewed the cracked visages staring blindly in the shadows: "Everyone who does evil hates the light, and will not come into [its presence] for fear that his deeds will be exposed." The emperor's fears, in the end, were not unfounded. Darkness cannot abide the light. Within a week of their exposure to sunlight after having been "exhumed," the soldiers' brightly pigmented colors simply flaked off and disappeared.

From the more distant viewing stand of my earlier visit, the terra cotta warriors had appeared remarkably well preserved, in keeping with the claim made by China's media at the time of their discovery in 1974. Yet once having gained access to the pit (abyss?), these hallowed icons proved to be little more than hollow shells that paled in comparison to the original perfection of God's last and greatest creation. The obvious imperfections of mortal restoration, painstakingly sealed with makeshift plaster of Paris, were no match for the deft touch of the Master's hand. Not that we should boast.... Through no fault but our own, we too have become fragile vessels of clay that only Jesus can repair to perfection—and resurrect for eternity. That's precisely what the Lord had affirmed to Jeremiah from the beginning: "Can I not do with you as [these] potter[s]? Like clay in the hand of the potter, so are you in my hand…"[9]

This conjured up a lamentation expressed by the same prophet who, like Isaiah, spoke not for an emperor but for God: "My people have committed two sins: They have forsaken me, the spring of living water, and have dug their own cisterns, broken cisterns that cannot hold water."[10] Now, some twenty-six hundred years later, God the Father was reminding me that His Son came to earth to connect us with His own *artesian* well, quenching the believer's spirit with a never-ending supply of living water. Why, then, would anyone choose to substitute such a priceless gift with cracked, empty cisterns—or fragile icons, for that matter? An artesian well, like an in-filled spirit, does not dry up. Broken cisterns do. Clay shaped by human hands will fail us in the end, just as it failed the first emperor of China. Only the Creator, who made man and every living thing, can provide sustenance that lasts.

Perhaps it was no coincidence that the first imperial capital of Xi'an was built at the junction of eight rivers, which have long since become arid valleys. The weathered, dust-laden figures that now stood before me spoke volumes about the parched environment. No one knows why the rivers disappeared; that remains one of the great geophysical mysteries of our time. Yet it's hardly a mystery to God, who perhaps foresaw the ongoing rejection of His Son in this region of the world—and with that, prophetically, the desiccation of north-central China's once thought-to-be "artesian" wells.

Still another image seared my subconscious as I wandered among these partially restored skeletons of imperial mythology. I'm referring to Ezekiel's valley of dead bones. It was as if, at that very moment, "the hand of the LORD was upon me, [bringing me] out by the Spirit of the LORD and set[ting] me in the middle of a valley…full of bones."[11] *Could these 'bones' of China's past live?* I wondered as He led me back and forth across the pit. Not in some futile attempt to resurrect them as Ezekiel had prophesied; that, of course, was impossible. But did the Lord have others in mind—such as their cultural descendants who came daily to pay homage in much the same way the Ukrainians had worshiped their relics for centuries? Might they exchange a moribund myth for the living Word, eschew the folly of dead history, and embrace a future of eternal life? Could they be resurrected by His blood from this wasteland of hollow men?

The apostle Paul had intimated as much to the Greeks at their Areopagus in Athens, although most failed to grasp his point. "I see that in every way you are very religious. For as I walked around and looked carefully at your objects of worship, I even found an altar with the inscription: TO AN UNKNOWN GOD." That was enough for the both of us, albeit in different times and places, to proclaim, "The God who made the world and everything in it is the Lord of Heaven and earth and does not live in temples built by hands"—much less in tombs of dead emperors. The take-home lesson for the Chinese, just as for the Greeks, was underscored by Paul himself: "From one man he made every nation of men…so that men would seek him and perhaps reach out for him and find him…"[12] In other words, the narrow gate always leads away from the memorials of men and toward the Kingdom of God.

There's eternal comfort in that, for only Christ knows the journey's end. His call, and the promise it entails, have never changed. Much as the terra cotta warriors had been arrayed in perfect formations, I was reminded with fresh certainty that God had strategically placed His own troops at this particular time and place for a purpose. Onward, then, Christian soldiers! Were we not standing face to face with an allegory befitting four thousand years of Chinese history? Just as the oppressed workers who had constructed this mortal myth were deprived of temporal life—casualties of a long-since-lost "war" fought to keep grave-robbers out—so are the poor in spirit of China today being deprived of salvation by those who stand guard against letting *eternal* life in.

Yet the Potter will have His own way in the end, adding just enough water to the mix to bring dead clay to life. That was Ezekiel's prophecy then and Jesus' promise today (John 7:38). That's *living water* only He can provide. Emerging from the pit, I cast a lingering glance over the rows of imperfectly reconstructed icons. There was work to be done! Bringing *real* men to life in Christ during what little time remains of the seventh day of Creation—men made from the same clay, but now targeted to be recreated in God's image.

Between that call and His promise, however, at least one as yet untested soldier stood in the breach. My trial by fire with Eric in El Salvador excepted, up until now virtually every seed had borne fruit in the mission field where I labored for His harvest. Yet, when faced with the adversity and even rejection Jesus warned His disciples would one day come, was I up to the task? Would my response as a professed "warrior" for the Lord be found wanting in His eyes? Frankly put, did I have the "right stuff" when the going got tough? Such was Jesus' challenge to me during this process of discovery preceding those trials by fire that lay ahead. Enter the Prosecutor, stage right[eous]…

The Prosecution's Case

"For we must all appear before the judgment seat of Christ, that
each one may receive what is due him for the things done
while in the body, whether good or bad."

2 CORINTHIANS 5:10

Prosecutors have a knack for drawing up succinct indictments that are painful and to the point. As regards our claim to being followers of Jesus, any defense we might muster depends solely upon how we've responded to His call while "in the body." Quite apart from God the Father's judgment of *all* mankind on His final day of reckoning, His Son will call each Christian individually to account for what he or she has done with the spiritual gifts bequeathed us in the time we were allotted. That promises to be a "close encounter of the third kind" with the second Person of the Holy Trinity. Not that we'll have the luxury of soliciting a "hired gun" to speak for us; nor will anyone but Jesus speak for the Prosecution. With that in mind, His list of indictments might be worded as follows:

I surrendered an exalted role in Heaven to be My Father's first Missionary on Earth.

Being omniscient, I knew from the beginning what this would cost.

But I did it anyway, because I also knew you couldn't pay a *just* price for your sins.

That is why your salvation had to be redeemed in full on My cross.

Sanctification thereafter was your own affair, albeit prompted by the Holy Spirit.

What fruit you bore serving others was a measure of your obedience to Me.

Now, you may think you "got by" for less and still found favor in My eyes.

That's assuming you understood the difference between cheap and costly grace.

Granted, you needed some instructions, and I was sent to give them to you.

Which is what my Beatitudes are all about—they were *meant* to be put into action.

Yet, to be sanctified through them applied solely to those who left all to follow Me.

Because the costly call you received was inseparable from the grace God freely gave.

His grace defined our relationship; loving one another was intended to nurture it.

That's what My sheep were *called* to do, created as you were in Our image.

My work was finished some two thousand years ago; yours began the day I called you.

So I must now ask you three questions:

(1) How could you, as one of My own, have done anything less for Me or the Father? More to the point,

_____

_____

(2) What did you do for Our Kingdom with the spiritual gifts I gave
you? Which leads to the only question that ultimately matters,

_____   _____
_____

(3) Do I *know* you—or not?"

_____
_____

Tough words—and costly! Not those of just any prosecutor, but the
Mediator and Judge Himself. Even tougher questions: Are *you* among Christ's
followers? If not, why pray? Who's listening? If God is, why worry? Isn't eternal life "guaranteed" by grace? Or can the fruit of one's salvation—perhaps
even *salvation itself*—be lost?

That provides food for thought—if not thoughtful prayer!—particularly
as it relates to this timeless truth to whet your spiritual appetite: If raising
Jesus from physical death was the ultimate demonstration of God's *power*,
rescuing His followers from spiritual death remains the supreme manifestation of God's *grace*. And that was costly because it cost God the life of His Son;
yet it's grace because God did not feel this too high a price to pay for our very
souls.

So we return, sheepishly, to the first of Jesus' incriminating questions:
"How could you, as one of My own, do any less for Me or the Father?" It all
comes down in the end to having nurtured the Relationship by answering
His Call. Which is why missionaries take their own calling so seriously. Now,
lest you think I'm ahead of you simply by virtue of what I have professed to
be, you're quite mistaken. Fellowship with Jesus begins right here at home; to
be more precise, right in the *heart*, where the Beatitudes first laid out Jesus'
terms from His own.

True, an intellectual assent to the reality of God was a necessary prereq-
uisite for my belated spiritual journey. What's more, having been granted a
Counselor and Intercessor through the resurrected Christ has drawn me
nearer to His Kingdom. Alas, the Prosecution will not rest until my case is sent
to the jury of One in Three Persons: Does Jesus truly *know* me—and, by
extension, *you*—as genuine disciples?

Blessed hope, to be sure. But where does the evidence lead? Are we "of the world" or "into the Word"—if not languishing in limbo somewhere between the two? "What's in *your* wallet?" the image-maker inquires, as if to refine our net worth as "consumers of consumption." Yet all the image-Creator requires to define our "net's worth" as fishers of men is "Who's in *My* Book?"

With that, the Prosecution has introduced its case. Who, then, will speak for us?

FIRST WITNESSES

Theirs Is the Kingdom of Heaven

The term "blessed" as it appears in Christ's Beatitudes refers to the spiritual well-being of those who already share in the Kingdom of God. As for the phrase "poor in spirit," Jesus was drawing attention in particular to His Kingdom as a gracious gift offered the humble-spirited, not an earned reward deserving of the self-righteous. Yet such poverty of spirit also applies to the crush of humanity beaten down by the world, to others who lack a redemptive sense of self-worth (there being a fine line between that and genuine humility), and to all the rest who dwell in darkness by choice more often than circumstance.

In a word, *deprivation* seems to typify the human condition. That has no boundaries, as I had confirmed for myself when the Lord first led me to Latin America to cut my "wisdom" teeth as a medical missionary. For the most part, however, its people simply refuse to allow poverty of whatever sort to define them. They are, by God's grace alone, at least reachable—and I, by virtue of the same, have been used as but one of His messengers in so doing.

In other parts of the world it can be much more difficult to convince the poor in spirit that they will experience Christ's Kingdom in eternity, not to mention here on earth. As opposed to my experience in South and Central America, where the people's hearts are so open and their spirits so hungry, I was woefully unprepared for what we would face in Albania two years later.

In one sense alone I was prepared, having been advised that my neurosurgical instruments would be superfluous in ministering to the physical and spiritual needs of Kosovar refugees caught up in the horror of the Serbian pogrom orchestrated by Slobadon Milosevic. That was small consolation for what proved to be the most distressing of some sixty medical mission trips I've undertaken during the past twelve years. Despite my inability either to meet their needs or fulfill my own commitment to the Lord, His boundless grace took me to the next level of affirmation—but not before confessing that I had failed them and nearly denied Him.[1]

You see, the refugees I ministered to in Albania were hardly interested in what my God had to offer. They were Muslims by birth—and the very thugs responsible for their oppression were Greek Orthodox Christians! Theirs was ethnic cleansing in the name of a triune God they had never comprehended to begin with, much less accepted. What use did they have for Jesus? Why would they even consider leaning on the everlasting arms of Christ my King? The only "arms" with which these Serbian Christians had embraced their neighbors were not those proverbial extensions of the compassionate heart; they were of a different sort, brandished to gun down Kosovar "infidels" and destroy their homes. If arms were used in the anatomic sense of the word at all, it was to strangle helpless Muslim women at worst—or as restraints during the course of raping them "at best."

All I had to offer, then, was an empathetic ear to the horrifying tales these women and children had to tell. For those, by and large, were my only patients. Virtually all their husbands or fathers had either been shot in the fields or unaccountably disappeared. Could Jesus provide these poor in spirit an answer for their suffering, or even a hand to hold onto in the dark night of their souls? Realistically, no. As for Allah, he had no answers either—only revenge, or cries of "Jihad," in keeping with the legacy of Islam now literally set aflame in the "Killing Fields" of Kosovo.

To compound their bitterness (and frustrate any thoughts of martyrdom some might have entertained), they were powerless to act—and I, equally powerless to assuage their anxiety and depression. As seemed to underscore the futility of our mission, the medications I had packed, including the antidepressants they so desperately needed, never arrived. They had been stolen, either in Italy before boarding the ferry that took us across the Adriatic or by customs officials in Albania to be sold on the black market. All I was left with was God's medicine—and at least here, perversely, that proved inadequate to meet their needs. Had I really believed I could explain to these poor in spirit the "why" so that they might somewhat endure the "how"? Is theirs to be the Kingdom of Heaven? For that, no Christian (at least on this side of the Great Divide) has an answer.

Contrast the Kosovars' lot with one of the poorest in spirit I've ever had the privilege of ministering to—in a shantytown on the outskirts of Guayaquil, Ecuador. Roberto had been triaged to my cubicle to treat his painful facial tic, for which the only effective cure was a medicine I did not have or an operation I could not offer. Disheveled and reeking of alcohol, he stumbled in clutching at his face as if laboring in vain to pull the eyeball from its socket.

"Armed" only with what the Lord provided, I grasped his contorted face in one hand and a Bible in the other. As my hapless charge continued to grimace in pain, I frantically began reading out loud: "Jesus went throughout Galilee,…healing every disease and sickness among the people…those suffering severe pain,…seizures, and the paralyzed…"[2] Over and over I recited the same verses. And louder and louder—as much to drown out his moaning as to "exorcise" the spasms. This created such a commotion that other members of the team began to filter into my cubicle, eventually swallowing the two of us in a bear hug of intercessory prayer.

Slowly and (at least to my way of thinking) inexplicably, the spasms subsided—and then disappeared! I was as dumbfounded as my grateful patient; for I had never believed in, much less used, so-called "laying-on of hands" as a healer. Roberto's doubts had even deeper roots. He simply could not comprehend that Jesus might have had a hand in any of this. To *his* way of thinking, such a pitiful life was unworthy of God's attention; by his own admission, he had to "change himself" first before turning to Jesus and asking for His help. It was at this point our interpreter began to sing in Spanish with a soft, soothing voice: "Come just as you are; hear the Spirit call; come receive Christ the King; come and live forevermore."

The lyrics spoke to this forlorn soul far more powerfully than I ever could have done—about what it means to be "poor in spirit," and the unconditional restitution Jesus alone has to offer. Swaying back and forth to the melody with eyes closed and hands raised, Roberto was suddenly overcome and dashed out of the cubicle. That left us perplexed and, I don't mind admitting, a little deflated—until he returned with his wife and three children. At that moment, five lost sheep, who had never found their way in this world, crossed through the gate into the Lord's pasture. And by week's end, husband and wife had taken their place alongside us as "runners" in the clinic, ministering to those who still remained outside, so that they too might enter into Jesus' presence. Neither servant nor sufferer had missed the turnoff Christ intended us to take that day. Not that He had chosen the "gifted" to take the higher road; rather, the Good Shepherd had *gifted* His chosen along the Way.

Others are simply too weighed down by guilt to risk embarking on this "road less taken" or are forbidden to do so altogether by their culture and its institutions. Whether imposed to direct, or merely control, the yokes of humankind are formidable burdens to shoulder alone. At least one in Latin America is attached to the reins of its established church.

Now, lest I'm accused of lashing out with the worst excesses of evangelical zeal—as in being a "spiritual elitist," if not an "anti-papist"—lend me an ear. That's what I did on two memorable occasions during my second year on mission in Guatemala. Merely taking the time to listen afforded me the opportunity to savor the harvest of God's Kingdom here on earth despite His "oxen," in effect, being muzzled while "treading out the grain."[3]

There's an old adage among physicians that has served us well: "Give a patient long enough to tell you what's wrong with him—and he usually will!" Whereas not interrupting his or her clinical history proves inductive in medicine, the doctor's empathetic silence becomes intuitive in missions. If the truth be known, fully one third of the patients we see in our primary-care clinics abroad don't come to have their diseases treated; they simply come to be *heard*.

One notable example was a mother of seven, whose oldest son was an alcoholic. Time after time the confession booth, a lit candle, or her precious coin dropped into a box at the foot of some icon had failed to exorcise the "demon rum" vicariously afflicting her own spiritual journey. Not that she was to blame; that was obvious to me—but hardly to this saint-in-waiting.

I'd heard such confessions before. How, she confided, could a self-professed "woman of God" attend Mass, much less take Communion, when the whole village seemed to be embarrassed by her son? Where could she find respite from her sullied reputation (and solace for her down-trodden spirit) in a cathedral so sparkling and holy? If anything, the reverence accorded the Blessed Mary there—that perfect mother of baby Jesus who had brought Him up so well—mocked her own perceived shortcomings as a single parent. That's why she had never even considered being baptized herself; though a fervent (if untutored) believer, the fear of further rejection was simply too onerous for her to bear.

It hardly mattered she knew the story of Jesus' own baptism by heart: about the beautiful dove descending; the sun breaking through; and most poignant of all, the voice of God proclaiming, "This is my Son, whom I love; with Him I am well pleased."[4] What could the Father possibly say by way of praise to this mother who, in her own words, had "failed so completely" as a shepherdess for her own sheep? Perhaps after her son was out of the house she might reconsider this "baptism thing." Until then, she'd continue to muddle through.

Such guilt-ridden reflections opened the door to a discussion of grace and the Holy Spirit, the latter as her intercessor. Knowing the profligate son's name to be Juan, I opened "his" book—the Gospel of John—for the mother to peruse. There she first learned about Jesus' gift of the Holy Spirit to all believers: "If you love me, you will obey what I command. And I will ask the Father, and He will give you another Counselor to be with you forever—the Spirit of truth…" (John 14:15–17).

Then there was the issue of baptism to consider. If not a commandment as such (nor, to be technical, absolutely essential for one's salvation), the Lord at least intended baptism to be an outward sign of an inward change—a change in her thinking she desperately needed to embrace. Consider the fact, I reminded her, that Jesus had been baptized, as His first act of obedience to the Father, with the ultimate intent of taking away the sins of the world. Surely such unmerited grace would extend to those within her own house! More to the point, the perfect Son of God had required baptism Himself as a rite of passage; how much more should we demand that of ourselves? As a bonus to the mother, following His example would demonstrate her love for the Lord to those skeptical neighbors in particular.

As for the love Jesus promised her, I then turned to John 16:21–23: "A woman giving birth to a child has pain…" We both grimly nodded; that obviously comes with the territory. All too often, however, a more difficult cross comes to bear down the road. Though a mother may have sublimated the pain of childbearing thereafter in the joy of childrearing, the same boy or girl who defined her very existence eventually falls to the temptation of sin over which she has no control. "And that's why Jesus came to earth," I paraphrased John's explanation, "to experience the very same anguish that all parents must bear at one time or another." Through His incomparable suffering, Christ was enabled to take on her grief as His own. But only if she truly *believed* that—at which point, John went on to say, she would rejoice. For "in that day…[Jesus'] Father will give you whatever you ask in [His] name."

And what this mother sought, I pointed out, was the very thing she had posed to me from the beginning: in a word, *freedom* from guilt! That was all she needed to hear. "Why, then, should I wait to be baptized?" she exclaimed. "Let's do it now!" There being neither pastor nor priest at the clinic, however, presented a logistical problem of sorts—or so the church had distorted her own perspective. But hardly mine! Trusting the Lord would not wish to see her opportunity pass, we prayed fervently for the Holy Spirit's guidance. And this is what we were told: if John had been a baptizer of the Lord, though hardly recognized by the established church of his day, why should I not reprise his role for the soul of another?

Behaving like two "in-filled" kids emerging from a candy store (where was the guilt when it felt so good?), we drew a bucket of fresh water from a nearby stream and ventured up the hill in a driving rainstorm to a small chapel. There, an unordained sheep of the pasture baptized another member of the flock belonging to the Good Shepherd. As if to affirm the act, at the precise moment of "sprinkling" (in reality, *dumping,* so as to "drown the past away" by her own request) a huge ray of sunlight broke through the cloud cover and came to rest on the chapel.

Though this "shining city" on a hill was no longer hidden, the clinic at its base remained blanketed in precipitation. "That's God's water," she exclaimed, pointing below. "Let's finish up my cleansing!" Whereupon she sprinted down the hill into the pelting rain like a child dashing through a sprinkler on a summer's day, "candy" in hand—the most carefree newborn daughter of God with whom I've ever shared a baptism.

Sometimes sharing is not all it's cranked up to be. An unborn child between unwed parents is a case in point. Realistically, that's become commonplace in Latin America; doctrinally, it remains an abomination for the local church there. Yet when Pharisaic principle becomes an institutional stumbling stone at the expense of a single soul seeking its very Cornerstone, Jesus takes even greater offense. Witnesses the expectant mother who came to our clinic for a prenatal evaluation. She had already been assured by word of mouth that the Lord alone was in charge of the work being done there. Which unmasked her real reason for coming: to receive *His* affirmation for her spiritual quest— a search admittedly quickened by the sin irrevocably committed some eight months before.

After interviewing the girl and praying with her, it became apparent to me that here was a heart wide open to where the Lord might lead her in the future—and an unborn baby as well! Sad to relate, the local priest felt otherwise. Her pre-baptismal counseling had been abruptly terminated once he discovered she was both unchaste and unmarried. The only way this expectant mother might legitimately continue to attend *his* Mass at all (not to mention ever being baptized), the priest informed her, was to cajole the absentee father into marriage. Without that sacrament, she was effectively barred from entering the church thereafter! *Strange*, I thought, *but there it is.*

Need she have reminded me that seeking God on her own initiative (and without a priest's oversight) was strictly forbidden? Those were the "rules of the house" and always had been—at least from the church hierarchy's perspective, which owns the place. Never one myself to suffer legalism gracefully, I boldly replied: "Only Jesus knows the *hearts* of those men and women He created to begin with, and in His own image. It logically follows that her salvation was *His* call to make." So it seemed to me at the time, for which I offer no apologies today.

Would that I could tell you our encounter had a redemptive ending for this disconsolate mother-(and seeker)-in-waiting. Such was not to be. She left the clinic satisfied in only one respect: her story had been told, and someone had listened. If there was any upside at all for myself, it was in knowing that I had taken the first step at Jesus' direction within my own very limited sphere of influence.

Regrettably, however, not the last! I should have found a pastor somewhere who would have baptized this forlorn sheep yearning to enter the Good Shepherd's pasture. That only made my hesitation in taking on the establishment for her sake all the more galling—which explains my boldness as a surrogate baptizer on behalf of the mother of an alcoholic who came to the same clinic just two days later. Whether the latter "precocious" act will have found favor in Jesus' eyes I'll one day find out for myself before the judgment seat of Christ.[5]

But this much I know for certain: simply because fallible men and their churches (i.e. those with a lower-case "c") have left the heart of Jesus' Beatitudes behind is precisely why He came—to give it a human face. Still challenged with such denominational obstacles today, Christ continues to enlist these same commandments from His heart to break them down. That's why His disciples continue to venture down roads where the ostensible "heart" of their church is already established—not to judge, but to *serve* the Judge of all things, who alone holds the key to *His* Church and the Kingdom of Heaven.

If only to test us, the Lord often leads His disciples down a road when we least expect it—and where there is no church at all to be found. One such journey entailed a literal mountaintop experience in the heart of Nicaragua, ministering to a subset of the population our medical team had not even targeted. That was the day we had encountered seven defiant youths loitering across the dusty road from our makeshift clinic enclosure. They had been there since early morning, obviously with far too much time on their hands and, by outward appearances, more than enough malice in their hearts. Their presence was something of a worrisome distraction for our team, what with their roughhousing and churlish behavior (spirited, yes— but hardly spirit-filled!). They pointedly stood apart from the rest of the villagers, who had been humble enough to stand for hours on end in the oppressive heat waiting to be seen.

Every so often I would emerge from my cubicle, ostensibly for a break—in reality, to fathom just what it was they were really up to. *Surely these rough-necks are beyond the pale*, I remember musing self-righteously, *and certainly beyond the reach of our ministry.* For all I knew, these were modern-day Sodomites lurking outside the clinic entrance, perhaps with an eye to defiling a few of those "angels unaware" we were ministering to behind our gated enclosure.[6]

The boys remained there throughout the day, for reasons I could only conjecture. *Odd*, I thought. *Did the Lord have something else in mind for them? Was their false bravado indicative of an unspoken need? Should I stay where I was, ministering to those who were following the rules—or go outside and meet them where, just perhaps, God was working?* Ultimately I resolved to call their bluff before the day was out—much to the chagrin of my youthful interpreter, who was about their same age and recognized "bad apples" when he saw them.

"No, not those," he cautioned me. "It's simply too dangerous to meet them on their own turf. Stay within the fence where there's some sense of order. If God wants them to be ministered to, He'll compel them to register like everyone else."

For eight hours I heeded the counsel of man—and not the mind of God that was painting my own into a corner—continuing to minister to those within the gates. At length, however, and empowered by the Holy Spirit (for there was simply no other way to rationalize my actions), I ventured outside with my frightened interpreter in tow. "A challenge awaits us—and them," I exclaimed with thinly disguised braggadocio. In truth, I had no other plan than to depend on my Lord's assurances not to worry about what I would say, but simply to rely on Him to guide me.

Venturing up to one of the toughs decked out in a stocking cap with a Chicago Cubs' logo, I offered an obligate high-five. That universal greeting among youths everywhere had the added, if unintended, merit of exposing the beaded power bracelet I was wearing, which I often used as a prop to tell the Gospel story. One of the others took the bait dangling before them and asked me what it was for. That was all the affirmation I needed to forge ahead.

But not before asking myself, *What would Jesus do in this situation?* More often than not, He would answer one question with another when encountering opposition. Using my best imitation of Him who was now speaking through me, I responded with a question of my own. "What do you they think these people inside the fence have come here to receive?" To which the Sammy Sosa-wannabe replied with a sneer, "To get some drugs." Nervous chuckles all around. Then silence.

"Because they've been chosen to play your game," mocked another, with eyes diverted as he kicked self-consciously at the dust.

"Perhaps," I responded. "Yet those who are truly chosen by the One who brought me here and gave me these beads to tell His Story are receiving something much more important—not drugs, but the Bread of Life."

More silence. That well-intentioned metaphor went right over their heads! Bemused (if not amused) by my earnestness, they began whispering in Spanish to one another, punctuated by more giggles and posturing. Despite what seemed an obvious misstep on my part, however, none as yet had turned their backs. Impulsively, I pointed to the first bead (a black one, signifying sin) and launched into an explanation of the story of salvation—God had come to Earth as a man to make them right with their Creator. The red bead was His blood freely given that made it all possible; the white, the end result of His forgiveness that washes us clean.

Whereupon their surly facade began to crumble. That some gringo would have taken the time to come out of his protective enclosure and meet these hardened skeptics where they were was mystery enough—for it was apparent that few, if any, had taken much interest in their lives up until then. Yet my extended hand of reconciliation withered in comparison to the notion that Someone far more important—none other than God's Son—had given His *own* life for their very souls!

That alone softened seven very calloused hearts. Antipathy gave way to curiosity. Soon they were all perched on a rock ledge in rapt attention. Seizing the moment, I beckoned for seven bracelets and placed one on each of their wrists as I walked down the line dispensing the Good News. With their hands now linked in a human chain of beads that positively glowed in the Christ-light, I silently beseeched the Lord to open their ears and eyes to His message. We then recited the sinner's prayer together. And, in the end, seven of God's children professed Jesus as their Lord and Savior.

As newborn babes in Christ, of course, they still had to be fed! Much to the dismay of the local pastor, who could hardly disguise his disdain for sowing such valuable pearls among swine, I distributed the few remaining Spanish New Testaments we had left. "All they'll do is sell them," he admonished me. No doubt he knew his own people better than I. Perhaps the man was right. Yet it wasn't for either of us to say whether the seeds Jesus planted that day would fall on the sun-baked road to be snatched up right away or among thistles that might well engulf them shortly after we left. This much, however, I vividly recall: at the end of the day, there they still sat with opened Bibles in hand, feasting on the Word and talking excitedly among themselves.

As we boarded the bus to leave, with the sun going down, my eyes met the ringleader, whom I had likened to Peter. He pointed upward and, with an appreciative smile, nodded to me in affirmation. A chill ran down my spine, accompanied by a flashback to that final scene from the movie version of *Jesus Christ, Superstar*, when the troupe of actors had boarded the bus, leaving behind one of their own on the cross as the sun set. What had been the director's literary license then was Jesus' literal legacy now. My only contribution to His encore in Nicaragua had been to obey one of those "God impulses" the Holy Spirit provokes, setting the stage to bring Christ down from the cross and into their hearts.

Not that these calloused youths had fulfilled our requirements for being ministered to, which was what registering in the clinic was all about. Yet Jesus suspends the rules of men to fulfill the needs of lambs whom He (not we) has summoned. Nothing more than obedience to one of those Spirit-driven provocations—extending the Shepherd's staff with bracelet attached to those who disdained the work Jesus was doing—brought seven of His kids to where they needed to be all along. From that day forth, we were brothers in Christ sharing an eternal inheritance.

They Will Be Comforted

Those who mourn in God's Kingdom here on earth have Jesus' promise they will ultimately find comfort. Soon after we left Nicaragua following my first mission trip there in 1996, I received word that the Lord had just such plans in mind for little Eric and his family back in El Salvador. As if to add to the pathos of our patient's plight, his mother and father had never married. God took that to heart—which is tantamount to saying He made the necessary amends to fit His divine plan.

Due in large measure to their shared travail, the Lord subsequently united Eric's parents in marriage. Thereafter, He prompted our team to build a house for the family that not only met our patient's medical needs, but gave his brothers and sisters amenities they had never known—a toilet, running water, and a refrigerator. More enabling still, the emotional support the family received (and the grateful manner in which they responded to it) became a profound witness for Christ's love. Most ennobling of all, the Lord was *glorified* when a vibrant church emerged in their village, where none had existed before.

Jesus provided some lessons and much needed affirmation for myself as well. As for the lessons, Eric's predicament underscores that the way people respond to tragedy is dictated in large measure by their culture. In the United States, for example, most responses are anything but ennobling. Here, the technology that kept Eric alive in the early going would in all probability be viewed as a "cost-plus" sociological disaster—not to mention the distressing legal ramifications such an unforeseen and inexplicable tragedy predictably evokes.

Yet for Eric's family in El Salvador, the newfound presence of Christ in their lives was all the comfort and compensation they desired. The downtrodden and dispossessed abroad are simply willing to accept less than what the proud and self-indulgent seem to require here at home when medicine has failed them. It was left for the boy's mother some two years later to put into words what they all had come to accept as a gracious gift from on high: "When we were the weakest, Jesus was the strongest." Acknowledging that we as physicians had been powerless to offer any medical cure, I certainly appreciated where she was coming from.

Perhaps an omniscient God, who alone could see the future, had kept me in El Salvador that second week for a preordained purpose: to serve as a mourner with (and minister to) the family, far more than as a doctor. In a word, to be a "carer" more than a "curer." Even so, Jesus alone had made a way when there seemed to be no way, ushering Eric through those first few days in a forbidding environment that was almost as trying for me as it undoubtedly had been for him. For we both intuitively realized—or so I believe he could—that as two who languished together in the darkest of valleys, neither of us had anyone else to turn to but the Good Shepherd. Blessed indeed were we who mourned—each in very different ways—because of His presence in our lives that fateful week in El Salvador.

The same could not be said, at first glance, for Eric's suffering counterparts in Russia. There the putrefaction of decay that characterized the former Soviet Union during the decade of the 90s sifted down, unconscionably, to its children. I caught a whiff of that up close and personal in Siberia. As something of a parody of our Wild West, that's where the dispossessed and politically suspect always seemed to end up by default. Those who mourn the most in this desolate land are the children—and, presumably, the few parents who can still be found that mourn for them. Orphanages are ubiquitous; street children even more visibly so. As for Siberia's newborns—a staggering number of which are victimized by a whole host of congenital anomalies spawned by inadequate prenatal nutrition and maternal alcohol abuse—no shunts are available to treat the hydrocephalus (water on the brain) so prevalent there.

Though we had been warned by the Russian authorities that our mission was to be medical and by no means "proselytizing," the Holy Spirit bolstered me with enough courage to pay lip service to the regime and still manage to speak the Good News to the people. At first surreptitiously (yet by the end of our stay there, openly), prayer became my undercover agent in Siberia. Regardless of why I was *told* I was there, let's just say, "I had my own agenda."

That it was to be Jesus' agenda as well became apparent during the first pediatric clinic I attended the day after our arrival. We had been asked to consult on some thirty-five children with various stages of untreated hydrocephalus. To comprehend the magnitude of the problem, that's far more than any neurosurgeon is likely to see in his or her practice in a year! Their plights, and those of the parents who bore their burdens stoically (while responding to me, at least initially, in the same way), were so heartrending that prayer became a natural extension of each examination I ministered. Knowing I had brought only twelve shunts perversely sharpened my diagnostic acumen as to which children would benefit from shunting and which would not. For the remainder, God's grace had to suffice. Yet that, as ever, proved more than adequate for their needs—and His designs.

As I had anticipated, praying with each of the families after examining their child and making recommendations raised a few eyebrows in the beginning. Wasn't that a job reserved for the Russian Orthodox priest—and certainly only while in church? My Siberian colleagues would respond by making a pretense of shuffling through the medical record or searching for the next set of x-rays while I indulged in such "heresy." Halfway through the afternoon, however, I began to sense the presence of lab-coated shadows gathering behind me during these prayer vigils. And by the end of the clinic, they were self-consciously joining in, hands linked with ours. The presence of the Holy Spirit in those prayer circles was palpable, as was His unspoken invitation. Planting seed was all that the Lord expected of me. Reconciling each of them to Himself was something He would take care of in His own time.

From a strictly neurosurgical perspective, my experience during the first leg of our Siberian mission in 1999 was more than I could ever have managed on my own: Seven aneurysms clipped, two tumors resected, and all twelve shunts successfully placed—in just ten days. That was my reward, I believe, for ministering to His children. However, with our transfer from the large regional referral center in Krasnyorsk to the much smaller city of Bratsk the third week, it soon became apparent I needed to be doing something besides operating. What few cases that had been set aside for our arrival were put on terminal hold pending "approval" from some unnamed bureaucracy, or (more than likely) reserved for its only neurosurgeon, who remained far less hospitable than my colleagues had been in Krasnyorsk. I therefore resigned myself to the primary-care clinic, trusting the Divine Physician had His own plans for me there.

My assignment was to be even more "primitive"—if ultimately more fulfilling—than I could ever have imagined. I was given the unenviable task of making house calls, visiting shut-ins who had no way of making it to the clinic, much less stand in an endless line waiting to be seen. Jesus opened their doors in His own ineffable way through my good friend, Sebastian Sosa, whom I had first met some four years earlier while on mission together and who now served as my interpreter in Bratsk.

That was no more of a coincidence than what our initial meeting in El Salvador had portended when, after introducing himself, Sebastian casually volunteered he was from an Argentine missionary family serving in Belarus. He had been given the opportunity to extend his education in the United States at Evangel University in Springfield, Missouri. "Had I ever heard of it?" he asked. Amazed by God's prescience, I replied with a chuckle, "I know them both intimately because I live there!" Though our friendship burgeoned during the next four years while he was in Springfield, I lost track of Sebastian after his graduation—only to find we had both volunteered, unbeknownst to each other, to go to Siberia with Operation Blessing. More "coincidental" still, as a result of his experience in Belarus, my friend now spoke fluent Russian. (Nothing more than the luck of the draw, I'm sure…)

It so happened that Sebastian had been visited by an elderly man at our clinic in Bratsk. He came on behalf of his bedridden wife, who had been confined to bed for eight long years following a severe stroke. The husband was now seeking a neurologic specialist to visit her in their apartment. Unable to walk or use her left side, she had not so much as seen the other two rooms of their cramped living quarters for almost a decade. That would have been the harshest perdition imaginable had not her loving husband tended to her day and night through the years. His world was confined to a wooden chair next to the bed, ministering to her every need.

Sebastian sought me out, and we agreed to go there immediately, accompanied by a nurse who was simply "on fire" for the Lord. During our cab ride out to the apartment, this prophetess in scrubs prepared us for what she believed would be a visitation of the Spirit by repeating over and over a single verse from the second chapter of Acts: "Suddenly a sound like the blowing of a violent wind came from Heaven and filled the whole house where [the disciples] were sitting. They saw what seemed to be tongues of fire that separated and came to rest on each of them. And they were filled with the Holy Spirit…"[1] It was only a matter of minutes before we three modern-day disciples would be a party to this description of Pentecost revisited.

Upon our arrival we were ushered by the husband into a tiny bedroom just large enough to allow for a bed and chair. A single window (barred, in keeping with virtually all apartments in Siberia) was their only visual contact with a world his wife no longer inhabited. There we began to pray over this destitute figure lying crumpled on the stained mattress before us. Whereas I merely laid my hands on her head and paralyzed side, beseeching that she be comforted, the nurse intuitively sensed as we prayed that the Lord had something greater in store. At length, she cajoled the women to stand despite my own unvoiced concern our patient might fall and break a hip—leaving her far worse as a result of our ministrations, and putting the credibility of the entire team in doubt.

Tentatively the woman took her first step as the others supported their charge, all the while continuing to pray over her. There they stood in suspended animation for what seemed an eternity, teetering back and forth. As for myself, the Doubting Thomas, I crouched down to catch her in anticipation of the inevitable fall. And then, with a dramatic flourish, she let go of their shoulders, brushed my friends aside, and limped off into a kitchen she had not seen for eight years! With her *paralyzed arm* (to which I, the "expert," had already attested), she reached into a cabinet and grasped a jar of jam, thrusting it into my hand as a gesture of thanks, with tears of joy streaming down her face.

Somewhere from the back of the room I heard the voice of God's spokesperson intoning from Psalm 16:8–10 on her behalf: "…Because [the

LORD] is [now] at my right hand, I will not be shaken.…my body also will rest secure, because [He] will not abandon me to the grave…" We had witnessed nothing less than a resurrection—and a revelation of the greatest magnitude for husband and wife. Through Sebastian we were informed that the patient's grandmother had told her something about "our" God before the communist takeover. That's why her husband had humbly approached a priest from the Russian Orthodox Church when she had been felled by the stroke, seeking God's blessing to heal his wife. Would this holy man intercede for them? To which the priest had coldly replied, "Once she is strong enough to come to church and light a candle there, then God will offer His blessing."

Our grateful, if perplexed, patient simply had no inkling the Divine Healer might choose to seek her out in their own apartment! Nor, for that matter, had the priest; after all, this was not a proper house of worship. That God would "lower" Himself to visit her there was a far cry from what they had been taught by the religious establishment. Still, the Holy Spirit blows wherever He pleases and takes us where even the church hierarchy cannot (or *will* not) go. At that very moment she was being personally ministered to by the Son of Man, who had come into this world to break down such manmade barriers between the Father and His children. Now, in a squalid apartment in the heart of Siberia, Jesus had made good on the promise of the Beatitudes to comfort those who mourn, right where they are.

One of the great ironies I've encountered while serving as a medical missionary in so-called "developing nations" is being taught far more about discipleship from those we minister to than I ever gleaned from my books, a pastor's sermon—or even the work itself. That "those who mourn" have something to teach us comforters about faith is a given; more often than not, faith is all they have to sustain them. To recognize (and then accept) that they might have something to teach us in kind about being disciples, however, smacks as a perceived affront to our calling. C'mon! Haven't *we* been designated as His "elect," sent out to proclaim the Good News? Ours is to teach; theirs to accept or reject. What could the discipler possibly learn from the discipled?

In the final analysis, this divinely orchestrated role reversal hinges upon *needs*—and theirs are invariably more pressing than our own. If the truth be known, of course, neither is arguably more important to Jesus than the other. Whether by choice or circumstance, what Christ ultimately requires of every follower is to become so *needy* that no alternative remains but to focus on His call and its promise. That's when "walking in faith" becomes the obligate reality. Only then does one *learn* to believe. What initially separates those who mourn from us, however, is that they're already there and ready to do.

Would it surprise you to know God might also have needs of His own? Okay, so that's an outlandish rhetorical question. But consider this: to "yearn for" is to be "in need of." And if one theme runs consistent throughout the parables, it's that the Good Shepherd is always *yearning* to find His lost sheep. By that measure alone, then, God "needs" His kids as much as they need Him. It's simply His nature—part of God's "genetic" makeup, irrevocably linked to the offspring He created in His image from the very beginning. As their doting Father, He first loved them before they ever knew Him.

Nor is God content to be a stay-at-home Dad. He takes the initiative by leaving His house cloaked in the flesh of mankind and seeking His lost children. Once finding them, moreover, He pays no heed to their apologies or promises to change, but graciously brings them back home where they belong. That has poignant relevance for us "grown-ups" as well. In the words of Henri Nouwen, drawn from his classic treatise on the return of the prodigal son: "The question is not 'How am I to know God?' but 'How am I to *let* myself be known by God?'"[2] Could it be that He's the One who's always looking for disciples, while we're the ones doing the hiding?

This brings us back to the "whethers" of choice and circumstance: one is elective; the other dictated. For those fortunate enough to have already been exposed to the Good News by virtue of the culture in which they grew up (a relative small percentage of mankind, to be sure), disavowing one's prior station or life's view to follow Jesus is little more than an exercise in free will. As for the broad majority of God's last and greatest creation, who has no choice in the matter, answering the call of anyone—or any god—that gives them comfort and hope becomes non-negotiable.

Mere circumstance therefore affords those who mourn a head start as disciples, simply because they're so *easy* for the Lord to find! Contrast their lot with the "joyfully in-filled" slouching unnoticed in their church pews, most of whom will take their fair share of Jesus' time to weigh the consequences before responding to His call. Lacking that luxury, discipleship may be thrust upon the destitute of the Third World in often unforeseen, even life-threatening, ways.

Perhaps no disciple-in-waiting ever "stood" before the Lord more isolated and needy than one terribly emaciated woman I was asked to consult on in Ternople, Ukraine. By appearances alone (curled as she was into a ball with immobile limbs and unable to do so little as lift her head off the bed to swallow), I assumed Prishtina had AIDS. Tragically, her doctors had assumed the same for well over a year, until someone had the hindsight to order an MRI. It revealed a huge tumor at the base of her skull that had been compressing the spinal cord all along, leaving this holocaust-like victim of medical neglect all but totally paralyzed from the neck down.

Even more "neglect" thereafter, insofar as no one dared operate on such a nasty tumor—harbored by this loving wife and mother of one—for legitimate fear of never being able to wean her off the respirator. As for the flip side of the coin, any treatment at all threatened to be worse than the "cure." For what little time she had left, while recovering from surgery she would be bound to her bed by a tracheostomy tube—its ties a noose from which there was no escape. Heads, the tumor wins; tails, she loses. Barring a true miracle, what quality of life could she possibly have? Better not to cross scythes with the Grim Reaper![3]

Yet the pathos of Prishtina's plight was such that the Lord compelled me to glean what little harvest remained. Given His often inscrutable nature to those of us who have no inkling of a given pasture's boundaries, perhaps Jesus had something more redeeming in store than some perverse prolongation of suffering alone in the field. By His grace, we managed to successfully excise the entire tumor after seven tedious hours of surgery. As everyone involved instinctively sensed, however, that proved just the beginning of Prishtina's inexorable "death by hanging." Though some early return of arm and leg function gave us grounds for hope, her diaphragmatic and intercostal muscles never regained enough strength to expand and contract her lungs in order to be taken off the respirator. So much, then, for being raised up on eagle's wings; our greatest fear had come home to roost.

Three weeks after returning to the States, I received an e-mail confirming that Prishtina had passed away. But not before she had exchanged her physical burden for eternal salvation at the Lord's beckoned call during one of many prayer vigils at her bedside. Perversely, that blessing (undisclosed in the e-mail) I knew nothing about until a year later. As I was soon to discover, Christ's living waters ran far deeper than I could ever have plumbed—or plummeted, for that matter. A single salvation was just the tip of the iceberg.

Having been immersed in ice floes of self-opprobrium from the day I left Ukraine, Prishtina's sad (albeit predictable) demise chilled my soul day and night. There was simply no warmth to be had; her own trial by fire sparked mere cinders instead, singeing the tinder of my fragile self-esteem. "What a grievous error in judgment," I berated myself. As Psalm 31 always directed me, I had prayed for discernment—and thought I had received it—for the sake of His name. Now, we both unaccountably seemed to have been put to shame. Or so it had appeared from my limited perspective across this frigid slough of despond.

To recross such a strait now frozen solid by remorse, I had to get out of the boat and make my way back on Jesus' shoulders, totally dependent on the light of the Son for guidance. That, in retrospect, was the lesson to be learned when I returned to Ternople—a lesson bequeathed to me by Prishtina's still grieving husband, who had shown up unannounced in the clinic with their ten-year-old son the day after I arrived. By all appearances, he was there to vent his lingering frustration over the alleged "poor care" his wife received after I left. I asked him to be more specific—at which point, unbeknownst to him, this grief-stricken man removed the goatskin that weighed so heavily on my own shoulders by recounting what had really happened in my absence.

To begin with, Prishtina had actually managed to be weaned from the respirator! In fact, for nearly a week preceding her sudden death, due to what's known as a pulmonary embolus, the endotracheal tube had been removed and she was able to converse with her family for the first time since their ordeal began. And what she shared with her husband in particular during that interlude provided all the reprieve the Lord required to reprise His encore.

Just before the sudden reversal in Prishtina's heretofore wholly unexpected improvement, she had eagerly witnessed to her atheistic husband about the wonders of a God who was merciful enough to at least offer her a second chance. No one else except "that disciple who had prayed with me before and after my surgery" gave her any hope at all, she had exclaimed to him. "And that's a God worth surrendering my life to; that's why I professed Him as my Lord and Savior. And now I'm assured of being with Him someday in Heaven!"

Upon hearing all of this for the first time, I tumbled to the realization that the husband's unanticipated visit had been yet another divine appointment. Despite what initially seemed little more than a failed physician's obligation to commiserate with a lonely spouse, to my surprise (and relief!) his real concern was being *left behind*. "My wife is in Heaven now, just as was promised her," he proclaimed. "I desperately want to see her again. But she never told me how to get there. What good things must I do to deserve a place beside her?"

Bingo! Preparing to pounce on his last statement with an explanation of grace, he silenced me in advance with a wave of his hand in exasperation. "I'm not done yet, because now that I've come to see you in a different light, as some sort of 'disciple' that my wife dearly loved, I want to hear what you have to say about something that happened to my boy, Yakov. There's a message here, I think, and I'd like your opinion."

He then proceeded to relate an incredible tale of their son's near-death experience some two months after Prishtina's passing. During a walk one day, Yakov had climbed atop a brick wall to impress his daddy. Suddenly the entire edifice crumbled, burying the lad completely beneath a pile of rubble. Frantically the father had dashed off to look for help before his son suffocated beneath the debris—only to return (shovels and pickaxes in hand) to find him scurrying around on top of the pile of bricks as if he were playing in a sandbox!

Yakov's miraculous restoration had unearthed a priceless revelation on his father's behalf. And, yes, he was right on target—albeit with me squarely in the cross hairs! "After my wife's experience, I think I understand why this may have happened," he exclaimed with more passion than I'd witnessed before in this stoic husband and father of one. "There I was, you see, running off to find mere men to help rescue my son from certain death, when others had already failed me before."

Catching my suddenly downcast and guilt-ridden eyes, he clapped me on the shoulder and chuckled. "But if we call upon Jesus, He will meet all our needs At least that's what the Bible says, which Prishtina had begged me to read to our son should she not be there to do that for him. And this is what I remember most of all," he went on to say, "'Seek ye first the kingdom of God,…and all these things shall be added unto you.'[4] Am I right in assuming that 'all these things' means making something good out of the bad, like what happened to my boy here? Because I do remember praying to Jesus, which is someone I'd never prayed to before until the moment that wall caved in."

I could only nod with tears welling up in my eyes. Whether from his joy reclaimed or my remorse revisited was not clear to me at first; after all, I had been the very man who had failed them both some nine months before. Hence my own revelation upon further reflection—an insight I owe to the street-smart wisdom of a Ukrainian plumber: If we earnestly seek the Lord's intercession, He will make the best of a bad situation. From the mouths of babes, indeed!

What else, then, was "added unto me" on that memorable day when an entire family had been reconciled eternally with God (and one another) through Christ as their Mediator? That two very lost sheep had found their Good Shepherd was reward enough. Yet added unto me as a bonus was a quart of vodka, its cap discretely resealed on a bottle half empty.

Okay—so it wasn't the fruit of the vine that Christ promised to share again with His disciples once they are reunited. I'm merely suggesting if you don't have grapes to celebrate when grace abounds, then potatoes will do! Moreover, neither of us as yet has been called to partake of that banquet, mired as we are in a far less Heavenly realm. What bears emphasizing is that a bottle of fermented spuds was all my new brother in Christ had to give— in exchange for one very repentant soul in a Kingdom that is as real today in Ukraine as it promises to be in Heaven for eternity.

They Will Inherit the Earth

"Be still before the LORD and wait patiently for him;…
Refrain from anger and turn from wrath;…
A little while, and the wicked will be no more;…
But the meek will inherit the land and enjoy great peace."

PSALM 37: 7, 8, 10, 11

Going on mission abroad is an invaluable hands-on expositor of the Word—especially so as regards Jesus' third beatitude in Matthew: "Blessed are the meek, for they shall inherit the earth." Whereas the other eight blessings/promises ring true and need no amplification, the third had always been an enigma to me. What possible relevance could an earthly inheritance have for those charged with seeking the Kingdom to come? Apart from some nebulous connection with Jesus' declaration that "the Kingdom is near," I hadn't a clue.

Even that seemed a bit of a stretch—until rereading Psalm 37, to which I believe Christ was referring as metaphor for the Promised Land bequeathed to Abraham and his descendants. His point being for future generations, just such havens exist for those today who are humble enough to first acknowledge their dependency on God's grace and then trust they'll be sustained by it with what little land they have.

I now know this to be true, because Jesus has sent me "there" so many times to reaffirm His promise for myself. Whether a small garden that feeds them or some remote village that defines them, those tiny slices of real estate are all they have ever known. And at least on this side of the Great Divide, that's all they'll ever need—as in "Trust in the LORD…dwell in the land and enjoy safe pasture"(Psalm 37:3). This is all the meek can do, while retaining a vision (however dimly perceived) of His Promised Land to come, which they will one day inherit for eternity.

The righteous submissive, therefore, arguably receive something far more tangible for their faith in the here and now, apart from Jesus' promised comfort afforded by the beatitude preceding. Yet this, the third of His blessings, comes with an occasional inadvertent "lien" superimposed by the servant on their property. Although God is always in the business of bequeathing parcels of grace to the "have nots," the "haves" may deprive them of their just due, despite having been sent in good faith to manage His estate.

That is a warning I believe, in retrospect, our organization failed to heed some twelve years ago after disembarking from our sleek, new "hospital with wings" in El Salvador. Amid the fanfare of a boisterous reception—complete with military band, a president who was using our arrival as a crutch to bolster his sagging popularity, and the crush of our own ever-present media—little Eric lost his inheritance here on earth. That was obviously not our intent; yet our pride got in the way. There was a certain air of Yankee "can-do" self-assuredness in our step rather than meekness as servants obediently seeking the Lord's guidance.

It's certainly not my place as a volunteer of Operation Blessing to air its dirty laundry. Many a naysayer within the organization, however, had already voiced fears of losing our focus on primary care in this rush to display the "ultimate" venue for medical missions work. As a very visible instrument that has opened doors to areas of the world we might never have gained access to, no doubt the plane has been a plus. Yet the question arose then—and has continued to fester to this day—was it God who opened those doors, or simply the plane? Had it been His blessing that brought us to El Salvador, or the pride of American ingenuity—being so sure of ourselves as to target in advance through the media those children who would receive the benefits of the Flying Hospital?

Our shared misfortune brings to mind a story found in the fourth chapter of First Samuel following the capture of the Ark of the Covenant by the Philistines. The prophet Samuel had warned God's chosen people that the descendants of their chief priest, Eli, would die because his sons had made themselves contemptible in the eyes of the Lord and their father had failed to restrain them. Yet God was speaking through Samuel about the devastating effects of sin in a corporate sense as well, the root of which is invariably collective pride. Neither sacrifice nor offering could atone for that. Not only did the guilty pay the ultimate price; the entire community could no longer drink from its spiritual rock—symbolically depicted once Eli's daughter-in-law gave birth to a son whom she named Ichabod, meaning "the glory has departed." The name alone underscored God's estrangement from the self-serving and prideful, when obedience and humility (a.k.a. "meekness") was all the Lord had required.

I, for one, believe it was precisely this lack of humility, far removed from the sacrificial offering of a plane we proudly made in the Lord's stead (with or without His blessing), that perhaps makes sense of an otherwise inexplicable tragedy. A little less self-assuredness on our part may have served Eric better. If there's an upside to this—and one that admittedly diverges from the fate of Eli's descendants—it's that the Lord was ultimately glorified in our scramble to supplant what pride had wrought. His seed, albeit at Eric's expense, eventually took root in the hearts of those who were impacted by the tragedy. And that has continued to grow to this day, nurtured by the meekness that comes naturally for the poor and dispossessed, so others might yet inherit God's Kingdom here on earth.

Not that I myself have completely taken this lesson to heart even now. It's difficult to point fingers at any organization of which you are but a volunteer, particularly when pride in one's own skills so often deafens the ear to those plans God has in mind. If the laying on of hands and intercessory prayer to heal a painful facial tic in Ecuador or to rehabilitate a stroke victim in Russia (when I thought I should be doing brain surgery!) had not been enough to alert me to my own hubris, yet a third encounter with God in South America continued to hammer home His message.

While in Brazil, the Lord convinced me a full embrace will make amends should the hand alone falter—whether that entails a failed operation or a laying on of hands in the absence of faith. Having encountered such spiritual warfare while laboring in vain to get cases done in the operating room at the local hospital in Brasilia, I opted for returning to the primary care clinic. If the truth be known, Jesus redirected me there because the Divine Healer had something more important He wanted to teach me.

We had been in the clinic only an hour when a distraught mother burst into my cubicle, dragging her writhing son behind her—that in the most literal sense of the word, as the boy was actively convulsing. This was but one of several grand mal seizures he had experienced during the early morning hours as they huddled together in a driving rainstorm with hundreds of others waiting to be seen. Yet, once he began to choke on his own secretions and turned blue, the mother's obligate meekness dissipated. She broke through the registration barrier to the examining stations within, demanding to see a doctor.

My cubicle just happened to be nearest the entrance. I'd like to think that was no coincidence in the Lord's scheme of things, as I was the only doctor there with the requisite "credentials" to treat epilepsy. Never mind that intravenous anticonvulsants are the only medication capable of arresting such repetitive seizures completely—and that we did not have. So much, then, for one's training and hard-earned degrees…

Impulsively, I grabbed the child and held on for dear life as if to somehow physically restrain his life-threatening rigors. Drawn by the commotion, a circle of support staff formed around the two of us, emitting a cacophony of prayer that gave new meaning to the term "Tower of Babel." They continued to pray—and I continued to wrestle—locked in mortal combat with a "demon" one-third my size, whose strength for the moment easily matched my own.

Some five minutes into this bizarre spectacle, I felt the boy go limp in my arms. *Would that this had been a "simple" case of demonic possession, and I the exorcist!* Yet my medical training told me otherwise. *My God,* I thought, *we've lost him!* For, as virtually all these patients eventually do, he had probably lapsed into a coma as the seizure ran its course before heralding the onset of the next. If so, he urgently needed an airway, and I prepared to lower him to the ground to begin CPR.

A strange thing happened, however, on the way to my first "Code Blue" in the mission field…Perhaps I should have taken more notice of the distinct impression I had that something *fled* the boy's body at the moment he collapsed in my arms. As I released my grasp and called for an endotracheal tube, he simply opened his eyes, blinked—and then walked over to his distraught mother with arms outstretched. There he curled up in her lap, yawning and staring at this entourage of strangers as if we had interrupted his afternoon nap.

The seizures had stopped, and then vanished without a trace—despite no medicine except "arms-around" (as opposed to "hands-on") prayer to account for such—and absent any of the residual side effects doctors invariably see following repetitive seizure activity. Far less worse for wear than the rest of us, the little boy then reached into the pocket of his mother's jacket and pulled out a plastic race car. Oblivious to our presence, he knelt down in the dirt and began pushing it around in circles—"vroom, vroom"—and then, right out the door.

I never saw them again. Yet the parting image still lingers: that of a mother who just had a pearl of inestimable value returned to her for safekeeping, and a boy who behaved as if the world was his oyster. Their shared inheritance was what the Lord had promised the meek; for he was her entire world—and her, his.

What I inherited was a strong dose of humility on the very morning that had begun with one self-absorbed brain surgeon sulking in a blue funk because the operations scheduled had been postponed. I can still hear Him at the end of that fateful day in the clinic: "My son, haven't we been here before? How many times do we have to take this walk around the desert? There's a world of difference between a surgeon and a servant. Do it your way, if you like; but you'll do it alone. Mind you, this is *My* clinic, and we'll do things My way!"

"Blessed are the meek, for they will inherit the earth." Plus humility and the hereafter—all of which the Lord had once again affirmed inside a dilapidated warehouse in Brazil.[1]

∞

Life is cheap in Africa. On a continent where tens of thousands fall prey to the twin pestilences of HIV and malaria every day, and thousands die, it can be painfully difficult to discern God's hand in what a neurosurgeon is called to do. Much less, *can* do. So when a concentrated surgical effort on behalf of a single newborn fails, it's tempting simply not to ask and just keep plugging the dike with another of His fingers directed elsewhere.

My very first mission trip to the Dark Continent in 1998 was a test case in point. Stepping out of the jeep that had transported me from Nairobi, Kenya, up the eastern escarpment of the Rift Valley to Kijabe, I was met by Dick Bransford, the surgical director of Bethany Crippled Children's Centre. It seems that they had reserved "a rather difficult case" for their visiting neurosurgeon. Presumably time had suddenly become of the essence, because our patient was already being prepped and draped in the operating room as I unpacked my surgical instruments.

Reflecting on the circumstances later, I could not help but feel that in some perverse sense this was a bit of a "setup," for reasons which would soon become obvious on the surface—or beneath the sheets, to be more precise. Understandably, Dr. Bransford and his associate had felt uncomfortable addressing this particular problem, for equally obvious reasons once I peeked under the drapes. There I found a three-pound infant with a grotesquely shriveled skull, on the back of which was attached a huge fluid- and tissue-filled sac known as an "encephalocele." What I ruefully recognized from my neurosurgical textbooks (though had never before seen in thirty years of practice) was a baby who had been born "without a brain." The little cerebral cortex that remained was immersed somewhere within this ominously pulsating appendage of sorts.

Inquiring as to the baby's neurologic status prior to being put to sleep, I was informed he had been moving all of his extremities and breathing on his own. That was difficult for me to reconcile, given a situation where there was, in fact, no functional brain. At the mother's request nonetheless (or so I was told, as I had not even met her), I was entrusted with reinserting what tissue there was into its intended enclosure and sealing the defect. This mandate I intuitively knew to be a perilous, if not impossible, task. And *that* was precisely God's point—more about this in a moment.

To say I was filled with angst would hardly do justice to the no-win predicament into which my colleagues had thrust me. Would I "lose face" by following my instincts and training, which clearly told me *not* to proceed—after having been invited on my first African adventure to do what only a neurosurgeon could do in such a distressing circumstance? Lord knows, no doctor ever takes a baby to surgery without weighing the risks and benefits of the case and thereafter discussing all options in detail with the parents. What I was assured instead as I scrubbed my hands bordered on medical paternalism, which in Africa is an all too common, albeit accepted, practice. For one thing, there was no father to be found. As for the mother, she was a thirteen-year-old who could hardly comprehend the implications of what we were about to embark upon.

Consequently this was our decision to make as medical professionals, not hers—or so it was confidently explained to me. And that decision had already been made, if our fully prepped and anesthetized patient was any indication. Recognizing me to be "new to the routine" there, the anesthetist on the other side of the drapes attempted to assuage my anxiety with a hint of resignation in his voice: "'TIA,' Brother"—as in "This is Africa." Presumably that was all the license required to proceed with what I sensed would be a disaster.

And so it proved to be. The overwhelming amount of tissue remaining in the sac was dead brain, in keeping with the few pictures I had studied during my rotation in neuropathology. To be more precise, those had been *autopsy* photographs—for no anencephalic (i.e. an infant born without a functioning brain) ever survived. *What in the world am I doing here?* I mused while suctioning away the formless mass, all the while anticipating the other shoe to drop and the baby to go into cardio-respiratory arrest. At length, however, a small remnant of seemingly viable tissue was separated from the rest and gently pushed back through the skull defect to complete the closure.

Having never lost a patient in the operating room, I was not about to do so now on my first case as a neurosurgeon in Africa. Managing to get the patient off the table and into the recovery room, however, proved to be small consolation for my own trial by fire. The infant died some two hours later. The angst I had felt during the operation now turned to anger. Why would God thrust me into such an untenable situation immediately following my arrival? Was this a harbinger of other failures to come? What factors prompted such a foolhardy undertaking, to which I had been an unwilling accomplice in this poor child's death? I wanted answers—and at the risk of fracturing a heretofore unestablished relationship with my new colleagues—I rushed out to confront Dr. Bransford.

Only then did God's merciful hand in what had transpired become apparent. It seems this unwed mother had been banished from her tribal village for having given birth to a "monster." Myself being altogether unaware of cultural taboos among the Maasai from which she came, Dick gave me a crash course in their beliefs. Such a birth was considered an evil omen for the fortunes of the entire community, he explained, a judgment passed on one or more tribal members who must have angered Enkai, their austere if ineffable god. That's why mother and child had been sent away—to protect the village from his future vengeance posed by this ominous threat.

To Dick's way of thinking (wisdom gained from some thirty years of self-less service to children from every conceivable culture within eastern Africa's melting pot), she had probably been forced into her unprepared role as a woe-fully "premature" mother. For her to have any chance of going home again—and perhaps one day having another child of her own under more acceptable circumstances—she could not have returned to the village with anything less than a perfect baby. Or no baby at all. As physicians, we could not deliver on the first. The second, for lack of a better alternative, was preordained.

What had taken place to cover our own failure was Jesus' signature prescription for the young girl's future welfare. It was not for us to rewrite that; only He is sovereign. We had done what we could within our own sphere of influence and limited skills, which by any other standard but the Lord's were sadly inadequate. Yet the mother's hand had long since been dealt a genetic mismatch that offered no future for an anencephalic in Africa. Lacking a social safety net such as we benefit from in more advanced societies, God had provided one for her in His own inscrutable way—thereby freeing this child from Enkai's curse—to drop back into her tribe in the Lord's embrace, and with His blessing.

So there you have it: "TIA," with all the trials and tribulations it implies for Africa's people, fully fifty percent of whom are under age fifteen. Yet the Christ-light cuts a wide swath across even the darkest of continents. Like modern-day Israelites being led through the desert, the meek who follow its lead there at least have *His* assurance they will continue to receive their entitlement to what family, village, and, yes, thin slices of real estate they possess as their sole sustenance. For the overwhelming majority, they will "make do" with that until their eternal inheritance, the Promised Land, comes due. As for the girl, she left the next morning for the only world she knew—her village and family—with nothing but a smile on her face and God's provision for the future. For her inheritance, and His purpose, that would suffice.

∞

"Submissive," "spineless," and "spiritless" are all synonymous for Webster's definition of the word "meek." Prior to 1975, "subsistent" (i.e. barely able to support life) fit just as well for a small town nestled in the highlands of western Guatemala. If ever there had been a people confined to such an existence on barren earth up until that year—only to be subsequently filled with the "fruit of the Spirit" so literally—it was the farm families of Almolonga. Theirs is an amazing testimony to which we as missionaries arriving "after the fact" were given the privilege of witnessing firsthand.

As often happens in medical missions work, their story (and ours) began with a reversal of fortunes. Just another case of God opening a door—and man, through his own ineptitude or cynicism, closing it as quickly. That's how our team ended up in Guatemala rather than Cuba. Nothing more than a tactical blunder, to be sure. Having had the good fortune of being invited to Cuba to pave the way for a much larger mission there later in the year, we inadvertently slammed the door on that opportunity by sending all of our medical supplies in advance of the team. That played right into Fidel Castro's hand. Possession being "nine-tenths" of *his* law—and now able to eschew the Christian message that was supposed to be the price paid for our admission—the Ministry of Health simply "disinvited" us two weeks before we were to embark.

It was a devastating blow. Being "all dressed up with nowhere to go," an alternative mission trip was hastily arranged for the team members who had already scheduled valuable time away from their work. Through the Lord's grace and networking skills alone, we managed to link up with a church in Quezaltenango, Guatemala, and arrived there late on a Saturday.

Now, as a "Type A" surgical personality, I've always chaffed at such downtimes before beginning work—which in this instance would be the following Monday. How, then, to spend Sunday? That brings me to Almolonga, one of three locales in the world featured in an inspirational video entitled *Transformation*. As a profoundly convincing witnesses to those blessings the Lord bestows on the meek who hunger for righteousness, theirs was a reversal of fortunes with eternal ramifications. For none has been so richly and visibly blessed as this farm village of some ten thousand inhabitants, situated, providentially, just ten miles from where we were staying.

More out of curiosity than anything, our team elected to spend Sunday there after watching the DVD. Having viewed secondhand such irrefutable evidence of the Lord's abiding presence in Almolonga, I was more than curious; "rabid" would be an apt description! Might that not afford me a huge measure of the affirmation I had been seeking all along, as one still caught up in a Christian walk guided as much by sight as by faith? No doubt. Yet we were all to receive affirmation in spades before the day was out—not to mention something far more important that accounted for the astounding success of our brief mission there.

I'm speaking of the privilege of being anointed by a true man of God, who prepared us spiritually for our appointed task. To understand that requires acquainting the reader with what had happened in this heretofore nondescript community. It all began some thirty-five years ago when an unemployed Mayan's life was changed forever and, by extension, the town where he had spent a lifetime. Out of the blue God spoke to him one day, bemoaning the idolatry that gripped Almolonga, where alcoholism was rampant, the jails were full, and the men refused to work. What few crops they planted were left to rot in the stagnant environs that resembled a modern-day Sodom and Gomorrah. God had taken their perfidy to heart. That's why He commanded this most unlikely disciple to pray and fast for a revival in Almolonga, a community split between pagan Mayans, who literally paid homage to a wooden cowboy, and Catholics, who worshipped icons in the local cathedrals by day and then staggered off as night fell to resume drinking in one of the town's thirty bars and saloons.

Night and day for months thereafter the young man fasted and prayed alone on the hillside overlooking his hometown: "In the name of Jesus, take this demon possession of idol worship out of them!" At length he received enough affirmation to brave returning to the town center, where (through no power of his own) three miracles occurred in quick succession and literally transformed Almolonga overnight. The first was his exorcism of a demon from the town's certified "crazy man" in full view of neighbors who had mocked both of them for years. The second was the healing of a paralytic simply by invoking the name of Jesus. The third was a miracle of Lazarus-like proportions: a woman brought back to life, who had been certified to have been dead as a result of gangrene after a botched Caesarian section. What made these miracles so compelling (shades of the empty tomb!) is that all three are *alive and well* today and members of the huge Christian church this chosen man of God now pastors.

That, however, is just a small part of the story. Overnight, a revival began that united all churches—Catholic, Prostestant and pagan alike—under the banner of Jesus Christ. The town was transformed. Alcohol disappeared; bars (and jails!) closed; men returned to the fields. On account of that, the fruits of the Lord's harvest became a wonder for all to see. Before, three or four trucks of produce a month had made the trip to market in Guatemala City, some four hours away. Now, more than *fifty* truckloads per *day* leave this bustling township, filled with vegetables whose size and quality defy scientific explanation: carrots and radishes two feet long; cabbages larger than basket-balls and so heavy both arms must be wrapped around one just to be able to carry it!

More convincing still, these crops are grown on some of the most diffi-cult terrain imaginable, with steep slopes that make farming tenuous at best—and where neighboring villages that have not experienced a revival in Jesus' name continue to eke out little more than a modicum of existence. For, you see, the town of Almolonga alone is Christian to the core. And not just nom-inally so; church services throughout the week are packed with believers. Indeed, the entire life of the community is built around them.

That Sunday we attended three separate services at different times and locations during the late afternoon and early evening. The third church is where we met the chosen man of God who, as Jesus' instrument, had been "responsible" for it all well over a quarter century ago. What struck me about this divine healer was that there was nothing noteworthy or appealing about him. If anything, he was decidedly *uncharismatic*. On that basis alone I remained skeptical of his alleged powers—that is, until the time came for him to confer the Lord's blessing through intercessory prayer on the team's upcom-ing mission.

One by one, a power outside this man dropped my friends in our prayer circle to the floor at the touch of his anointing hand. Intuitively sensing my own skepticism, he passed me by time and again as he ministered to the other members of the team, now littering the floor like so many limp rags. I don't mind admitting that this whole exercise was something I both disbelieved and actively resisted—until, like the others, I found myself unaccountably dropped to the ground by the mere touch of his hand on my forehead. One of the members of the team described in her own inimitable fashion what happened on that Sunday: "Well, I guess we all went 'church hoppin' until everyone finally got drunk on the Holy Spirit!"

Never had I been privileged to witnesses the fruit of that Spirit so literally as was apparent in Almolonga. That carried over to the entire mission for the remainder of the week. What had transformed this erstwhile farming community steeped in idolatry and alcohol simply has no other explanation than the Good Shepherd's involvement. And I, the greatest skeptic of all, had been empowered by His touch through a man of God who himself had been chosen against his will. Rather than chaffing under the boredom of a "down" day before we began work, the Lord had led us through an intense afternoon and evening of spiritual preparedness, the likes of which none of us had ever conceived—much less partaken of—before ministering to the poor in His name.

The end result was a clinic experience that set records for Operation Blessing, which by numbers alone will probably never be surpassed. In just five days, nine doctors both treated and ministered to over 3,500 patients! Surgically, I witnessed results that defied the odds in such a primitive setting: an all-but-blind young man with cysticercosis of the brain (a tapeworm infestation) that I shunted, who inexplicably regained his vision; a woman with a perversely recurring brain tumor that had been operated on unsuccessfully on four separate occasions, who finally had it completely removed; and an anesthesiologist at the local hospital (and a classical guitarist by avocation), who was left without any discernible deficits in his dominant hand after having a treacherous nerve-sheath tumor resected from the brachial plexus without benefit of an operating microscope. None of this could have been possible without the Lord's abiding presence there and our intense spiritual preparation the weekend before.

Far more important, over half of the patients we treated in the clinic gave their lives to Jesus in the process of having their physical needs met. The latter were little more than discarded leftovers compared to the table of plenty the Lord had prepared. For God knew that each in his or her humble way hungered for a righteousness only the Bread of Life could satisfy. Just as King David had discovered in a far different place and time, it was the *seeking* that made all the difference—as in "seeking after God's own heart." Whereas the caregivers had their way prepared by seeking out the Lord's proven disciples among His own people, the care-receivers were simply seeking to be filled. And for those with empty yet open hearts, the Divine Physician never disappointed.

Nothing underscored this more than the testimony one of our team physicians from Mexico gave to the group the night before we left. By everyone's admission, Dr. Ariel was the most diligent of the physicians there. He had spent an inordinate amount of time the first three days painstakingly examining each patient and giving them the best medicine we had to offer. By his *own* admission, however, he was perplexed by the fact that when he would emerge from his cubicle to call for the next patient many of those waiting said they preferred to see one of the other doctors.

His curiosity aroused, our friend peeked into the other cubicles to see what his colleagues had to offer that, by word of mouth among those waiting in line outside, captivated them so. What Ariel saw were doctors and nurses huddled with their patients in prayer. As he so humbly put it: "They didn't want the medicine I had to offer; they were hungry for the Lord's medicine. Why else would they have come?"

"Blessed are the meek, for they will inherit the earth." That was Jesus' unmerited gift for doctors and farmers alike during this brief but bountiful harvest the Lord had arranged in Guatemala—despite man having closed the gate to what was thought to have been a missed field of labor for Him elsewhere.

They Will Be Filled

If darkness cannot abide the Christ-light in the heart of Guatemala, His remittent flame smolders halfway around the world in the hearts of the Vietnamese. To be sure, it must first be ignited—and that only in the safety of private conversation. Take, for example, Bao, the son of my dear friend, Dr. Le Gnoc Dzung, both of whom I first met and began working with in 2001. Bao is a junior faculty member in the neurosurgery department at Da Nang Hospital, which his father had chaired for some twenty years following the Vietnam War. He epitomizes the youth of his country who, quite unlike their counterparts in Almolonga, know a great deal more about the world than do their elders.

What sets Bao apart from his own generation, however, is that he *questions* everything. As a gifted pianist, nothing exemplifies that more than the melodies he prefers to play, his favorite being Sinatra's signature tune "I Did It My Way." Always open to new ideas, the only resistance Bao harbors to accepting Jesus is that his mother is a staunch Buddhist. Or so I surmise to be the problem, as his father had once been a practicing Catholic before the Christ-light went out for the moment in 1975 and darkness descended on the country.

Yet, here and there, I've been able to kindle a spark in Bao. Like the time he asserted with the self-assuredness that typifies most opinions offered at that impressionable age: "The Christians I've come in contact with behave as if they're *better* than others who don't share their views." To which I replied, "Bao, being Christians doesn't make us better than anyone else; it just makes *me* better than I once was." That hallowed precept obviously resonated with one whom, by his own admission, was "always on the make." Yet to recast the "making" in such a unique *light* was something he had never before considered.

One thing Bao and a few of his colleagues never questioned after my first mission trip there, paradoxically, was the value of prayer. Ever since I first started working in Da Nang, I've always made a point of praying with my patients. Those who go to surgery also receive a second prayer once asleep and before we make the incision. Perhaps you think the staff never notices something so "trite" as inviting Jesus into the operating room with you, or that your prayers have no impact on those who as yet haven't felt comfortable enough to practice it openly themselves? Well, excuse my impudence—but think again!

That's what I was compelled to do on one memorable occasion when I found myself in the middle of a neurosurgeon's greatest nightmare: being unable to locate a tumor lurking beneath the brain's surface. In the typical American hospital today, such a problem has been rendered moot by computerized neuronavigation that allows us to localize the smallest lesion deep within the brain. Yet no such expensive technology exists in developing countries. All one can rely upon are imprecise coordinates determined visually during the surgery, assisted on occasion by the threatened-to-be lost art of palpating the surface to detect differing tissue consistencies or, failing that, the searching probe of a blunt-tipped needle.

"Thinking again" was something I had to be reminded of during this threatening-to-consume trial by fire. My Vietnamese assistant, Dr. Choung, respectfully made clear that I had neglected one critical step in the procedure. "You didn't take the time to pray today like you always do," he whispered to me so as to save face for his professor in the eyes (and ears) of others in the room. "You've shown us so many times that prayer is very important. I remember the last occasion we operated together some two years ago," his voice now nearly inaudible as we stared at the swollen, unforgiving brain. "You took my hand, prayed over the patient, and everything was then okay. That patient did very well—as all of yours have done who had the benefit of prayer."

So there was my lamb, prodding the shepherd with his own staff concerning the merits of "hungering and thirsting for righteousness" in all things—operations included. Make no mistake, Choung is hardly a professed Christian. Yet he could not help at that moment "to speak of what he had seen and heard" before. And in that sense, he had been *filled*. Chastened by his reminder (and my oversight!), we halted the case for some much-needed intercessory prayer.

Well and good…Yet I still had a formidable problem on my hands, above and beyond my failure as a shepherd directing his sheep along the narrow path. Hopefully I was not about to duplicate that as a surgeon. My obvious frustration was an inauspicious start—until the Holy Spirit whom we had just invited into our midst came to my rescue with a Godsend of an idea. "Do you happen to have an ultrasound machine?" He prompted me to ask. "Perhaps we can locate the tumor that way."

Choung shrugged his shoulders and replied they had never done that before—but, on the strength of the prayer we had just uttered for guidance and discernment, thought it worth a try. He broke scrub and scurried down to the OB-GYN floor to commandeer a decrepit ultrasound machine gathering dust. Wrapping a sterile glove around its unwieldy probe ("hardly suitable for delicate brain surgery," I remember grousing), we immediately located the tumor and "delivered" it safely. At the end of the case, my would-be disciple deferentially bowed to me, and with a knowing smile then said in a resolute voice, "Jesus is very happy that we depended on Him!"

Shortly thereafter we ended the day by partaking in a celebratory meal with the hospital staff. Not on account of the Lord's surgical success; rather, this was the Tet holiday, Vietnam's equivalent of ushering in the New Year. Ancestor worship remains the cornerstone of their spiritual tradition, as shrines erected to deceased loved ones in virtually every home attest. During Tet, candles are lit and incense burned to reconnect with one's predecessors, more so with their wisdom and advice for the upcoming year. Seeking such righteousness, the petitioner *will* be fed—spiritually and literally! Lush banquets in the workplace and at home are staples of this month-long celebration given in honor of deceased coworkers and family alike, whose spirits they believe are still with them. Hence the shared meal with the hospital staff that afternoon.

While gulping down another soy-soaked dumpling, I happened to belch up one of my socially suspect musings: Perhaps this traditional fete was one of those divine appointments during which He expected me to witnesses *en masse* about breaking the Bread of Life. Why not run that one up the flagpole and see who salutes? Inquiring as to the purpose of this gastronomic largesse in a country of such limited means, I was startled to learn that these banquets were intended to "speed up the reincarnation of those who have passed on."

Praise the Lord and pass the mustard! Here was a door thrown wide open by the Lord of Hosts in advance. What a unique opportunity to contrast ("with gentleness and respect")[1] the Buddhist concept of reincarnation with the *reality* of Christ's resurrection—and with that, His promise of reunification of body and soul every believer will experience at the end of the age. Or so I phrased the Good News. Though the collective giggles and nervous glances at first seemed to suggest a rejection of what I had said—if not a cultural *faux pas* of the first "rank" (as in *bad taste*)—two members of the staff later sought me out individually to inquire about this "interesting philosophy."

"Blessed are those who hunger and thirst for righteousness, for they *will* be filled." That was the intended upside of my impromptu sermonette. Yet the downside of perhaps having taken a cultural misstep in the process is all too familiar to me, predisposed as I am to foot-in-mouth disease. Particularly so when it comes to "thirst"—if not always in search of more righteousness, at least for sake of mere protocol.

As regards the latter, I recall one comical gaffe during yet another of those interminable Tet banquets (this one outside the hospital) when I was asked by our host what I would like to drink. Now, missionary or not, it is a cultural slight of the gravest sort to refuse an alcoholic beverage. The Vietnamese (like the Chinese) relish their booze when celebrating, and to stand apart from the revelry is deemed an affront to all. Plus, there's the added benefit of loosening a few of one's inhibitions once the staple of partying among the Vietnamese—karaoke—consumes the crowd, as it inevitably does.

Which brings me to my libation of choice, resurrected from my former life as a party animal in the guise of an earnest medical student during the late 60s and early 70s, when the Vietnam War was in full swing. To commemorate that bygone era (and lifestyle) I dredged up my old standby, the hallowed "John Collins"—a heady concoction of bourbon, Collins mix, and a dash of egg white to enhance the drink's signature foamy consistency. So, turning to the waitress hovering over my shoulder (and with strains of the Doors' classic "Light My Fire" blaring in the background to mark the occasion), I ordered my drink.

Whereupon she wagged a gnarled finger at me and sternly replied, "No, GI Joe; chicon sic en foo." Or so I interpreted phonetically the guttural reprimand I had just received. Not wishing to resurrect images of the "Ugly American" for this mama-san who had obviously borne her share of intemperate soldiers, I opted for my best Hugh Grant imitation from *Notting Hill*: "Uh, right!" and proceeded to order the next best thing, a "Tahitian Mama." It was left for my dear friend (and earnest karaoke partner), Dr. Le, to connect the grunts and make the necessary translation for me. "Chicon sic en foo?" No, what she was laboring to say in her best English was "Chicken is sick with the flu"—an obvious reference to the bird flu ravaging Southeast Asia at the time. Ergo: no chicken, no egg white, *no* John Collins. End of conversation!

Still other blunders I've committed, mercifully, have had more redeeming value. For one, I'm an instinctual "hugger"—and nothing is more *inappropriate* among the Vietnamese than embracing someone, regardless of gender, family excepted. That conditioned practice, ironically enough, afforded me some much needed affirmation once I learned of my error—but not before my *fourth* visit in a five-year period.

Both the belated realization and redemption came about at a time when I was questioning the value of continuing to return to teach neurosurgery at Da Nang Hospital. After all, the Congress of Neurological Surgeons (our international body) was now sending an academic professor there once a year—someone with admittedly far more credentials than I—to give lectures in the time-honored Vietnamese tradition. On my last visit I frankly inquired of the team whether my presence was still needed.

"Oh, yes," they replied in unison. "They're just visitors; you're family. And besides," one of them went on to say, "what you teach at the bedside is far more enlightening than any lecture. We can get their kind of knowledge off the Internet, but not the wisdom from your heart. The best thing, however, is the love you bring us in the hugs we've never received before except from our families!"

So Jesus had made good on His promise, far beyond filling those who hunger for righteousness. They had also been filled with a thirst for love only He could deliver, albeit with arms only we can provide. That's what Paul was driving at in 1 Corinthians 13:1. Transposing a few words, though not surrendering the gist of his intent, aptly characterizes my own: "If I risk eschewing the cultural traditions of men, but have not love, I am only a resounding gong or a clanging cymbal." May the Lord forgive me for taking such liberties with His Word. As for but one of the many ways He will continue to express His love through me, however, I offer no apologies.

∞

This last bit of self-characterization brings me back full circle to 1993, when I'd first been summoned by the Divine Conductor from my solo improvisation, "Renaissance Man," to play third fiddle with His "Gospel Philharmonic." The reason Jesus' invitation took so long in coming was understandable; the real mystery is why I was chosen at all. Not only had my spiritual instruments to play the type of melody He required been left untuned for forty-seven years; more unforgiving still, I'd often relished striking discordant notes during my former life, despite what I smugly believed to be a virtuoso performance. "Virtuoso" as in Webster's obsolete sense of "being learned in the arts and sciences;" "performance" as in an "act" that had been pleasing to no one but myself—much less to the Lord, who stood silently in the wings waiting for the curtain to mercifully fall.

To be both precise and metaphorically consistent, that fell with a crash at 10:30 PM on March 27, 1993, when I first began dying to self and living for God while attending a Broadway musical. During the grand finale to *Les Miserables* (and appropriately so, as I was among them), Christ knocked the props from under my one-man "chamber [of horrors] orchestral suite." That Victor Hugo's masterpiece by comparison, when set to music, would have such a profound impact on my life's view this particular night should have come as no surprise; *Les Miserables* is nothing less than the retelling of a story Jesus had been orchestrating for some two thousand years. Nevertheless, a single thunderbolt from above during the duet of Jean Valjean and Fantine finally dropped me to my knees; for they had seen the face of God through nothing other than the eyes of unconditional love.

The music in tandem with the lyrics conveyed to me an awe-inspiring vision of Christ's agape *love*—not our own concept of the term, which pales in comparison. That insight invoked not only my own sense of love's labors lost at the time, but mankind's for one another through the ages. Unaccompanied by His "unchained melody," the resonance of our lyrics threatens to fall on deaf ears. That's what my friends in Vietnam had been saying in their broken English. That's how music transcends cultures. That's why, when "played" (or hugged!), His Story becomes as universal as it is compelling.

Made as we each are in God's image, to love one another unconditionally as He does is to *see* Christ. Paul was intimating as much both in his oft-recited love soliloquy of 1 Corinthians 13, and its lesser known counterpart in 2 Corinthians 4:6 ("For God…[gave] us the light of knowledge of the glory of God in the face of Christ"). These timeless truths were meant to be exercised by (and for) us all. Live those, and they *see* Him—but only if we love them in kind as His own.

Though the scales had fallen from my eyes that memorable evening in 1993—at which point the Divine Physician scrubbed His hands, put on gown and gloves, and embarked upon the time-consuming operation of remaking my head and heart—it wasn't until some six months later that I openly professed to the first and silently consented to the second. Which brings me in a circuitous fashion back to those "resounding gongs and clanging cymbals" that continue to intrude on the melody I've played both before and after my rebirth. Let me give you but one of many examples.

The profession to repent of my first life came during an interview for a feature article in our local newspaper extolling the virtues of my alleged "good works" as a neurosurgeon, during which I happened to share this heretofore private if sacred moment at the theater. Justifiably, my spiritual musings came back to haunt me. Such pretenses often do when divulged in the cynical atmosphere of an operating room, where someone had taped a copy of my interview on the surgery desk bulletin board. Appended to the margins was an equally justified sarcastic note scrawled in magic marker: "Park finds *God* on Broadway!" BONG! Knowing me as that individual did mocked the self-contradictory pretense of my own statement. CLANG!

It was an abject lesson in humility. Yet even today I remain thankful (and seek no apologies) for that in-your-face slam dunk at my expense. For in a very real sense, I knew what I professed to be true! Pretentious? Yes; especially for one who as yet had not given his head to the Lord.[2] Far more important for my future, I grasped for the first time that night the distinction between being a carer and a curer as a physician. Only Christ can bridge the gap between the two—with nothing more than unconditional love. That's what He had already given me. It would be the least I could do for His own thereafter.

June 2007: Eleven years earlier (and some three years after my Great Awakening), I had first ventured to El Salvador. As a fledgling medical missionary there, my spiritual rebirth had borne more than its fair share of both suffering and fruit. Vicarious involvement in Eric's anesthetic misadventure aboard our Flying Hospital notwithstanding, a number of other Salvadorian children experienced God's grace of healing in a far more primitive setting. At a crumbling edifice disguised as a hospital in rural Zacatecoluca, I had performed my first brain and spine operations outside the United States. And there I met Juan Alfero Rodriguez, a genteel, middle-aged neurosurgeon from San Salvador who greeted me with an affable handshake and agreed to assist me in surgery thereafter.

Far more important from Jesus' perspective, some seven hundred Salvadorians had professed salvation in Him as their Lord and Savior that week. The "soul" encounter I recall most vividly, however, was ending our final day of work by sharing a late evening meal with my new colleague in a small cantina on the way back to San Salvador. Juan came across as the most worldly of men. Consequently, he was not among the fruit of that particular harvest, despite my most enthusiastic testimony shared over tamales and a pitcher of beer my friend had ordered to celebrate the occasion—after which we hugged goodbye, fully anticipating never seeing each other again.

What I initially perceived a failure for Jesus as His witnesses was attributable in large measure to my unbridled earnestness. Having turned over my life to the Lord just a few months before, as newborn babes in Christ are prone to act, I behaved accordingly. That had nothing to do with the beer. Far from being "in my suds," I was simply "over the top" in eagerly relating to my bemused (if ever polite) friend the unspeakable joy of surrendering one's life and career to a higher calling.

No doubt my teetotaling team members who had ridden the bus back to San Salvador would have been appalled had they been privy to such a "last supper," sharing the Bread of Life with Latin America's version of the fruit of the vine! Not so for my urbane friend, who quietly drank in my new birth experience with appropriate head-nodding—if not thinly disguised befuddlement. Though nothing of what I would have deemed "concrete eternal value" came out of our conversation (seeking as I was yet another immediate convert!), in retrospect it had still been one of Jesus' altar calls on behalf of a lost soul seeking righteousness above all things. Call that "intuition," but of this much I was certain: Juan's response would have to be consummated at the Lord's appointed time, not my own.

Although we lost track of one another over the years, I remained forever grateful for the brief time the two of us had shared together, and yearned to see him again. Providentially, in 2007, the church in Kansas City that Vicki and I were attending organized a mission trip to El Salvador. Signing on with a team drawn together for the purpose of door-to-door evangelism and preaching in the public square of San Salvador, as ever I sought out some venue in which my surgical "gifts" might be utilized as well while there.

True to form, the Lord's memory proved more enduring (and His networking skills far greater) than my own. Our resident missionary family in the city just happened to be acquainted with one "Juan Alfero Rodriguez" by reputation, and reconnected us through e-mail before the trip. In all honesty I had been surprised Juan even remembered me. Not only do I have the kind of face one would forget in a crowd of two, I had suffered keen embarrassment recalling our last one-sided conversation together more than a decade removed. Equally surprising, Juan assured me he had tried to e-mail on several occasions thereafter—of which I remained unaware, thanks to one of many cyberspace glitches of my computer through the years.

Once the two of us had been "reintroduced," my friend proceeded to make meticulous preparations for the visit. I inquired in kind as to any equipment needs his surgical team might have at the indigent general hospital where he was serving as department chairman. That was a Godsend: Juan was in dire need of a headlight, and his hospital an expensive stabilizing frame for brain operations—both of which I had access to and brought along to donate.

Sad to relate, our reunion as neurosurgeons serving the poor had an inaus-picious beginning. The surgery schedule quickly ground to a halt, falling vic-tim to the bureaucratic sloth that seems to pervade such publicly "funded" institutions in the Third World. Having led the team through a technically difficult removal of a high cervical cord tumor that morning (thanks in large part to their new Mayfield operating frame), I was chagrined to learn that the salaried government anesthesiologist had found an excuse to postpone our second scheduled case that was to follow. And that's when things got inter-esting.…

Invoking that time-honored dictum of Central America—"If you don't have bread, then tortillas will do"—we did what Latinos do: passed the time in conversation, sharing each other's few triumphs and far more frequent tra-vails. As regards the latter, my friend confided he had been wrestling with a life-changing career choice framed as a challenge to his sense of self-worth—whether to abandon his often frustrating role serving the poor in a govern-ment hospital for the allure of fortune and fame he was rapidly acquiring in his private practice.

Recalling that I had been embroiled in the same conundrum when we first met eleven years earlier, I reminded him of the challenge that had posed for me at the time: how to reconcile what we are and do with what God *cre-ated us to be* from the beginning. For good measure, I then added scriptural references to similar choices that Abraham, Moses, and Paul had to make. To my surprise, not only had Juan become well-versed in the Bible, but those very references the Holy Spirit had conjured up resonated with my friend to a degree I found encouraging. Whereupon, our conversation took a propitious turn on the Lord's behalf.

Though we had been informed some forty-five minutes into our exchange that the operating room was now available, Juan seemed far more interested in bringing our relationship full circle. Time literally seemed to stand still as he recounted in great detail our first such talk in the cantina so long ago. With tears suddenly welling up in his eyes, he grasped my shoulder and said: "You'll never know what that evening we shared together meant to me." Which, he then went on to explain, accounted for his turning to Bible study as a response to something I long ago forgot I had told him: "Don't concentrate on the work you do, but on the Word that calls you to do it." Juan

then concluded with a profession of affirmation he had received by my returning to El Salvador, describing that morning as a "divine reconnection."

And so it was. Gently taking me by the hand in the middle of a walkway
at the heart of a bustling metropolitan hospital, this heretofore austere chairman of the Department of Neurosurgery—paying no heed to the quizzical
stares of passersby in white coats—looked resolutely into my eyes and said, "I
want what *you* have through Christ." Scarcely able to restrain my own emotions, I blurted out the first thought that came to mind, Romans 10:9—
prompted, as ever, by the Holy Spirit Himself: "… if you confess with your
mouth, 'Jesus is Lord,' and believe in your heart that God raised Him from
the dead, you will be saved."

"Juan, it's really that simple," I concluded, but then added a caveat: "To
make such a profession entails a life's change that begins with sincere repentance. Christians refer to this as the 'sinner's prayer.'" With that, one very contrite sheep clothed in surgeon's garb fell on his knees and pleaded, "May I
pray that with you?" And he did—in full view of more than a few startled colleagues, who paused with rapt attention to witnesses a spectacle the likes of
which had probably never occurred in such a sterile (if career-threatening)
setting.

As one measure of the impact such a profession of faith might have on
others, coming as it had from someone so influential within his professional
community, fast forward to the following evening when I had been scheduled
to speak to the El Salvadorian Association of Neurological Surgeons. Somehow Juan had managed to pander, cajole, or perhaps even *bribe* (if the quality of the steaks served were any indication) every member to attend on their
valuable evening off call. A command performance? You bet—though my
presentation added nothing to the occasion.

Rather, it was Juan's introductory remarks that such a well-heeled assem-
blage needed to hear. And they did—stealing my tepid thunder in the process.
Gesturing toward me, he began by saying, "I have in my heart tonight such
a huge sense of *release*! That I owe not so much to 'John the Baptist in the flesh'
seated here beside me, but to our Lord Jesus Christ, who willingly gave His
life for each of us in our place." Knowing Juan as they did, that salutation
was met with stunned silence—and then scattered applause from the back of

the room, which built to a crescendo as everyone rose to celebrate the chairman's new birth.

What remarks I made thereafter I scarcely recall. Nor, I wager, does anyone else. Those would have been superfluous. God's Word—the Good News—had already been spoken.

Apart from allowing for at least three visits per year to Tenwek Hospital in Kenya as the prospective site director for our East Africa neurosurgical residency training program, I've probably made more visits to Nicaragua than any other country. Not because the neurosurgical needs of Managua's poor at the Lenin Fonseca Hospital are so overwhelming (invariably, they are); not on account of the huge numbers of operations done (sadly, they don't); not that a thirst for learning among the staff is so acute (thankfully, it is)—but simply because I repeatedly find myself being "recalled" (like Peter) as a disciple to share the Gospel.

No doubt Jesus' preoccupation with seeking out the spiritually lost of Israel was forever being interrupted to address the physical needs of those he encountered along the way. In like manner, when making rounds on my first day back in Managua, I'm always faced with a whole host of difficult cases that require urgent treatment. Yet the numbing bureaucracy this particular government hospital labors under never fails to frustrate my best humanitarian instincts. It all boils down, sadly but predictably, to human nature—both theirs and mine.

"Why go the extra mile," its salaried anesthetists and OR personnel rationalize, "to see that those cases needing to be done *do* get done, when there's no such thing as overtime pay?" Just because some visiting professor has come doesn't make their particular workday any different than another. That sort of mindset runs counter to my own inbred nature as a "can-do" surgeon (if not, perhaps, my fragile ego!)—until Jesus invariably reorients me to *His* call, not my own. First and foremost, I've been called as a fisher of men for Him, not just as a surgeon for them. Whether tending a net (or "mending" a brain), lending an ear to the lost—and then befriending them—is what a genuine disciple of Jesus does. Like His first followers, alas, I am a slow learner.

Let me cite but one memorable example.

At the beginning of our third operating day, a comatose patient with a life-threatening brain hemorrhage happened to have "an accident" on his gurney just before being placed on the operating table. Such stool contamination was deemed reason enough for someone—anyone—to shut down the room, send the patient back to the ward, and put the remainder of the surgical schedule on interminable hold—at which point the entire OR crew then broke for lunch!

It being just 10:45 in the morning, I resorted to what I often do best when encountering such passive-aggressive behavior: not shouting, but quietly sulking. Perhaps sensing that my frustration had become too obvious, at that very moment one of the neurosurgery residents by the name of Carolina asked if she might speak with me in private outside the room. I was about to apologize to her for having to make amends for my own impatience (and others' sloth!) when she revealed what was really on her mind.

"Yesterday, you were kind enough to give us a different sort of lecture apart from neurosurgery," she began. "Something about the role of grace and prayer in a Christian's life. And that's my problem," Carolina tearfully confessed. "Right now, I'm really struggling with prayer, because I'm haunted by feelings of unworthiness. The priest says I should never approach God without him to intercede for me, and I'm beginning to think he's right. Because every time I try to pray when I'm alone I become afraid. I feel a presence of something cold in the room, something forbidding—as if my attempt to pray is making this thing beside me angry. Is it real? Why do I feel this way? And how can you speak of having a 'personal relationship' with Jesus," she concluded, "when the church says a priest must do the speaking for me?"

Could there have been a more compelling example of God's grace for us both than this open-ended invitation to witnesses on the heels of such a painful confession? There I stood, so wrapped up in my own agenda, so awash in self-pity—so *misdirected* that Jesus had sent a lamb to rescue the shepherd from himself! Having been summarily stripped of my breastplate of [self-] righteousness (for I was certainly no priest to whom she "owed" a confession), the Lord had anticipated this very moment by immersing me in the book of Hebrews the evening before to cull out a few memory verses for that week. As a consequence, rarely if ever had He armed me so well with "the sword of the Spirit"[3] to address Carolina's specific concerns.

To begin with, it was apparent to me she was engaged in genuine spiritual warfare. Her description of the "cold presence" she felt was as close to an encounter with the demonic as I had ever heard. Only the Holy Spirit could combat that, which He did with Scripture, assuring Carolina she *already had* a High Priest—One who supersedes all others and serves in the only sanctuary built by God, not man, in Heaven. For Jesus alone had ascended there to sit at the Father's right hand, specifically to intercede for her and all His children.

That led us to His second point. Since she was "now surrounded by such a great cloud of witnesses" (i.e. several new brothers in Christ within her own department, apart from myself), the time had come for her to "throw off everything [manmade] that hinders…and fix [her] eyes solely on Jesus, the author and perfecter of [her] faith." It logically followed that since Carolina had such "a high priest who [alone] has gone through the Heavens,…let [her] hold firmly to the faith [she now must] profess." Only then could she approach the very throne of grace of which I had spoken the day before with confidence, rather than some manmade confessional booth with guilt (Hebrews 12:1–2; 4:14, 16).

Having been raised in the Catholic tradition, this last benediction of sorts struck home. Carolina finally found the strength in the Lord's Word to surrender herself to Him—which she did at that very moment just outside the operating room while reciting the sinner's prayer. Once again Jesus had brought me face to face with the irresistible power of the Holy Spirit—and an answer to this soldier's prayer at the beginning of every day to be vested in the armor of God with the sword of His Word in hand.

Others, like the chairman of her department, had taken more measured and cautious steps to salvation. In that sense, Dagle Daviles and myself are kindred spirits—both of us question anything that smacks of dogmatism. From the very first time we met, he was forever weighing the merits of what his priest had been "requiring" of him versus what the Bible made explicitly clear. And for this thoughtful seeker, there was simply no reconciling the two.

The end result of this quest eventually brought us together in nightly Bible studies. Long after I would depart for home, moreover, Dagle continued to e-mail me with old questions and new revelations from his ongoing search of Scripture. Despite my obvious shortcomings as a human being, the Lord had prepared me for these encounters with a thirst for teaching His Word. By His grace, to this particular sheep of His pasture I had become something of a shepherd—and nothing has filled Dagle and I with more joy than seeing him grow in knowledge and faith through the last six years. One of our favorite shared verses, from Romans 1:11–12, depicts best of all the relationship we share with Christ as our mediator: "I long to see you so that I may impart to you some spiritual gift to make you strong—that is, that you and I may be mutually encouraged by each other's faith."

This relationship has borne more fruit than I could ever have fathomed. If one definition of a successful ministry is transferring the spiritual gift of teaching the Word to another (such that he in turn becomes a teacher to his own people), then Dagle Daviles has fulfilled that role to the letter. Not only has he brought his best friend and neurosurgical colleague, Harvey Sosa, to the Lord; Dagle now insists on group Bible study being an obligate part of every visit I make to Managua.

Our last such gathering was by far my most memorable. Having shared a late supper in a local restaurant, prior to my 6:00 AM departure the next morning, the lighthearted revelry of the evening (band and beer included) rendered our planned Bible study to follow an indiscretion sadly lacking in decorum. Or so it seemed to me, and I alerted Dagle to my concerns.

Yet my friend and disciple was not to be denied. A take-charge sort of fellow, he sought out the restaurant owner for some privacy—whereupon we were ushered upstairs, Bibles in hand, and feasted on the Good News until the wee hours of the morning. The irony of our impromptu devotional was not lost to either of us–closing the joint down over beer and the Beatitudes in Christ's Upper Room!

Would Jesus, Himself accused at one point in Matthew of being "a glutton and a drunkard," have objected? I think not; if anything, Dagle's wisdom was proven right by his actions. The lamb had taught his shepherd what it means to seize the moment. And that one was sacred.

They Will Be Shown Mercy

If one theme typified my experience in Siberia, it's that things in this dark recess of the former Soviet Union are never quite as bleak as they seem. Or might have been, for that matter. Jesus had a great deal to do with both while we were there—as shown by His unanticipated healing of the elderly stroke victim shortly after our arrival in Bratsk. That I had arrived there *at all* was something of a miracle in itself, attributable only to the mercy Jesus extends to the merciful as promised in His fifth beatitude. Presumably He makes allowances on occasion for the foolish as well; for the very night we were to leave Krasnoyarsk for Bratsk, I managed to fulfill both criteria by misplacing my passport!

That was no small matter in the eyes of the Russian authorities. One of our other team members had already been detained for entering the country with an expired passport. He spent the next three days in the Moscow airport waiting for the American embassy to free him from house arrest. The sobering realization that the Gulag had once been but a stone's throw away now added a touch of drama to my own predicament. More unnerving still, I'd drawn the short straw and "volunteered" to ride on a chartered Russian cargo plane with three others who, like myself, had been asked to stay behind in Krasnoyarsk to deal with some political fallout that had arisen there in the press. We were scheduled to leave in an hour, at which time my lost passport was certain to be of interest to the priggish airport security.

Enter the merciful, stage "righteous," whose spiritual ministrations to

me kept the focus on God's door so as to prevent other men from closing it. For that, in a very real and frightening sense, now applied to the
heavily guarded doorway separating me from the cargo plane sitting on
the tarmac outside. That's when Jesus and my three brothers came to the
rescue.

Embracing me in a prayer circle with laying on of hands, they anointed
my forehead with oil. Such a gesture seemed little more than some pious
ritual to me—until our time came to board the cargo plane. Inexplicably,
my passport (or lack of same) was not checked as I went through the security gate! It was like Paul and Silas finding their jail cell mercifully open
after spending all evening in prayer and praise, and simply walking to freedom, bringing their jailer to Christ in the process.[1] The last, sad to relate,
I did not take the liberty of doing. Not that this made the open tarmac
before me any less of an escape to the "Promised Land."

As so often happens after experiencing such a spiritual high, I should
have steeled myself to go back down into the valley. Nothing had prepared
me for the journey I was about to take on a rickety cargo plane piloted by
two less-than-sober Russians, who just happened to have a stash of vodka
in the cockpit. That I was being taken up in the air and not down in the
valley offered no more comfort than the "seating" arrangements, relegated
as we were to the tail section jam-packed with medical supplies. The plane
cabin was not only unpressurized, it also had no heat. Nor did we have
any way of orienting ourselves during the takeoff, there being no windows
in the tail. With ears exploding, the four of us sprawled out on our Action
Packers enshrouded in nylon webbing like hapless flies caught up in a spi-
der's web, acutely attuned to any changes in the engine's vibration that
might herald impending disaster.

For two interminable hours we clung to the netting with hands
numbed by the bitter cold, enduring the roar of the deafening engines and
the stench of diesel fuel filling the air. More prayers were said during what
we perceived as an "ascent" into hell than during the rest of the mission
combined. I sensed how a drug smuggler must feel—wedged between
cargo boxes, his heart in his throat, and his passport in absentia. Yet, God
had plans for us in Bratsk, and we lived to tell the tale.[2]

∞

As one other measure of His mercy shown the merciful, our arrival there coincided with a huge neurosurgical triumph on the Lord's behalf—something He made possible by compelling me to take some specialized spinal instrumentation along. Though I originally intended to use this equipment for teaching purposes, Jesus had a more important demonstration in mind. That began to unfold during our first day on rounds in the Bratsk hospital, when I was asked to consult on a middle-aged lady who had suffered a severe fracture-dislocation of her cervical spine with resultant quadriplegia. She had been bedridden for three months, waiting to die of pneumonia or a pulmonary embolism the majority of such patients eventually suffer. Her MRI revealed one of the most devastating injuries I recall ever seeing: the sixth vertebra had been so dislodged it sat in *front* of the seventh, with no remaining canal left through which the spinal cord could pass.

The woman's diagnosis was in keeping with my perception that things are never quite what they seem in Siberia. It had probably been weeks since anyone had done a neurological examination on this all-but-abandoned soul. What I found on my own was a huge surprise: she had some retained sensation in her left foot and was able to detect applied pressure to both legs. Though unable to move any of her extremities voluntarily, these meager findings at least indicated some neurologic function inexplicably remained. Not wishing to embarrass my Russian colleagues with these "new" findings, I reviewed the MRI scan on my own after rounds. A single view suggested that, just perhaps, the spinal cord was not transected after all.

Insofar as her dislocated vertebrae had already fused, that seemed but small consolation. The problem being, her doctors had been unable to mobilize this poor lady into so much as a wheelchair because of the intense pain engendered by such a grotesque deformity. If for no other possible gain than to get her out of bed and perhaps forestall the inevitable, I volunteered to operate in hopes of somehow reducing the fracture and stabilizing it with the titanium plate and screws the Lord had thrown into my bag at the last moment. The truth of the matter was, without an operating microscope, a power drill, or even traction to reduce the dislocation,

that would be a formidable and (at least by traditional neurosurgical standards) foolish undertaking.

Yet not by God's! He will always make a way if that fits into His plans.
Despite the overwhelming odds against even completing the operation,
He led me safely through it in full view of a host of skeptical Russian nurses
and doctors literally looking over my shoulder. At the close of the procedure we had a nice-looking x-ray, with a realigned spine secured by the
only plate I had brought, which *just happened* to have been the precise size
required! Another one of those amazing coincidences, I'm sure…

Such a *minor* manifestation of His mercy to me hardly compared with
what the Lord had in store for everyone the following morning. Inquiring
on rounds as to how our patient was feeling, she broke into a huge, toothless grin and gave me "two thumbs up" (literally) with hands that had been
lifeless the day before, then proceeded to raise both her legs off the bed!
Here, but for the grace of God, was an otherwise totally inexplicable reversal of fortune in the face of cataclysmic adversity—in, of all places, Siberia.
She would walk again!

I fell on my knees in thanksgiving, numbly reciting over and over the
one verse that seemed so applicable for the moment: "Blessed are the merciful, for they will be shown mercy." Through no merit of our own, Jesus had
bequeathed this blessing to servant and sufferer alike. What had seemed a
fruitless undertaking on my part, He had orchestrated. As for our patient, the
Lord had chosen through His mercy to acknowledge yet another paralytic's
suffering and answered it with the command, "Take up your mat and walk!"
Never have I been so filled with awe in the presence of His healing power
than at that moment—not to mention astounded by the timeless truth of
His Word, which the Beatitudes once again affirmed.

My Russian colleagues, of course, simply perceived this miracle as little
more than a show of Yankee ingenuity blessed with some much-needed technology they did not have. Though hardly surprised by their reaction, I knew
better. This was *His* doing, not mine. Time after time, the Lord had made it
abundantly clear to his disciples that miracles don't lead to lasting faith; rather,
faith merely affirms the miraculous.

Shortly thereafter He would remind me of that elemental truth through
the faith of the nurse who accompanied us to the apartment of the elderly

stroke victim (see "They Will Be Comforted"). Unlike the skeptical neuro-surgeon who had assisted me in this spinal operation, the nurse had not been dissuaded a miracle was in the works on that occasion without surgery. And the truth of the matter is: Both healings merely affirmed God's ability to suspend the laws of probability if it served His purpose.

Nothing prepared me, however, for how such abiding faith can still transform lives even when physical healing is not God's choice. The last night before leaving Siberia for home, I made my final house call, still reeling from the miracle I had witnessed two days before on my first homebound consultation. An articulate, well-dressed lady had come to the clinic, asking specifically for a neurosurgeon who might visit her friend. Some two years before an intruder had broken into the friend's home and slit her throat with a bowie knife, rendering her immediately paralyzed from the shoulders down. The fact that there was little I could do for either of them now as a doctor was immaterial; drawn by the pathos of this tragic story, I and three others agreed to go to her friend's apartment that evening.

Adhering to the Russian tradition of removing our shoes when entering a home, there we found our patient surrounded by three ladies plus the messenger I had met in the clinic. For the past several months each had been taking turns tending to Ludmilla's needs in shifts, twenty-four hours a day, seven days a week.

Such steadfast faith conjured up visions of the paralytic described in all three synoptic Gospels[3] who had been brought by four companions to Jesus to be healed. Finding the doorway too crowded to enter, they climbed up on the roof, cut a hole in it, and lowered their charge down to Jesus below. The parallels were so striking, I immediately opened my Bible to the fifth chapter of Luke and read the account to them through our interpreter. What bore emphasizing was Jesus' statement that it was because of the faith of the *stretcher bearers,* not the paralytic's, that their friend's sins would be forgiven and his paralysis healed.

Now, some two thousand years later, we stood face to face with four like-minded angels of mercy. That was the bridge we used to cross over into a discussion about Jesus. Proudly nodding to an icon sitting on the mantle, Ludmilla affirmed she "knew something about God," but could not worship Him unless she was able to go to church. Reflexively, I responded by picking up my guitar I had brought along and singing them a song that seemed so aptly titled for the moment: "Surely the Presence of the Lord Is in This Place." Although everyone else in the room grasped the concept, Ludmilla was still perplexed. She confessed to somehow sensing Jesus at her bedside through us, but didn't know how to communicate with Him.

Taken aback, I responded, "Well, you pray."

"I'm willing," she replied. "I know I cannot be healed, but to have my sins forgiven is more than I deserve. How, then, do you pray?"

What a Heaven-sent request, as if (once again) "prescripted!" Quickly I turned a few pages further to Luke chapter 11, where one of the disciples had asked in all earnestness, "Lord, teach us to pray." We then read together the very words with which Jesus had instructed His disciples: the Lord's Prayer. That evening four merciful stretcher bearers and a paralytic came to the Lord, each spoken to across the barriers of language through the timeless truth of His Word they had waited a lifetime to hear: "Blessed are the merciful, for they will be shown mercy."

Jesus had made all the preparations necessary for just such a moment when, as a neurosurgeon, I had nothing to bring to the table. Certainly He hadn't chosen the gifted, for none of us had gifts of our own to offer. Rather, the Lord had gifted the "chosen" with specific instructions to complete the Father's work: "Do not take a purse or bag or sandals;…When you enter a house first say 'Peace to this house.'…and tell them 'The kingdom of God is near you'" (Luke 10:4, 5, 9). That, in retrospect, is what my fumbling fingers on the guitar in His presence were meant to convey.

As we prepared to leave, I glanced over at the neatly placed row of shoes next to Ludmilla's apartment door. They spoke as one, in silent reverence; "sandals" aside, surely we were standing on hallowed ground. They had been removed for that very reason. Through us—not because of us—Jesus had made *His* way there when we could see no way forward. Yet those shoes had brought us to this very place, bringing Ludmilla with her four stretcher bearers precisely where Jesus wanted them to be. "Gifted" indeed were the feet (and shoes) that night, bearing the Good News in His presence.[4]

∞

Speaking of gifts, had not the apostle Paul made it clear that all spiritual gifts are of equal worth to the body of Christ? And insofar as he alone was responsible for two-thirds of the New Testament, it's hardly surprising that Paul's perspective (no doubt inspired by the Holy Spirit and, therefore, not to be taken lightly) constitutes the "majority opinion" in the court of Protestant doctrine. Having said that, are there grounds for an appeal? Risking blasphemy, my own read of the Gospels themselves makes me wonder whether Jesus might not value the gift of *mercy* most of all. He always seems to makes allowances for those who manifest it, despite their shortcomings otherwise.

Why do I believe that? Well, for starters, rarely has His mercy been extended to one as undeserving—and yet so often—as to myself. Were I to give the remainder of this chapter a subtitle, it would be "Mistakes I've Made." That also explains its length; Lord knows, there's no shortage of material to work with! Which, as regards Jesus' never-ending capacity to forgive, is precisely the point. Not only did He erase that subtitle from this page, it won't be found in His Book of Life. That's His promise.

Far more ennobling, few qualities better define the inherent nature of our Lord and Savior for all eternity—or consistently characterized His three-year ministry here on earth—than being merciful. While many so-called "Pauline evangelicals" today would limit legitimate spiritual gifts to those listed in Ephesians 4, Romans 12, and 1 Corinthians 12, perhaps we'd be better served to simply take the Lord's word at face value: "…wisdom is proved right by her actions" (Matthew 11:19). He alone, as the Son of God, is the personification of all wisdom. The Vine is known by His fruit. As such, Jesus' actions arguably spoke louder while alive than His words admittedly ring true beyond death—notwithstanding His resurrection, which legitimized both. The same should apply to us, regardless of what label we place on them.

Assuming my surmise regarding the gift of mercy in particular is correct (yet who am I to question the church's premier saint among ostensible equals?), at least two truths stand self-evident to me: (1) How like God to lend a merciful hand to the humble when they least expect it—or even to the proud when they scarcely deserve such an unwarranted gift; and (2) perhaps the *last* place such a "gifted" neurosurgeon should attempt something as delicate as clipping a bleeding aneurysm would be in Mongolia.

Blasphemous musings aside—and before I stand accused of being schizophrenic as well—what do these seemingly unrelated "pearls of wisdom" have in common? For those like myself ("blessed" with such hubris as to place a Mongolian sheepherder's fate in the lap of the gods), the Lord *our* God occasionally lends a dark sense of humor apart from mercy to make His point.

Like the time I insisted my Mongolian colleagues resurrect their Soviet version of an operating microscope that had not seen the light of day for more than a decade. Now, insofar as optimal lighting and enhanced visualization are deemed essential when clipping an aneurysm in the brain that's poised to rerupture, it naturally follows that the intrepid surgeon makes sure his rusty scope is in proper working order. (Sort of like kicking the tires before buying a clunker, if you catch my drift.). Which I did—albeit neglecting to ask whether they had an extra xenon bulb "just in case" the light source on their microscope blew. Which *it* did (more about that conundrum, shortly).

Such an unmitigated disaster in the middle of an operation is not unheard of, particularly when depending upon mothballed Russian technology. I had already learned this through painful experience in Siberia where not one, but two, of our operations had been interrupted by just such an occurrence. Take my word for it: donning a carbide lantern in a room full of flammable anesthetic gasses is an improvident substitute (though having been required on one occasion in Bratsk when reconstructing the cervical spine of our profoundly paralyzed patient, who subsequently recovered completely).

Better that the surgeon recognize he has an equipment failure before the operation begins—and nothing can be quite so temperamental as a hand-me-down operating microscope, let alone one that hadn't "swung into action" since the Cold War. To invoke the golfer Tiger Woods' description of a perfectly functional golf swing as metaphor: "It's tough to make it work, because there are just so many moving parts!" If you're lucky the breakdown is obvious (though, just like the golf swing, not always "fixable").

Take, for example, the forty-thousand-dollar scope we crated up in Missouri for donation to a hospital in Western Ukraine just two years before. It had miraculously survived its seven-thousand-mile odyssey by air, ship, train, and truck from the middle of the United States to the far reaches of Eastern Europe. After prying open the shipping crate, however, we were crestfallen to find our scope had a broken arm. That extension was essential for stabilizing the optics of its mount—as in "maintaining one's 'swing plane'" or simply "keeping the bloomin' head down," to extend the golfing metaphor.

Here was a bolt of lightning out of the blue that threatened the entire "round" of some eighteen cases (yes, eighteen) we had prepared for over the next two weeks. Being without a functioning scope was like heading back to the driving range to brush up on one's pre-scope, 1960s-era skills and wait out the storm, trusting your patience doesn't falter—and your patients don't suffer the consequences. To complete the metaphor, there are simply no mulligans in surgery; you have to do it right the first time. Otherwise, it's just another "good walk spoiled."

Having not even gotten into the swing of things, as it were, we each resorted to what we did best: they tinkered—and I prayed. What else could a missionary neurosurgeon, who was "all thumbs" as a mechanical engineer, do? Not so the entrepreneurial son of my Ukrainian counterpart; within twenty-four hours he had taken the broken arm to a light factory, soldered the piece together, and reinstalled it to perfect working order!

God *does* answer prayer, of that I was once again certain. Still, He pays no heed to unrepentant seventy-five-cent fuses that have minds of their own—in this instance, a tube of glass the size of a fountain pen cartridge that proceeded to "blow" the moment we turned the scope on. A replacement bulb was not the problem as it had been in Siberia; I'd learned my lesson well and had prepared for that eventuality. No matter—and no problem! Lacking a Western-made fuse, what my friends decided we needed as a substitute was a good ol' Eastern Bloc transformer.

So we set off for the town market, it being a Saturday. After rummaging through what seemed like piles of junk for an hour (interspersed with booths peddling clay pots, clothes, chickens, and whatever else Ukrainians need to survive), Mikola stumbled upon a bona-fide World War II vintage transformer! Hardly to my skepticism and surprise, our cunning purveyor of mechanical bric-a-brac (disguised as a snake-oil salesman, or so I thought) guaranteed this antique curio would suit our needs. Plopping down fifteen U.S. dollars (for what man would not sell all he had for a pearl of such inestimable value discovered in a "field of dreams"?), we rushed off to the hospital transformer in hand and, with hearts in throats, plugged it in to the scope. Voila! Let there be light! And there was…

The reward? Eighteen patients received life- and limb-saving operations, thanks to a borrowed soldering iron, a fifteen-dollar transformer—and a ton of prayer. As a poor imitation of Christ, I can only speak from personal experience; yet I can *stand* on scriptural truth. It all hinged upon a Divine Hand of mercy extended to the merciful who labored in Jesus' name and, ultimately, for His glory. Equally rewarding, such largesse from a God they did not know (but had heard so much about during my two previous visits there) was not lost on my Ukrainian friends. Apart from the many healings they had already witnessed in the past, this singular mechanical triumph not only "transformed" the scope but their minds as well. That very evening the entire family opened their hearts in kind to the Good News during the first Bible study we shared since I had ventured to Ukraine as the Lord's caddy some three years before. A "good walk bettered"—but only by following His lead, not my own.

So much for God's benevolent hand in Ukraine. But I've digressed from the nearly disastrous technological tryst I started to tell. Now I was in Mongolia some two years later. And there a reprise of divine "dark humor" beckoned (literally!) in the austere environs of a government hospital in the capital city of Ulan Bator.

Don't get me wrong; any mischievous purpose that might lurk in the mind of God would never be exercised at a patient's expense. That usually manifests itself instead when He deems it necessary to "discipline the disciple." Like that memorable occasion in Troas when Paul had been droning on for so long that Eutychus fell asleep and toppled from a third-story window, only to be mercifully revived.[5] Though some may fail to find humor in that story, I still do every time I read it. For I see myself, by His grace alone, falling asleep safely ensconced in a pew rather than precariously perched on a window sill.

Whatever the Father's method, disciplining His children is the intended (and all-too-frequent) result—much as Christ Himself had done in remonstrating His very first disciples who had neglected the use of prayer to exorcise a demonic spirit in a young boy.[6] To be sure, that archetypical demonstration of the power of prayer was given without a trace of humor. His cleansing of the temple aside, this was as close to anger as our gentle Lord ever came in Scripture. What does strike me as darkly humorous about that particular incident was the brazen dullness of some intellectually challenged disciples who should have known better.

Yet, that had been in Galilee of the Gentiles. This was Mongolia of the communists.[7] I'm thankful to relate their decrepit scope functioned admirably during the delicate dissection leading up to defusing the bomb itself. In the broad majority of cases, to be sure, the clip is then successfully applied and the aneurysm's gossamer-thin, cherry-red dome shrivels to impotence. The occasional alternative scenario, however, portends disaster: the bomb explodes in one's face and a frightened surgeon suddenly finds his operative field awash in blood that, failing a rapid and proper clip adjustment, begins to spill out of the cranial vault onto the floor.

Not that such untoward drama unfolded that day; but for the grace of God "would there have gone I"—as in to hell and back (the return trip assured only if you've been appointed to witnesses His ultimate plan unfold). No, a disaster was not in the hand of cards the Lord intended to play; rather, His bluff would suffice to gain what He really wanted: capturing our attention.

With a knowing smile, Jesus stood back and watched at that moment of truth when I applied the clip—at which point the xenon bulb that had been lighting our way suddenly blew! To add insult to injury, the overhead lights in the OR had already gone out some five minutes before, attesting to the fact that the hospital power had been on generator all along and had finally overloaded. For all intents and purposes ("intent" being His *operative* word), we were in total darkness from the moment the clip was placed.

My fingertips still grasping the applier lodged somewhere at the base of a brain I could only feel, I awaited the explosive, telltale gush of blood welling up in the field while calling for a replacement bulb. Now, it's one thing to ask for equipment under duress when the circulating nurse doesn't speak your language, quite another to frantically wave with the opposite unoccupied hand she cannot see! Not that it mattered. True to form in Mongolia, there was no other bulb to be found in the whole country, much less in its only operating room.

Critical seconds ticked away. The same could not be said for my once-beating heart. Gently I palpated the retracted recess of an invisible brain in our pitch-black field under the drapes. Mercifully, it remained dry. But had my clip been applied accurately? Was the aneurysm's neck secured? Or had an adjoining artery been kinked (perhaps even incorporated) by the spring-loaded jaws now closed? Alas! The absence of profuse bleeding notwithstanding, none of these questions could be answered by Braille.

"Bring on the light of the world," I remember praying, "or at least in this particular operating room!" An eternity later (in reality, some two minutes), the generator kicked in and the overhead lights flickered back on. That was small consolation, considering their quality. As best as could be done, I examined what little of the field we were able to see with the naked eye and—mercy upon mercies—the aneurysm had deflated.

Still, I could never be sure the surrounding vessels had been saved. That would have to await my sheepherding friend's awakening in the recovery room, at which point any vessel occlusion would have already been heralded by an obvious stroke. And by then, a revision of the clip application would probably be too late. Never mind the scope necessary to pull that one off was already dead in the water.

"Fortune smiled on us that day!" or so my Mongolian assistant would later assert once our patient awoke within fifteen minutes of the procedure and with no neurologic deficit. So we had successfully defused the bomb. But on account of "good fortune"? Hardly! For a God who alone can see the past, present, and future, He *knew* the bulb would blow—but not before gently guiding my hands to complete the necessary dissection with just a split second added to properly apply the clip. Only the presence of a far more gifted hand than my own could have orchestrated this—which provided a God-given opportunity for me to witnesses on behalf of His presence beside us that day. And for those with eyes to see, no microscope was required.

That message, I'd like to think, struck home. For the remainder of the time I spent there, my Mongolian colleagues (former communists all, who had never considered inviting any god— much less Jesus—into their operating room) kept asking me about this "amazing fellow" from Galilee. Admittedly, the only aspect of Christ's character I chose not to touch upon was His enigmatic, if rapier-sharp, sense of humor—as in *manifest to make a point*, and more than once at my own deserved expense. Though I was unable to reference it chapter and verse for them in Scripture (and still can't!), they appreciated the take-home lesson: "Whatever it takes," says the Lord, "I'll always find a way to capture your attention." Amen. Point taken!

⚭

Speaking of making a point, whether as an instructor in surgery or a disciple of the Word, at least one has withstood the test of time. If from God and for His glory, it will bear lasting fruit; if manmade and self-serving, it's just another bite from Satan's apple. On the rarest of occasions it can be a bit of both.

Like the less than dignifying occasion when I was "hell-bent" (a not inappropriate choice of words) on demonstrating to my Chinese colleagues the latest innovation for draining blood clots off the brain. Rather than drilling away a large segment of bone and reflecting the brain cover underneath to remove what's known as a subdural hematoma, the prevailing wisdom in America is to make a half-inch twist-drill opening and insert a small drain that slowly evacuates the fluid. Such a "minimally invasive" technique has the added merit of being performed under local anesthesia, with the patient awake, thereby avoiding a general anesthetic.

This presupposes, of course, a hematoma that has been there long enough to have at least partially liquefied. By all appearances, that applied to an elderly farmer who had recently taken a fall, striking his head. He was transported to the Shaanxi Provincial People's Hospital some two weeks later in a semi-comatose state with a paralyzed right arm and leg. Once his family had bundled enough yuan together to pay the hospital bill *in advance* (as all hospitals in this communist country require), a CT scan could finally be done. This revealed a large, water-density collection of fluid compressing the underlying brain far to the opposite side.

What timing! I remember thinking. *A perfect case to show off my new technique—for which I 'just happened' to have packed all the necessary equipment in my travel bag of instruments.* Was this to be another one of those "God things" revealed at just the just the right moment—a reprise of His Siberian orchestration using a cervical plate as a baton to heal a paralytic? Not in the sense He had intended. Jesus recognized my motivation for what it was: little more than tooting my own horn, as in "check out the skills of that American doctor."

A deft slight-of-hand governed by a daft brain (mine!) would prove a more apt description once we took our patient to the OR later that day. There I anesthetized a small area on the scalp and drilled a tiny hole to insert my drain. "Well done, good and faithful servant!" the Divine Physician might well have said, but didn't…He led me instead down the primrose path of self-incrimination using His best Columbo-imitation line of questioning.

"Say, good buddy, that certainly was a nifty maneuver you just performed! But there's one loose end I can't quite tie up, and wonder if you might help me out. Did the translator who took this fellow's medical history let you in on a little secret before you trotted out on stage to display your skills?"

"And what might that be?" I would warily ask, sensing a setup—but only after having already committed ourselves to the procedure just described.

"Well," he replied with a wink, "it turns out your patient is on a *blood thinner,* and that's where I need your help. Though I'm certain you were aware he was doing fine for some thirteen days after striking his head, it wasn't until this morning that he took a turn for the worse and presented to you as he did. So I must ask you, my merciful friend who has come halfway around the world to do good (and not harm): What did his *repeat* CT scan show just before you operated?"

Tah-dah….For that I would have no answer to give the Lord, who was now assuming His role as my Attending Physician. Perhaps on the basis of some nuances in translation (and I'm being merciful here—to myself!), I was unaware of this critical gap in the clinical history. Consequently I had not been prompted to order a second scan following the precipitate change in my patient's condition. That permitted a gleeful Satan into the operating room, apple in hand—a huge chunk of which I would consume in short order.

Were this America and not China, it might just as well have been crow….For what I was now faced with was a *solid* clot, not the crank-case-oil-consistency fluid I had anticipated. That signified a rebleed just eight hours earlier, for which a mere twist-drill sized hole and drain were woefully inadequate. Having taken the liberty to make a big production of performing "delicate brain surgery" under local, would that I have taken the precaution instead to have the patient intubated and under a general anesthetic. Then it would have been a straightforward matter to simply extend the incision circumferentially, remove a large portion of bone, and extract the tenacious clot with suction and forceps. As matters now stood (and my patient now lay), that alternative was not open to us. With as much embarrassment as resignation,

I forced the tiny tube through my small opening (akin to hammering a square peg into a round hole) and silently, if fervently, prayed for the Lord to cover me—lest our patient have to return later to have the very operation he needed all along!

Which brings me to the fruit of the Spirit that would shortly be served, accompanied by a prodigious helping of grace. The next morning I made my way to our patient's bedside with an interpreter in tow to gently break the news that further surgery was required. Yet he had some "breaking news" of his own! Now wide awake and with full recovery of his previously paralyzed arm and leg, this delightful old codger understandably demanded to know why another operation was necessary. And to make his point, he then stood up from the bed with both arms outstretched in thanksgiving that the prayer I had offered on his behalf before the surgery had been answered.

To say that I was "dumbfounded" by such a turn of events would hardly do justice to the moment. Then again, it *did* justify the self-opprobrium of one knuckleheaded brain surgeon. Not only had I been "dumb" in not insisting upon a more precise history from our translator in my rush to tailor a disease to fit my special operation; Jesus "found" me wanting as a circumspect physician in not preparing for every eventuality beforehand. So, "dumb" and "founded"? You bet! My condemnation was totally justified. Yet what I had lost the previous day (i.e. "face") had been regained on the following through no other intervention than God's merciful hand.

Not that the Lord ever revealed His hand in a manner my skeptical Chinese doctors would have required. The only point He *would* make was that such mercy must simply be accepted in faith. I, for one, had no other explanation for what we had witnessed. My patient, for another, had no more money for a repeat scan to prove us wrong. After all, his family had barely managed to scrape enough yuan together to afford the first one; a second was simply out of the question. No matter; Lord knows (literally) that would have been superfluous and beside the point. Not so, His mercy; it's never too much for Him to give. That's what I should have known all along. Which was *His* point from the very beginning.

∞

"In you, O LORD I have taken refuge;
let me never be put to shame;…
for the sake of your name lead and guide me."

PSALM 31:1, 3

"…Mercy triumphs over judgment!"

JAMES 2:13

Acromegaly is a bad disease. The coarse physical features induced by an excess of growth hormone from a tumor of the pituitary gland are bad enough. The havoc that wreaks on the body's inner workings are far worse: insulin-dependent diabetes, uncontrollable hypertension, and consequent heart failure—not to mention impaired vision, should such a tumor also compress the overlying optic nerves.

Gilbert is a case in point on all counts, a young man I first met at Tenwek (a Christian mission hospital in Kenya) after surgeons in Nairobi had failed to slow the disease's inexorable progression. Faced with a remnant of secreting tumor, while losing his vision in the process, Gilbert and his family prevailed upon me to attempt a removal of the residual.

Armed only with a vaginal speculum(!) to pass through his sphenoid sinus to the base of the skull where the tumor lay, I first had to administer diluted epinephrine to shrink the swollen nasal mucosa blocking our way. That's standard procedure at the beginning of what's known as a "transphenoidal approach" to the pituitary gland. Mind you, as the proverbial "captain of the ship" in the operating room, the surgeon is responsible not only for the operation, but for all drugs administered by (or delivered from) the anesthetist. And here I made a critical error of omission, which, in any other circumstance, would have cost my patient his life.

For it seems the epinephrine I requested had not been properly diluted. Shortly after its administration Gilbert's heart (already weakened by hypertension through the years) began to beat erratically and then stopped completely. That horrifying development brought me face to face with my first real Code Blue in the mission field, complete with manual cardiac compression to propel blood to Gilbert's oxygen-deprived organs in what seemed a vain attempt to keep him alive. For more than an hour we labored, struggling to restore a sustainable rhythm that might rescue us all from a single careless oversight superimposed on a failing heart.

In the course of straddling Gilbert's chest while directing the efforts of the resuscitation team, I had plenty of time to ruminate. What blind trust my patient and his family had placed in me—an American doctor they hardly knew—a trust woefully misplaced despite all the prayers I had ministered to them immediately preceding the operation. More degrading still, my wife, Vicki, (a cardiac nurse practitioner) was there to witnesses my failure. In all our past experience with Code Blues, never could we recall a single patient recovering from one that lasted so long. My oft-recited prayer for redemption taken from Psalm 31 now came back to haunt me: "In you, O LORD I have taken refuge; let me never be put to shame;…for the sake of your name lead and guide me."

So many times in the past that prayer had provided my patients safe harbor. Why not today? Perversely, just that very morning I had noticed a framed needlepoint hanging in the guest bathroom: "A life stitched in prayer is less likely to unravel." *Hollow words*, I remember thinking, as Gilbert's life seemed to be unraveling completely before my very eyes. Worse yet, at my very hand.

Thankfully, at length we finally managed to restore a normal cardiac rhythm and output in Gilbert's weakened heart—but only after a full hour of artificial support to diseased organs starving for blood. Had our herculean efforts been enough to sustain them? Probably not—or so it appeared at first. Gilbert did not regain consciousness, and for two days thereafter seemed to have "tapped out" in the clutches of what everyone believed would be a persistent vegetative state.

As if to make matters more galling for my auto-focused, if tattered, ego, the entire community was well aware of the tragedy—culminating with a church service dedicated to intercessory prayer for Gilbert's healing on the morning we were scheduled to depart Kenya. I certainly didn't decry the need; what concerned me was whether we might be setting God up for a "fall" should our communal petition not be answered. *False consolation of religion,* I shamefully confess to pondering as I shrank lower in the pew, while prayers of mercy not only for Gilbert but his guilt-ridden doctor echoed against the walls. Should mercy triumph over judgment (the latter "poor," as in my own; or "righteous," as befit His)? That was hardly justified in this case; my condemnation was deserved. But why should Gilbert have to pay the ultimate price in my stead?

Equally shameful to relate, I railed against God during my twenty-four-hour flight home, the longest I ever remember taking, or so it seemed. Mercifully, there was an e-mail waiting for me, and it was encouraging. Gilbert had begun to show signs of emerging from his coma! Not that this promised a return to meaningful function of vital organs, among them his optic nerves. Undoubtedly they had been so compromised by the prolonged hypotension during the Code that most likely he would now be blind. Much less did I hold out any hope of my colleagues ever weaning Gilbert from the respirator.

Fast forward some six months later. With foreboding I had made plans to return to Tenwek, fully prepared to reap the chaff of what I had sown. For I'd lingered in my own self-induced expiation ever since, aided and abetted by a technical glitch that kept me in the dark. The hospital's Internet server had gone on the blink in the interim, precluding my learning anything further concerning Gilbert's progress—or, more than likely, lack thereof.

To my amazement upon arrival, I was informed our patient had not only regained consciousness, but enough strength to come off the respirator—though he did require a tracheotomy to bypass his scarred windpipe. Even that proved another diabolical bridge for him to cross, which, prophetically, meant meeting me for a second time on the other side. Providentially for *my* sake, that very morning Gilbert had come to the hospital to have his tracheotomy removed. Marveling at the Lord's timing, I was overcome by the merciful hand extended by his still-grieving mother. Breaking her own cultural taboo, she embraced me in the warmest hug imaginable—matched only by the toothy grin of her son who waved at me from across the room where he sat on his bed.

"That's impossible," I exclaimed to her. "When I first met Gilbert, he could hardly see his own hand in front of his face!" If anything, his profoundly compromised vision had *improved* since our frightening shared ordeal—an otherwise inexplicable miracle apart from the intercessory prayer that had clothed Gilbert like a blanket, if not stitched him back together again, in his surgeon's absence.

That tender morsel of mercy was but an appetizer to precede a banquet-full bestowed upon us all during my next visit to Tenwek some nine months further removed. On my first day back, I strolled into the holding area of the OR—and there sat Gilbert and his mother! I did a double-take, recalling a pearl from Yogi Berra's infamous lexicon of wisdom: "It was like déjà vu all over again!" Surely this was just another one of those "extraordinary coincidences"— were if not for those of us who recognized God's merciful hand in this second divine appointment in as many visits.

With no advance planning on anyone's part but the Lord's, Gilbert "just happened" to be there that very morning to commission the most fulfilling week I've ever had in the mission field. More merciful still, his mother proudly related that her son had been weaned from his tracheotomy and had a portion of his scarred trachea reconstructed by my good friend, Russ White. That was something of a miracle in itself, as two visiting ENT physicians heretofore had declined to attempt such a technically demanding and risky procedure.

To be sure, only Russ could have pulled that one off, being the most fearless and skilled surgeon I've ever known. But no doctor could account—much less take credit—for what else Gilbert's mother had in store for me. Not only had his vision continued to improve; most inexplicable of all, Gilbert's blood pressure was now normal and his diabetes had mysteriously disappeared. Oh, the riches of God's mercy! What my ill-conceived and aborted surgery could not do, the Divine Physician had done Himself.

Perhaps most merciful of all—on a very personal level—God had seen fit that my daughter, Brittany, should accompany me on this particular trip to reverse some spiritual backsliding that often occurs during those impressionable university years when one "tests the waters." Yet Jesus had something just as important to reinforce in her thinking: Brittany's earthly father, the doctor she knew to possess a merciful heart (but occasionally fallible skills), would forever pale thereafter in comparison to the real Healer and Father of all. Apart from that, He also wanted her to remember He is a God who *bears*. Some 2,000 years ago He had borne our flesh, our sin, our cross. Now Jesus graciously bore His own disciple's mistake, taking a bad situation and making it not only better, but best, for everyone involved.

It was left for Brittany to speak for us all later that evening during the first devotional she ever had the courage to lead. The gist of her remarks centered upon love and forgiveness; yet one thing she said spoke volumes to an earnest father charged with discipling his daughter. I will cherish these words for eternity: "The more merciful we are to others, the more we ourselves are treated with compassion."

As for Gilbert and his mother, yet another of Jesus' refrains continues to light their path to this very day, taken from Luke 18:27. "What is impossible with men is possible with God," if only we have ears to hear and eyes to see. And by His boundless mercy and power alone, a young Kenyan literally resurrected from the clutches of a terminal disease is now able to *see* that most clearly of all.

RECESS

Reality Check

Thirsting for righteousness has its downside when judged by secular standards. In the earliest phase of my spiritual rebirth, all I had been looking for was affirmation of the Christian's life-view among other believers such as my father. Yet it was the Beatitudes that riveted my attention thereafter. Why? Because they mirrored my own perspective, as opposed to what the "real" world values. Well and good, intellectually. A less than contrite *heart* was another issue entirely. Only one remade in Christ's likeness could compel me to truly *thirst*, which was what my aforementioned "operation" had been all about. Sad to relate, that was something Dad never quite understood.

Following my "recovery," I had responded to the call with a singular passion that befit the *Braveheart* portrayal of Robert the Bruce. He had been warned by his father that all men lose heart when it comes to seeking righteousness. Dad had essentially said the same thing. Yet the dictates of my conscience counseled otherwise: "But I don't *want* to lose heart; I want to *believe* as [Henry] Wallace does!"

Still another motivation was even more egocentric: Affirmation of my own self-worth. Though a far less laudable goal than the first, that makes it no less real for believer and agnostic alike. What I'm tangentially referring to is reward. Whether one terms that an "inheritance" is in the eye of the beholder. On this, however, virtually everyone agrees: to banish all motivation of reward (or of at least avoiding rebuke) either in this life or the next is to render our very being an existential exercise in futility. The only choice for those outside the faith is to have one's reward "paid in full" from society in one lump sum now—as opposed to believers, who also receive a return on the principal—God's first fruits here on earth and His treasures in Heaven forevermore.

That was a choice with which I had been confronted sooner than I would have liked. At this pivotal time when the Lord was turning my own table of plenty upside down, opportunists lying in wait underneath scrambled for any scraps that fell to the floor. What ephemeral rewards I had obtained financially, or "memorials" I had built by way of professional reputation, were threatened to be consumed by a few colleagues I had come to trust.

It was, perhaps, a fitting end to the pretension that had characterized my original life's quest to become a "Renaissance Man." All the more fitting because the alter ego of my pre-Christian existence, a college professor by the name of Reynolds Price, had already alerted me to the pitfalls of placing one's faith in other people—in particular, catering to the false praise of men seeking to advance themselves on your dime. Price had been a professor of literature at Duke University when I was there as an undergraduate back in the Dark Ages of the sixties. The undergirding thesis of his life's view was that man should seek affirmation only in his work, because personal relationships are bound to disappoint in the end—casualties of deception, divorce, or death. I swallowed that view "hook, line, and sinker" for the next twenty years and eventually came to appreciate where Price was coming from.

What I did *not* bank upon, however, was that my vocation was subject to the same vilification. That became manifest immediately after declaring myself for Christ—which, parenthetically, is the type of setback Jesus had warned His disciples would befall them. Genuine followers refer to that as "the cost of discipleship." What made this all so ironic is that a year or so after being reborn (and long after I had lost track of Professor Price), I discovered my mentor had abandoned his own cynicism for a more virtuous perspective. One of the many books God put in my hands at that particular time was Price's *Three Gospels*. This seminal work reflected a quarter-century of his own search (and those of his students) for the *historical* Jesus, much as I had done over a much briefer period of time before exchanging a head of knowledge for a heart of worship.

That, I now believe in retrospect, was no accident. Long before then,

God the Father had ushered us both along the same road in different vehicles, knowing full well our pilgrimages would ultimately lead us to a life-changing encounter with His Son. Though facts arguably more than faith fueled our respective journeys, only the Lord knows which hearts He can change at the Crossroad—and both of ours were on His list! By seeking affirmation in an environment far removed from the one in which I had been placed, Reynolds Price's quest eventually dovetailed into my own: two shepherds of a sort, serving their flocks in very different ways, who met Jesus face to face on a road rarely taken by academicians and physicians alike.

What we both had discovered, after a number of false starts, is that the Lord's offer—and our reward—centers upon a loving relationship between Father and child. That's a far cry from the praise and affection extended to one another in the workplace, which usually ring hollow and are always subject to withdrawal. Such is not the case for God's divinely sanctified relationships, because Christ's love is *unconditional*. Even when we fail Him, He's always there—much like those endearing friendships of childhood, the likes of which are rarely recaptured as adults.

Out of gratitude for the ultimate price paid on our behalf, any affirmation a Christian seeks is based on the approval from the benefactor—in this instance, Jesus. By way of contrast, those who actively seek—and happen to receive—the ephemeral approval of mankind during this lifetime have already been given their just reward. Yet the beauty of Christ's offer is that those who thirst for righteousness receive a double draught: His affirmation now and eternal life thereafter. It's a win-win situation, one that speaks to the very heart of Jesus' unmerited gift to those who seek His will as unconditionally as Christ extends His love: "But seek first his kingdom and his righteousness, and all these things [one's daily concerns and needs] will be given to you as well."[1]

That promise had been put to the test after returning from one of my earlier mission trips. Waiting for me on the desk was a letter from my two associates dissolving our partnership of fifteen years. Thereafter (and in league with a third neurosurgeon whom I had naively trusted at face value as a professed Christian), they conspired to destroy my practice, and nearly succeeded.[2] Was this the just reward the meek were to inherit in the Lord's service? If ever I needed affirmation on God's terms and not man's, it was now.

Jesus ultimately made good on His promise, because He knew He had my heart. Immediately following my "divestiture," the Lord called me to Nicaragua, where a whole host of rewards awaited both Master and son. By virtue of the work I had been consigned to do, a windfall for Christ's Kingdom was returned to its rightful Owner. Those two weeks produced a rich harvest through no merit of my own—although more than adequate remuneration for myself in knowing I was finally on the right path.

Along the way, He also provided a fellow pilgrim with whom to share a love of missions work, a few triumphs, and many more travails. Through his own Christian walk and mature witnesses by example, Dr. Mark Axness reconciled my professional "losses" with the spiritual rewards I had received. Insofar as both of us were being tested at the time, God provided a soul mate to share the load. Being equally yoked in shared adversity is entirely consistent with Jesus' nature. Knowing beforehand we will experience hardships and even persecution for His sake, the Lord will never give us more of a burden than we can bear—or share.[3] What He *does* provide, as Father to child, is a reprise of those long-lost, unconditional friendships of youth.

That comforting bit of Scripture was put to an even greater trial over the next six months as I balanced the rigorous demands of a solo neurosurgical practice with subsequent mission trips to Ecuador and Brazil. Despite having been pushed from the nest amidst whispers swirling about me in the hometown where I had grown up, the surgical volume of my practice only increased— much to my former associates' dismay. Consequently they tightened the screws by alerting the hospital administration I had left my patients back home "unattended" while on mission in China. Though that was hardly the case, I was no longer able to take any time off for other trips on His behalf, lest I be called on the carpet for alleged "bylaws violations"—at which point they would be more than willing to testify against me.

From Jesus' perspective, of course, such trials in the workplace at home were not nearly so important as what impact they threatened to have on my commitment to serve Him abroad. He therefore made a way where there seemed to be no way by "covering" for me Himself. It was His way of saying, "Bert, you're going to far-off places to shepherd the sheep of My pasture; for that, I'll take care of your own flock in return. What's more, I'll see to it that it grows during your absence!"

No greater comfort and assurance could have been given me than Jesus' very words: "Blessed are you when people insult you, persecute you and falsely say all kinds of evil against you because of me. Rejoice and be glad, because great is your reward...."[4] By obeying the Lord's call and going to where He was working, I was promised to have all my worldly needs and concerns—and, more importantly, those of my patients—provided for in kind.[5] In exchange for having lost the financial security of a group practice in which virtually one hundred percent of the patients were medically insured, I had been given an inheritance of inestimable value. Apart from that eternal blessing, I was now able to minister to my patients in a manner of the Lord's choosing, without having to face the caustic, secondhand comments I used to hear in reference to my associates growing weary of this "Christian crap" that allegedly impacted unfavorably on the group's reputation in our community.

Others were more polite, yet just as skeptical. A few were even kind enough to respond to my enthusiasm for medical missions on behalf of the poor with comments like "It must be nice to finally be able to do what you want to do," or "I'm sure you're helping." Yet none were willing to acknowledge the Source from which these seemingly destitute patients derive their peace of mind—or, for that matter, my own.

This brings me to the debt I also owe Dr. Robert Coles, yet another mentor-from-afar. As a child psychiatrist and lecturer at Harvard University, he identified the crux of the problem (albeit in a far different context) in his Pulitzer Prize-winning, five-volume series entitled *Children of Crisis*. "Rich kids who tried to break out of their sheltered surroundings and respond to the call of conscience [or God] presented a threat to others." At age forty-seven, I too was a rich kid surrounded by rich peers. When Jesus' call came to cast my lost with the poor, apparently that was every bit as threatening to my colleagues as the thousands of children Coles interviewed for his work. Why? Because their perceived wealth had become an impediment to what matters most.

Such unfounded (if not childish) fears aside, a different sort of unexpressed angst applied to the academic community in my hometown—although here the threat was not so much to status and wealth as to "academic freedom" or lack thereof. Let me give you an example. A mutual friend in the history department at the local university attempted to arrange a debate between myself and a member of the so-called "Jesus Seminar" pertaining to the reliability of the four Gospels and Acts as primary source materials on the life of Jesus. Two roadblocks, however, quickly emerged. For one, the chairman of the department of Religious Studies, where the debate was logically to be held, feared controversy and, conceivably, retribution since this was a state-supported university—or so it was lamely expressed to me. For another, my proposed opponent ultimately refused to debate someone who was "clearly an evangelical advocate" (rather than, one must presume, an unbiased scholar like himself).

Now, as opposed to the track record of a truly esteemed scholar such as Robert Coles, my paltry résumé is such that no one need have taken notice. I understand and accept that. What's more, Dr. Coles has the added distinction of being as meek as a lamb and sly as a serpent, using the less obtrusive course label for what he terms "spiritual literature" as a vehicle for his message. As he so humbly (if presciently) observed: "That's how I [smuggle] the Bible tradition into the university, for it belongs there and it is a privilege to call upon it as a teacher."

Why, then, does Harvard continue to invite Dr. Coles into what he acknowledges to be a "citadel of secular humanism," while I was denied the same at Missouri State? In his own self-deprecating if incisive words: "for idolatrous reasons…a name [with drawing power] listed on a brochure." No mystery there—Dr. Cole's credentials are impeccable. It should not pass unnoticed, however, that his calling as a witnesses for Christ unfolded far removed from the social constraints of the community in which he now resides. Taking the Good News into such hallowed halls as an "outside" honored guest is therefore less threatening for audience and speaker alike.

Contrast that with Springfield, where peers from among both the medical and academic communities viewed my own spiritual transformation firsthand. The overwhelming majority, accordingly, perceived me as some sort of "infected alien intrusion" (as one of my colleagues so colorfully put it) into a professional world that offered them safe harbor. This I could handle. Far more difficult for me to reconcile, none were swayed by my enthusiasm for Christian apologetics, being too "busy" to examine the compelling evidence for themselves. So they would not fall victims to the same infection, I had in a sense been "quarantined." That's the reality. Far from being some sort of prophet without honor in his hometown, however, I simply saw myself as a donkey carrying the King's message to His people. In Springfield, alas, that was a tough stretch of road to navigate. Balaam wouldn't listen; would that he have beaten me instead.

Perhaps the Lord allowed all of this to happen, because it was His way of reminding me I was now supposed to be doing the Father's work—not what I perceived to be my own. He also changed my thinking as to where my *real* spiritual gifts lay—not as a teacher, but as an evangelist always and a healer on occasion when granted the privilege. As such, rather than fulfilling a business contract for a fee, my new contract—no, covenant—was with Jesus on behalf of His lost sheep. By declaring war on my practice, He nudged me toward greater commitment in the mission field abroad and among the poor here at home. This was, after all, what God had called me to do, what He had planned for me from the beginning, recreated as I was in His image.

That was a huge assignment, and required a character to match. Given the silver lining of privilege during my "first" life, which had isolated me from the gathering storm, Jesus had every reason to question whether I was now up to the task. True, God will always take the time necessary to develop one's character to match the call. Yet therein lay the problem: I was *already* out in the mission field doing His work. My character needed maturing—and fast! Christ alone prompted me to recognize the situation for what it represented: I could fight for my professional reputation as the secular world would have me do in the courts, or I could yield to the Holy Spirit as He reworked my life in preparation for His next, and bigger, assignment in the Lord's pasture.

It was a painful yet profoundly valuable lesson. His purpose for me, as for all believers, had been revealed in no uncertain terms: to do God's will and complete His work. And there is more of the latter on behalf of more grateful patients than the "real" world and my former colleagues will ever know. Each mission trip abroad only adds to that, what with more cases, more effective witnessing, and better surgical results in the most difficult and challenging environments imaginable. All of which defies any explanation other than Christ's presence in the clinics and operating rooms where He works beside me.

Jesus offers no greater affirmation for those who labor in His stead than this: seeking *first* God's Kingdom and wherever He is at work is the key to both personal and professional fulfillment. The very Source that Professor

Price, Dr. Coles, and myself had been seeking all along—and which we each discovered in very different ways through our respective walks—has changed our lives immeasurably for the better. Not, most assuredly, because of anything we have done; rather, solely on account of the Lord's righteousness paid in our behalf on the cross. And nothing other than Christ's resurrection has made that a *reality* in the lives of every believer who answers His call, despite all the persecution and spiritual warfare this necessarily entails.

SECOND WITNESSES

They Will See God

"Seeing is believing," or so the old saying goes. It can be reaffirming as well for those who already believe. If ever I needed affirmation for what I thought God had called me to do, it had been during my first mission trip to El Salvador in 1996. Having turned tail on the values of my former life, and acutely aware of the problems that had created for me back home, Eric's tragedy had been a sobering introduction to the mission field. Though Jesus had clearly shouldered my burden down in that dark valley, I was having trouble seeing the Christ-light within as His sixth beatitude promised. "Pure in heart"? I'd like to think so. Troubled in mind? You betcha! And this was preventing me from *seeing* God and focusing on His plans for my new life.

That's but one reason, I now believe, the Lord brought an angel in disguise to our walk-in clinic outside San Salvador on the final day of the most trying week imaginable—to affirm once again why I had been called there in the first place. His other reason had more important and *unforeseen* consequences. Although the sixth beatitude promises the pure in heart shall see God, some assistance on their behalf is occasionally required. Like a two-dollar pair of reading glasses. Let me explain.

For several days I had noticed an elderly peasant woman waiting patiently in line to be seen by one of the doctors. Somehow she always managed to "miss the cut" at the end of the day and would find herself back where she started on the next. Eventually I lost track of this persistent soul—only to have her return on the final day of the clinic shortly after we had already closed and packed up our gear. Through an interpreter, her daughter explained she had come for an eye examination and a pair of glasses.

That had been a pervasive request throughout the two weeks; everyone, it seemed, wanted glasses. The ophthalmologists had been so overwhelmed doing refractions in the early going that a huge backlog of patients at their station prevented many others from being evaluated for more serious eye problems. My solution for this logistical nightmare was simple: rather than wait for a formal eye examination, I commandeered a hundred or so pair of reading glasses from the ophthalmology storeroom. Whenever someone asked to see an eye doctor thereafter, I simply took three pairs from my knapsack and would have the patient try them on in labeled sequence—weak, medium, and strong. Once their faces lit up, it was all we needed: diagnosis and treatment in one fell swoop! As an added bonus, the lines in the eye clinic were reduced considerably.

That had been then; yet this was today. The little lady was inconsolable in her grief, having been told by the registration team our eye clinic was closed and the glasses were already stowed away onboard the bus waiting to take us to the airport. Now it just so happened I had been the last to board, and there she caught up with me standing in the door well. The driver opened the door while I dug into my knapsack to see if there were any glasses left. At the very bottom I found one pair labeled "strong." She grasped them eagerly in her gnarled hands, tried them on—and immediately broke into a huge grin. Fumbling in her coat pocket, she then pulled out a dog-eared copy of the Gospel of John and began reading out loud. Tears of joy streamed down her face, as I stood there with a perplexed look on my own.

After all, such an emotional response seemed out of keeping with her quiet stoicism throughout the week, and I mentioned that to the daughter. "But you don't understand," she replied. "There are fourteen members of our extended family, all of whom found the Lord through my mother." And as it turned out, she had been the spiritual head not only of her own household, but for many of the neighbors as well. Rather precipitately, however, her eyes began to fail some ten years earlier and she could no longer read to them from His Word. "This is the first time she's been able to see print since her descent into darkness," the daughter went on to say. "The Bible is her bread of life. Please forgive her for overreacting. She's been very hungry—and so have we. For you see, no one else in our family can read."

Forgive her? Awestruck silence in the presence of a saint was all I could muster! Here was an erstwhile "pillar of fire" in the wilderness, whose flame had been snuffed out for a decade, with all that portended for her starving sheep bleating to be led—and fed. Lack of reading glasses was the only thing that had kept her from "seeing" God and allowing others to see Him through her eyes. That's why Jesus had delayed my boarding until the last moment, and why He had seen fit that I had not given my last set of readers away. "Blessed are the pure in heart, for they will see God." A blessed assurance, to be sure; yet sometimes we have the privilege of assisting those with hearts far purer than our own to find their way.

On rare occasions the disciple is given an opportunity to be a conduit of light in a more sanctified setting than the door well of a bus, as the Lord did for me one evening in Argentina. That's when He took me to a higher level of unearned reward at a revival attended by some two hundred new converts to Christ whom we had ministered to in the clinic that day. There had been an altar call at the end of the service, and the pastor graciously invited members of the medical team to come down to the front to share in our patients' professions of faith.

As we mingled among the crowd of newborn believers gathered at the altar in prayer, I instinctively laid a comforting hand on the head of one elderly farmer who was trembling and sobbing. Others apparently saw my gesture differently. The moment I touched the man his eyes rolled back and he fell into the arms of his son, who gently lowered him to the ground. Immediately thereafter I felt the tug on my sleeve from a little girl, who beckoned me to come over and "bless" her mother in like fashion. The same thing happened! In quick succession others gently guided me to their friends or loved ones. I began to pray with each, then laid hands upon them while family members gathered behind in anticipation of the "fall."

And so it continued, one right after another, as the Lord accompanied me on the most humbling spiritual journey I have ever had the privilege to take. It was His way of leading me, if only for the moment, to a higher level of affirmation by allowing me to *see* what He had been to the sheep of His flock for two millennia. Imagine! An unordained layman with no other credentials than a heart for the Lord, who had been granted the privilege of wearing His robes as a pastor, apart from the physician I was.

As the praying continued, the ground around us became littered with bodies in various stages of spiritual repose. It was as if a great battle was being waged here, and the "casualties" were growing with each passing minute. A battleground? Absolutely! For men's souls. And Jesus was the victor, with whom I was standing (by grace alone) in His hour of triumph. For the Lord knew my heart—and though by no means as pure as originally conceived in His mind's eye, I had been called into my Creator's presence to share in the vision He had for mankind from the beginning. Blessed at that moment were we all; for we had truly *seen* God, just as He had promised.

While the youth praise and worship team continued to play up on the stage, I marveled over the countless ways Christ gives us affirmation. This presupposes, of course, that we recognize and accept what our own unique spiritual gift is—and mine most assuredly was not as a song leader. Why, just that very morning I had brought my guitar to our devotional and led the group through a smattering of hymns I had learned. Though my motives had been as pure as my love for the Lord in so doing, that certainly had *not* come across as a spiritual gift—an admission I'm forced to make each time I rekindle the fantasy of serving in that capacity. After removing His earplugs, Jesus gently reprimanded me in His own inimitable fashion: "Bert, why don't you leave the music to others and use the gift of compassion I gave you? I think you'll like the fit, because *My* heart is what I want others to see in you. Only then might they seek out the Father and find Me."

Such a revelation wasn't what I had envisioned when I joined Him at the altar; yet it was enough for others to witnesses—and Jesus to approve— that sacred evening in rural Argentina. That's why the pure in heart are so blessed: they *see* God in our service to them.

"In the past God spoke to our forefathers through the prophets…but in these last days he has spoken to us by his Son…sustaining all things by his powerful word…."

HEBREWS 1:1–3

In the Old Testament era God spoke to His chosen people through visions of prophets sent to legitimize the timeless truth of His utterances. Yet the Father of *all* mankind chose to reserve His final revelation for the incarnation, death, and resurrection of His Son, Jesus, so that everyone might *see* the Word as living history transcribed in flesh and blood.[1] That's why "His Story" from the perspective of Scripture begs the question: Do prophetic visions, in and of themselves, have any value for the body of Christ today—notwithstanding those self-proclaimed "prophets" who profane that spiritual gift for their own self-aggrandizement?

In a word, can visions of any sort allow us to "see" God? For the pure in heart with open eyes, the answer to our question is a resounding Yes!—assuming the vision truly fortifies God's Church and sustains His believers. To defend the point, let's begin with a controversial example.

During my first three years as a born-again believer, I attended an Assembly of God church. Every so often (on average every third or fourth Sunday) the service was interrupted by someone speaking in tongues—followed immediately thereafter by another "translating" the message into English for the congregation. Now, as a newcomer to the faith, I don't mind admitting initially being put off by such a practice. Nevertheless, the amazing thing was that the cadence and inflections of the interpreter's version invariably *matched precisely* that of the "prophet." My point being, either these two individuals were charlatans who had gotten together before the service to practice—or their words were bona-fide prophetic utterances that conformed precisely to what Scripture requires (see 1 Corinthians 14, mandating that someone other than the original speaker must interpret the utterance for the congregation's benefit; otherwise, the said prophet is only edifying him- or herself). Being a skeptic by nature, it may surprise you that I believe these to have been genuine manifestations of a unique spiritual gift.

That's also what a passing knowledge of Hebrew suggests to me. The Old Testament translation of the word "prophet" [*nabiy*] extends far beyond some solemn pronouncement accompanied by thunder and lightning with angels flitting about. A prophet in its more generic sense is simply one speaking from and for God—His messenger, if you will, carrying the King's Word to all peoples.

Whether we call them "prophets" or merely "servants," they wear coats of many colors. True, Jeremiah was a priest and Samuel an anointer of kings; but Amos was a cowboy—which is what I wanted to be as a young boy (and, some skeptics would assert, have become as a born-again Christian riding apart from the denominational herd). For present purposes, my "designated identity" is beside the point; as an impartial observer, what missions has taught me is that a few visionaries today come from ostensibly hostile quarters to the Christian faith. One I met in my work abroad was a card-carrying Muslim orthopedic surgeon in Basra, Iraq.

By secular standards, Thamer Hamdan was a powerful man—perhaps the most respected bone doctor in the Middle East. Two qualifications in particular warranted his distinction as a mover and shaker among the elite. To begin with, Dr. Hamdan's formidable reputation as a healer caught the attention of Saddam Hussein some four years before the fall of this would-be "king of Babylon." Never one to trifle with the suffering of others, Saddam had summoned the good doctor to assuage his own once Udai, his infamous son, survived an assassination attempt that left this antithesis of Jacob[2] with a shattered long bone in his leg. Just because my soon-to-be acquaintance had been out of political favor at the time as a Shiite (and had close personal connections to their most powerful imam or "holy man") was of no concern to Hussein. He recognized Dr. Hamdan to be the leading Iraqi expert in orthopedic trauma and enlisted him for a "command" performance—which Thamer fulfilled admirably.

This leads me to my friend's second richly deserved qualification as a "medical guru." I witnessed that firsthand the day Thamer presented his prodigious wartime experience with extremity trauma to the Orthopedic Academy of Iraq. By virtue of numbers alone—some *twenty thousand cases*—garnered over the course of three devastating wars in a mere twenty-year period (the Iran-Iraq War of the 1980s; the first Gulf War in the early 90s; and the vendetta that followed in 2003 at the hand of Bush the younger), no one in the world has had the "benefit" of such a wealth of experience.[3]

Yet I digress from the real story to tell. In 2003, shortly after "Operation Flight Suit,"[4] I was asked by Operation Blessing (no pun intended) to go to Iraq with a team of doctors for the purpose of treating war casualties and civilians alike. The latter, it seems, had been dismissed from the hospitals in Basra to accommodate the huge number of casualties anticipated during the lengthy war—neither of which, parenthetically, materialized. It was in one such hospital that I first met Dr. Hamdan and heard the aforementioned presentation.

Although the breadth of Thamer's experience would prove mind boggling during the course of his lecture, nothing prepared me for this devout Shiite Muslim's first slide. He showed a picture of *Christ on the cross*, accompanied by the doctor's very words: "Praise be to Jesus, the Prince of Peace." I was astounded! How could a man of such influence risk alluding to my Lord and Savior in an auditorium full of Muslims (many of whom, to my surprise, seemed to be nodding in affirmation)?

After the lecture, I introduced myself and, dropping all pretense of diplomatic savvy, asked Dr. Hamdan about the slide and his potentially incendiary comment. To which he replied with a shrug of his shoulders: "We are all sons of Abraham, and both Jesus and Muhammad we consider to be God's greatest prophets. What's more, who can dispute that Jesus possessed a God-given gift that we as doctors in Iraq must all emulate? Make no mistake, my friend, He was the greatest physician to ever walk the earth. That's why I begin all my lectures with this same slide. It's the very least I can do for Him."

Which brings us back to this delicate matter of visions. "You should not have been surprised," he concluded with a chuckle. "For you see, I recently had a *vision* [emphasis mine] that a true man of God—a brother such as yourself—would be sent here to work and teach us His ways." That lofty prophecy was to be fulfilled beyond measure during the subsequent week of work we shared together, for we both had much to teach one another. Insofar as spine surgery had become a recent preoccupation for Thamer, naturally I assumed my familiarity with the latest in spinal instrumentation techniques was why I had been invited to operate with him in the first place. As so often happened to me before in other venues, however, screws and plates were simply to be used as keys to unlock closed doors.

By his own admission just before our final workday together, what technical skills I brought to the table were small potatoes compared to the invaluable lessons "the Lord" (*his* words, not mine) had taught him about the physician-patient relationship. The irony being, my bedside manner was merely a reflection of the Western-style medicine in which I had been trained—prayer, of course, excepted! What made "treating patients as opposed to 'cases' so 'enlightening'" for Thamer (again, his words) were simple gestures, like following my lead by sitting on the beds of our patients, taking their hands, and praying with them.

Appreciating where I was, such prayers were always delivered in the name of "Father God." Yet Thamer had no difficulty making the real connection. He fully understood (and appreciated) in whose Name I was speaking. And to this earnest disciple with the purest of hearts, his own culturally dictated practice of standing at the foot of a patient's bed, chart in hand, and *pronouncing* treatment was no match for the Divine Physician and His ways. As for myself, merely donning Jesus' lab coat and reflecting His light (both of which I knew myself to be unworthy) proved a singular witnesses worth a thousand words.

Yet the question remains: For one so accustomed to exercising diplomacy in high places, was my new Muslim colleague stretching the point merely to nurture a fruitful collaboration? Or, just perhaps, had his vision been real? I have no way of knowing for certain, though this much we would affirm from our week spent working together: Jesus was—and remains—the Divine Mediator between men. As our Mentor as well, He had something to teach us both.

Granted, but would Thamer ultimately risk his reputation among Iraq's ruling elite to bear lasting fruit for God's Kingdom here on earth, if not in Heaven? The answer to at least the former became apparent the day I was scheduled to return home. Taking me gently by the hand (virtually unheard of among xenophobic Muslim men), Thamer inquired with solemn humility whether he might be allowed to come aboard Operation Blessing and work with our team. To put that startling request in his own words: "I want to do what you do: to hear His call and know I've answered it…"

What an incredible opportunity for God's Kingdom—and with Christ as my witnesses! Not that the leadership of Operation Blessing perceived it as such. Despite our own willingness to respond to Thamer's vision and God's call together, my sponsors from the so-called "religious 'right'" could not bring themselves to think outside their boxed-in presuppositions. That bore the stamp of an all too familiar, if pharisaical, refrain. Might not Christ justifiably respond to those well-intentioned evangelists today from the other side of "their" door, just as He had scolded the Pharisees of His day: "Woe to you…[who] shut the kingdom of Heaven in men's faces.…nor will you let those enter who are trying to.…You travel over land and sea to win a single convert, and when he [wishes to] become(s) one, you make him twice as much a son of hell as you are" (Matthew 23:13–15)? The last phrase seems a little harsh to my way of thinking—but there it is. Sadly, what I believe to have been Jesus' personal invitation for Thamer to join the team never saw the light of day.

Contrast that myopic, knee-jerk boardroom disclaimer with but one patriarch's open-ended response to another seemingly "threatening invitation" some four thousand years ago. Within our present context, how ironic that it's Abraham's *vision* on Mt. Moriah to which I'm referring. Mind you, no one else had heard the Lord speaking the day God instructed Abraham to sacrifice his long-awaited "son of the promise"—least of all Isaac or the men accompanying them. Yet at the very moment this anguished father raised his dagger in obedience to the Call, everything he had surrendered to that point was returned to him.[5] Why? Simply because Abraham, pure in heart and with eyes to see, "*believed* God, and it was credited to him as *righteousness*" (Romans 4:3; emphasis mine). Merely venturing out on the limb was not enough; rather, he was willing to cut it off altogether for the sake of remaining engrafted to the taproot of his very being.

Who of us today would have done the same? Should that somehow "make *us* right" with God, perhaps; but on account of some hypothetical offspring in promise only? Unlikely. Posing our question another way: Can one man's itch cause millions to scratch? Thamer's "itch" to share the blessing (and others' "allergic reaction" to the very notion!) aside, the passage of time has answered that in the affirmative. For it was through Isaac (a personification of Christ Himself) that *all* whom God created in His image were to have been reckoned.[6] In the words of Paul, reflecting on that seminal event some two thousand years later, "it is the children of the promise who are regarded as Abraham's offspring" (Romans 9:8).

So where does that leave Thamer? A Muslim, yes—but most assuredly a descendant of Abraham and arguably just as righteous. My own sense is that our team would have done far better than Paul but to reflect on the words of Jesus to the Samaritan woman at the well: "If you knew…who it is that asks you for a drink, you would have asked him and he would have given you living water.…A time is coming when you will worship the Father neither on this mountain nor in Jerusalem. Yet a time…*has now come* when true worshipers will worship the Father in spirit and truth, for they are the kind of worshipers the Father seeks" (John 4: 10, 21, 23; emphasis mine).

Like the Samaritan woman, Dr. Hamdan had willingly given what offerings he had to secure the Lord's blessing—but did so, apparently, on the wrong mountain! That's what the silence told him. Nevertheless, Christ had spoken loud and clear some two thousand years before that the time for true worshipers to emerge had *already come*! And I, for one, believe this was Thamer's time, seeking him out as God did. Had His grace been extended by faithful (albeit fallible) men to a searching "Samaritan" brother instead of reacting as the disciples often did in Jesus' day, where it might have led is anyone's guess. Only God knows for sure. Yet in view of my friend's potentially powerful witnesses after having been immersed in "such a great cloud of [Christian] witnesses,"[7] I fully anticipate being called before the Lord on my day of reckoning to account for such a missed opportunity on behalf of His Kingdom.

In the interim, I'll continue to follow Christ's lead alone for the sake of those who seek His righteousness above all things, lest they fall prey to the enmity of F. Scott Fitzgerald, the quintessential spokesman for the Lost Generation: "So we beat on, boats against the current, borne back ceaselessly into the past"[8] of our fundamentalist preconceptions that continue to frustrate the Lord's intent for *all* mankind. Peering out into the church's self-imposed darkness like a modern-day Gatsby (seldom righteous but searching nonetheless!), I still catch a glimpse of Spirit and Truth on a distant shore, and wonder what might have been. That vision cannot be dispelled, and haunts me to this day. There stands a solitary figure beseeching Christians to "come over to Macedonia [Iraq] and help us!"[9] Sadly, after all these years, Thamer Hamdan and his people are still waiting.

They Will Be Called Sons of God

Making peace with a former enemy is a delicate proposition. It can be chastening as well when guilt by association renders the peacemaker vicariously responsible for a whole generation of youth being led like lambs to the slaughter. Whether invoking Cold War polemics to justify some ill-begotten "Domino Theory" in Southeast Asia, or the barrel of a gun to foist democracy on the so-called "nation" of Iraq (where three irreconcilable sects have no such tradition, much less alleged "weapons of mass destruction"), the price paid by innocent civilians accelerates one's recompense markedly.

Having opposed both conflicts from their very inceptions made my own task as a missionary in Vietnam and Iraq at once fearful and humbling. "Man's inhumanity to man," the poet laments. What credibility could the proverbial olive branch possess when offered by one of its own ilk? Absent an infilling of the Holy Spirit, little if any. Only Christ can successfully mediate between men and God—and man to man.

Representing the United States as some sort of lay ambassador to war victims was never my intent. Being on "a mission for God" as a twenty-first century Blues Brother was why I had been sent—hopefully to more redeeming effect than turning handsprings down the aisle at some trumped-up revival…Rather, I'm referring to "blues" in the sense of being called to share in their sorrow while reflecting the face of Jesus, tears and all.

On the "face" of it, representing Christ in Muslim Iraq on the heels of our self-proclaimed victory in the summer of 2003 seemed an ill-conceived venture from the start. Particularly so once I learned that the counterpart to whom I was offering His branch of reconciliation was none other than the most influential Shiite holy man in all of southern Iraq, Mohammed al-Sadr. Thanks to the relationship I had developed during my first week of work there with Dr. Hamdan, who happened to have been a former classmate of the younger Sadr and remained his close friend, I (of all people!) was granted an audience with "His Excellency," the elder.

Dressed in appropriate Muslim garb graciously supplied onsite by his entourage, I was ushered shoeless into the imam's presence. Lining the wall of the chapel on either side of us were a dozen or more servile attendants. Among them was his son, Muqtada al-Sadr, whose militia (as of this writing) vigorously opposes the United States' presence in Iraq. The sad irony being, in June of 2003, flush with U.S. "victory" there, the lines of division separating us had not become so entrenched as they are today.

Following a polite exchange of platitudes, Mohammed launched into his two-point presentation: (1) it seems "His Excellency" had been apprised of my bedside manner with patients, which differed dramatically from the traditional practice of Iraqi physicians. Consequently, he was inviting me to return in the near future "to teach surgery and *ethics*" [emphasis mine] to their doctors in a surgical hospital he was building for his Shiite people in Basra, whose medical needs had been ignored by the former Sunni regime; and, (2) like my orthopedic colleague, Mohammed perceived us both as "sons of Abraham" who had far more in common spiritually than any "rumors" of Jesus' resurrection as the "Son of [Allah]" could dispel.

Far be it from me to know for sure today, but I believed at that time the imam's latter point to have been much more than a mere diplomatic panacea. I was also of the opinion that his son, who sat at our side intently listening to the conversation, may have harbored other sentiments (as subsequent events in 2007–2008 now attest). Yet I remain convinced that Mohammed's untimely passing shortly after we left Iraq—irrespective of the skeptical reception my optimistic report received from our team leadership—prematurely closed a door that had intentionally been left open.

Even today I can't help but think this was an opportunity missed, at least insofar as it *could* have impacted subsequent tragic developments in the southern half of the country. No doubt Mohammed was but one of many powerbrokers in the amorphous mix of oil and water that typifies Islamic culture and politics within Iraq. (Indeed, have the two *ever* been separated?) Nevertheless, by all accounts he was the most powerful Shiite cleric of his day. Among many other credits, Mohammed had constructed the largest mosque in all of Iraq with his "own" [read: followers'] money and remained until his death their spiritual head.

By pale comparison, I was but a lamb sent into the lion's den to do my Shepherd's work. And for that moment at least, the southern end of the lair was quiet—its alpha male satiated by an all but stripped Sunni carcass felled at the hand of some headhunter from the Bush leagues. What few scraps remained were left for Mohammed's deprived Shiite pride of cubs. Thanks to American largesse at the expense of its *own* pride, the lion alone was content to lay down with the lamb. Had the insurgency not gained such momentum after 2004 (perhaps because its ravenous cubs had not been allotted their fair share?), I might still be returning to Basra yearly to put a human face on the Christ they knew only by reputation.

That particular lamb, of course, was then (and remains) a very poor imitation of his Shepherd. Mine was but a lone, and probably inconsequential, voice—a single drop of living water that might well have evaporated on its own accord in the arid sands of Bush's "post-war, mission-accomplished" Iraq. Yet, this much I know for certain: At least my Shepherd's "social gospel" is alive and well in Islam as a whole, if providing for the poor and believing in the redemptive power of good works are any indications. And that, most assuredly, remains common (if rocky) ground to lay an olive branch on—if not to build a bridge over.

Which is another way of suggesting that "the stones still cry out"[1] to be heard today on behalf of the broad majority of Muslims I've worked with in Kenya and Albania/Kosovo (to name but three venues in general) and Iraq in particular. To be sure, that refrain differs markedly from other less than God-fearing "principalities," such as China and Russia, where those in power with hearts of stone politely defer to Christ's message simply to gain our technology and teaching. Once pruned of any useful produce, their heads of state then discard His branch of reconciliation and trample it underfoot.

And yet, in a sobering but paradoxical sense, I also recognize *myself* as perhaps having been little more than grist for the mill while in Basra—if not the real stumbling stone. Had I possessed more compelling credentials; had I bothered to network more with my own leadership (both spiritual and professional) through the years rather than remain a "cowboy" as suited my nature; had I not been just a garden-variety neurosurgeon from Springfield, Missouri, who simply sought to exercise my spiritual and professional gifts within the sphere of influence the Lord had bequeathed to me; had I *been* and *done* more than that—a few things in southern Iraq, just perhaps, may have turned out differently.

Then again…although His Scripture has been fulfilled for every believer, the Lord's script has not entirely played itself out in the Middle East. Granted, on both points. Would that my role as peacemaker, however, during that 2003 springtime of optimism in Iraq have borne more fruit. To this day that remains, at least from my limited perspective, a God-sent opportunity missed for His Kingdom.

Seeking righteousness is one thing; suffering persecution for doing so, quite another. That's what two former warriors on opposite sides of the Vietnam conflict taught me. Both had been drafted to fight in an unjust war and had been "through hell and back," while I was safely insulated from this bonfire of national vanities by an equally unjust deferment as a medical student. But for the grace of God, I too should have been baptized in their shared trial by fire.

One had been singed and simply left it at that, accepting his experience as part of life's rich pageantry; the other had been burned beyond recognition, only to be resurrected from the flames. The former was a sixtyish-year-old acquaintance of my good friend Dr. Le. Having been a foot soldier for the "victorious" northern side, Dr. Thieu moved south after the war. For twenty years he had endured more than his share of persecution by the time we met, serving Da Nang's "vanquished" people as a gynecologist. That meeting was not without incongruity; he was wearing an American helicopter pilot's bomber jacket. Whether donated (or commandeered) during America's hasty withdrawal from the city at war's end was not something he chose to volunteer. Nor did I ask.

Assuming I too had been a war veteran, it was logical for Thieu to open our conversation with what proved to be a rather compelling metaphor phrased as a question: "What *wind* [emphasis mine] brought you back to Vietnam?"

My first thought was to offer an effusive apology for not having rendered the same type of conscripted service that in all too many ways had redefined his life. Yet Thieu's propitious choice of words prompted a totally unscripted (though scriptural) response on my part. "The wind that first brought me to Vietnam in 2001," I replied, "has a mind of its own—and for the last two thousand years, at least, blows where it chooses." That caught my new acquaintance off guard, and he asked me to explain what I meant.

"Please understand that the type of wind you're referring to is not what my Benefactor had in mind when He sent me here. To be more precise, the Greek word for 'wind' is *pneuma*, which Christians equate with the Holy Spirit—the very Force that swept over my life some ten years ago and graciously redirected me to Vietnam in order to meet you."

Well, you could have blown the good doctor over with a feather (or the Spirit, depending on choice of metaphor—and point of view)! Reflecting for some time upon what I had said, the silence was finally broken when he raised his glass and proclaimed: "I want to know more about this 'wind' of which you speak."

The seed had been sown. Christ had come to reap the whirlwind. The rest, as the trite saying goes, is history—as in *His Story*, a glowing tribute to the transforming power of the Spirit with a mind all His own, choosing that particular night to usher my new acquaintance into a Kingdom he had never fathomed.

That's but half of the story. And to my way of thinking, its less ennobling half—like some gaudy reversible liner on the underside of the very jacket Thieu had been wearing the evening he exchanged his earthly coat for an eternal crown. I had seen such a jacket one time before; it was worn by our team leader during my first mission to Da Nang in 2001. The difference being that Dwight Lohrenz was the "real McCoy," having served as a helicopter pilot during the war.

Several years thereafter (and "two lives later," as he often referred to his spiritual transformation), this erstwhile warrior had heard Christ's call and answered it with both guns blazing. When the opportunity arose to return to Vietnam in the Lord's service, he jumped at the chance. After all, it had been but four miles from Da Nang that Dwight had endured his greatest trial by fire in the most literal sense of the phrase while fighting over a mountain of marble in nothing but a tin can with rotors. Returning to the embers long since grown cold some thirty years later as a peacemaker for the Lord was selfless surrender of the highest order.

Although no man was better suited for the task at hand (being truly anointed with the spiritual gift of leadership, as everyone who served under this soft-spoken saint would attest), few if any had to carry the emotional baggage that accompanied him. That became sadly apparent the day the two of us climbed Marble Mountain and ventured into the grotto filled with memorials to North Vietnamese war dead.

Unbeknownst to me, at that very site one of the bloodiest helicopter battles of the entire war had been fought. Dwight related the horrific details as we made our climb and then descent into the cavernous expanse that had once served as a refuge and hospital for a battalion of Vietcong saboteurs. Having stumbled upon this beehive of enemy activity in 1969 just a stone's throw from the American airbase at Da Nang, a fleet of helicopters armed with rocket launchers had been dispatched to blow the top off its nest.

Hundreds died there that day, poignantly attested to by any number of shrines and plaques lining this bombed-out remnant. The pathos of it all was brought home to me as I stood respectfully by while Dwight, tears welling up in his eyes, read one such plaque: "Erected to commemorate the destruction of eight American imperialist helicopters and their crews in defense of the Fatherland."

Those "imperialists" had been his buddies (fifteen in all), mere boys who had plunged to fiery deaths prematurely. Yet Dwight had been spared to become a modern-day Daniel as Christ's fire-tested witnesses for eternal life.

Quite frankly, I don't recall a single word being spoken during our painful retreat back down the mountain together. And to the day of Dwight's tragic passing at the hand of colon cancer a mere three years later, I could never bring myself to discuss what we had experienced atop Marble Mountain. Yet his enduring legacy is an eternal flame that was never intended to be confined under a bushel. Rather, like that at the Tomb of the Unknown Soldier, it continues to cast a ray of hope over all God's house, including the darkest recesses of Southeast Asia.

Memorials to fallen warriors are an honorable afterthought—and Vietnam is chock-full of them, revered on many a street corner and in virtually every provincial village both North and South. Memories of fallen saints are something else again, and certainly deserve equal billing. Though Dwight no doubt would have admonished me that recognition by His Lord and Savior was more than enough for him, I certainly appreciate where my friend was coming from—but would respectfully beg to differ. He was simply the very best Jesus had to offer as a Christian Soldier, and others needed to know that.

Hence my resolve to make my own "amens" for him in the end: both for the suffering and rejection Dwight occasionally had to shoulder from those few Vietnamese old enough to still harbor resentment over the devastation "his" war had wrought, and for the equally unwarranted rejection he suffered at the hand of the very ministry he tirelessly served in good faith. A mere six months before his painfully abrupt and all-too-premature death, we shared our last conversation while on mission together in Basra, Iraq. There, Dwight confided to me he had been deeply wounded by a nefarious form of "corporate downsizing" that affected every business after 9/11, whether secular or faith-based—in this case, forced upon our ministry by the shortsighted de-emphasis of the primary-care outreach clinics that had been its lifeblood.

"They're simply not talking to me anymore," he lamented, "and I don't know why." Nor did I. No one brought more to the table as a leader of men and women than Dwight Lohrenz. None better prepared us with the "full armor of God" before a day's labor in the field than did he. After all, my brother had been there in Albania at the time I first met (and, sadly, abandoned) him, while he ran the race to the end of what proved to be one of our few ill-conceived missions. He was there in Vietnam to shepherd his discouraged flock once we found ourselves embroiled in true spiritual warfare of the basest sort. Now, he was here in Iraq as a mere "logistics volunteer," having paid his own way—only to be swept under the rug in some perverse form of corporate housecleaning.

Mark this well: *No one* deserved more from mankind—but arguably received less—than Dwight Lohrenz. Yet God's Word would not return to

Him (or him) empty; it would achieve the purpose for which He sent it. And I would be sent back to Vietnam on my friend's behalf to reprise that Word—but only in God's time.

That opportunity came during my fifth visit to Da Nang in 2007. As for His Word, it spoke loud and clear on the plaque I had commissioned a skilled Vietnamese sculptor to craft. His studio stands at the base of Marble Mountain—as does the stone marker upon which is inscribed Dwight's last will and testament as I believe he might have written it:

> "'Come, let us go up to the mountain of the LORD,…'
> He will teach us his ways,…'
> He will judge between the nations…
> They will beat their swords into plowshares
> and their spears into pruning hooks.
> Nation will not take up sword against nation,
> nor will they train for war anymore."

> ISAIAH 2:3–4

The eternal flame of just another "unknown" soldier? Not for those huddled masses in Southeast Asia, yearning to be free. Only the best and brightest of Jesus' warriors could have kindled the flame to light their way in the darkness. That's how the Lord came to know my dear friend as His very own. That was enough for Dwight. That's all *he* ever needed to know.

Despite one's best of intentions and even the Lord's blessing, sometimes the bridge of reconciling others to Christ simply cannot be crossed. Those to whom the missionary witnesses may be so lost, unreachable, or just plain callous—and the cultural/political milieu in which they labor so oppressive—that it's difficult to justify the effort being expended on their behalf, much less for God to *justify* them on His. Or so it often seems. It's at this point the Lord reminds us what we've been called to do, "despite" them, is for Him—and in a time and place of His choosing. Jesus alone is the Great Reconciler. Only He knows which hearts can be changed.

That's why the Lamb of God came into this fallen world to begin with: as a peacemaker. The missionary merely carries His offer of restitution to the destitute and devious alike. Yet only to the extent to which we are at peace with ourselves—and Jesus' call—determines how effective we are as His messengers. Whereas true peace of mind is nothing more than a fleeting chimera for the so-called "realist", the presence of the Holy Spirit makes that blessing an ongoing *reality* for the called. Which is what I believe Christ was driving at when He told His disciples: "[M]y peace I give you. I do not give to you as the world gives."[2]

Nor as the world receives. Hence the difficulty of witnessing today, particularly so in communist countries. The Gospel is hardly welcomed, much less received, by the leaders of such bastions of secularism as Vietnam, China, and Cuba, to name but a few. As that pertains to medical missions in particular, what their ministers of health give and take is "as the world gives" (and takes)—as in "giving" themselves permission to *receive* our gifts. Any justification for you being there, despite pure and unselfish motives, is weighed self-servingly by theirs.

By definition communism remains the state "religion," and the depth of the people's commitment to that is in direct proportion to the control of their minds. The gifts their leaders receive gladly. The implied message is merely tolerated—and that only *pro forma* at the negotiating table before entering the country, not once you're out on the street or seeing patients in the clinic. These, then, are the most difficult and challenging frontiers in which a missionary seeks to find affirmation, if not for him- or herself, at least for the Lord.

To my chagrin I had ignored that harsh reality after leaving North Vietnam following what initially promised to be a bountiful harvest for God's children in Hanoi. While there as members of an advance team for a later mission, two of us had been invited to work with a surgeon at the National Hospital of Pediatrics. What made this joint venture so ironic for my companion, Ron Oates, was not only the fact that he and the North Vietnamese surgeon had fought on opposite sides of the conflict; they had faced *each other* on the same battlefield near the demilitarized zone! To share the privilege of healing a few of its children some thirty years later represented peacemaking of the most gratifying sort for everyone involved. Having exorcised more than a few demons from the past in so doing, it still

went without saying that finding acceptance as "sons of God" from those
we served was not to be.

Far from it in the end. That unspoken edict was handed down from
somewhere above: hardly Heaven, of course; rather, a wary Politburo less fearful of the United States than the *real* Kingdom we represented. Their proverbial "rice-bowl mentality"[3] was never enough to assuage such paranoia despite
the gifts we had to confer. For one, I had arranged to return to Hanoi the
next year and donate an expensive operating microscope to the hospital. In
this day and age, microsurgical techniques are considered essential for achiev-
ing satisfactory results in the removal of brain tumors and the like—particularly so among the pediatric population. Though her children would have
benefited immensely (as there were no operating microscopes in all of North
Vietnam at that time), the promised invitation to return to Hanoi never sur-
faced.

Peacemakers? Most assuredly; even the rigid Vietnamese leadership was
willing to acknowledge that. But "sons of God"? Not in their eyes! While the
silence from Hanoi remains deafening, Jesus understands. Having "been
there" so many times before, He can offer us reassuring counsel: "If people do
not welcome [the Good News], shake the dust off your feet when you leave
their town," and let my peace return to you (Luke 9: 5; John 14:27). More
bluntly put—and humbly accepted—should they spurn the *real* gift, then
keep it for yourselves.

China would seem another case in point at first glance. Yet even there the government cannot disavow God's intended inheritance for its people altogether.
Let me give you an example. Speaking one evening at dinner with a former
army officer who had taken a job in the bureaucracy as director of the Hand-
icapped Association in Wuhan, I sensed that even the most hardened of hearts
had softened in spite of itself by caring for these unfortunate wards of the state.
No doubt this man was willing to indulge my witnesses (if only face-to-face)
simply to reap any potential benefits. But a single offhanded comment he
made that evening spoke volumes to my suspicion that the Divine Reconciler,
unbeknownst to him, was working on his heart. "There's something in what

you Christians have to say," he conceded at the end of our conversation. Considering its source, that was an astounding admission.

In one sense, however, his comment had not come as a complete surprise. An elderly man whom I had met on the street the day before (dressed in characteristic Maoist garb of his generation) unconsciously betrayed how such sentiments could occasionally surface even in one of the world's most mind-controlling regimes. Recognizing me to be an American, he had asked me three things: How old was I? What did I do for a living? Was I a Christian? The last question caught me off guard, and I later sought out an expatriate who taught English in the school system there to explain what the old Maoist had meant by that. She informed me that such is often asked of Americans, and for one reason. Throughout the twentieth century, which had begun with the distasteful intrusion of foreigners across China's closed borders, its people had learned through harsh experience that the only "good" outsiders were Christians. All others had their own self-serving agendas.

Buried somewhere within these two exchanges lies a seed for God's Kingdom here on earth, one that has been planted in the rockiest of soils overgrown with thistles of autocracy. Yet it's a seed nonetheless, and has survived despite no conscious effort on their part to cultivate it. In just such subtle ways the Gospel is making inroads into the fissures of communist China's resistant bedrock, one root at a time: an aging Maoist on the one hand, a middle-aged bureaucrat on the other—the one subconsciously monitoring the Lord's work, the other unwittingly laboring in His field.

Many of China's younger professionals, openly envious of the West, wish to labor in fields of their own choosing. A few are even willing to put their trust in God to make that happen. Just ask Zhang Wen Ben, an admitted agnostic with whom I'd worked in Xi'an. This gifted doctor had passed a very stringent examination in order to further his training at an esteemed neurosurgical hospital in Beijing. Only ten percent of such candidates make the grade. Despite such an exemplary performance, a recent e-mail from my friend assured me that oppression is alive and well in China. As Zhang sadly confessed: "I've wanted to tell you for some time that I passed the doctoral examination, but as soon as I knew the results and reported to the hospital director for my transfer, he informed me they would not let me study in Beijing. He simply said, 'We had allowed you to take the examination, but had not necessarily agreed for you to train elsewhere if you passed.'"

Zhang was thrown into a severe depression, and even considered resigning from his hospital. In the Chinese medical system that would be tantamount to committing professional suicide. Yet hope springs eternal, whether in the breast of humankind or its e-mails. One of the latter suggested that, just perhaps, my witnesses to this former skeptic had not been in vain. Having slipped him a Bible before I left, Zhang had apparently digested it and taken Moses' "let my people go" appeal to heart. "This is very important to me, as you know, but is a situation I don't want to face alone," he confided. "Therefore, *let us pray to God together* [emphasis mine] for His guidance and deliverance from whatever is blocking my path." Staring at this poignant plea on my computer screen, I was suddenly overcome and fell to my knees—as much with thanksgiving as for intercession. For you see, one must never underestimate the power of the Holy Spirit. When used as a wedge, it can roll even the largest stone away.

"Blessed are the peacemakers," the Good Book says, "for they will be called sons of God." Apparently not in Jesus' hometown—and scarcely in Russia's hinterland. Any act of kindness done there on purely humanitarian grounds, and then judged by them, is as fleeting as the writer of Ecclesiastes had warned us it would be: "I have seen all the things that are done under the sun; all of them are meaningless, a chasing after the wind."

Our surgical team learned this painful lesson firsthand on the day we were to leave for Bratsk, blithely unaware we had been identified with the wrong end of the political spectrum from the moment we set foot on the frozen tundra of Siberia. If the truth be known, our Russian sponsor had in mind a "humanitarian" gesture that would fulfill his own aspirations—carving a niche for himself in the field of presidential candidates angling for the post shortly to be vacated by the ailing Boris Yeltsin. From this Jewish entrepreneur's perspective (whose keys our Christian organization had shamelessly used to open the Kremlin door), this particular mission was nothing more than a down payment on his campaign promises.

Accordingly, the public perception of what our mission had accomplished was grossly distorted by the press, which happened to be controlled by the opposing political party. We were crestfallen to learn through an interpreter that their media had cast our work in a very dim light. The newspaper headlines told the tale: our "heart team" had lost four patients, and one of my own aneurysm patients had died. Though both claims were untrue, that wasn't the half of it. We didn't even have a heart team doing operations in Krasnyorsk!

"Vanity; all is vanity!" As seems to be typical of the media everywhere, theirs was more intent upon "making" the news rather than reporting it. It was left for me to set the record straight, having been promised an opportunity by the hospital administrator where we had worked to respond at a press conference that afternoon, while the remainder of the team flew on to Bratsk. As befits the political chicanery that typifies virtually everything Russian, however, the press conference never materialized.

Nowhere does politics interface more harshly than with Russia's antiquated medical system, given the pervasive influence of the Mafia and those few in power that hold the purse strings. Moscow excepted, among the system's many failings is the inability to capitalize on the skills of its healthcare workers (some of whom are quite gifted), simply because of the shortage of medical equipment.

That's probably the only reason I had been invited to work with a team of five neurosurgeons and a neuroradiologist in the regional medical center of Krasnyorsk—provided I brought with me the necessary surgical and radiology supplies to treat an astounding backlog of patients with aneurysms, brain tumors, hydrocephalus, and the like. Although the work was some of the most gratifying, if challenging, surgery I have had the privilege to undertake abroad, my Russian friends were hardly open to what I had to tell them about Jesus. The neuroradiologist who doubled as my translator would always cut me off when the conversation veered in that direction. "We're just trying to make it day by day, and don't have the luxury of thinking about spiritual matters," he chastised me on one occasion. "Need I remind you that God doesn't put bread in my children's mouths?"

His comment struck me as ironic, if not altogether sad. For it's precisely when political, economic, or social circumstances leave people nowhere else to turn that faith in God so often flourishes to fill the void. That's but one of many black holes in the former Soviet Union into which the spiritual vitality of its people has disappeared; some three-quarters of a century deep to be exact, as reflected during the communist era when not only the Russian Orthodox Church but all religion fell into disfavor. For all intents and purposes, fully two generations of Russians have never known God.

This contributed in large measure to the impenetrable darkness that enveloped Russia's floundering capitalist experiment during the 1990s, lorded over—and gutted—by the black market where only the fittest (read: selfish) survived. As for its government hospitals, doctors invariably closed up shop and left at mid-afternoon to tend to their vegetable gardens at home— not as a hobby, but as a necessity; otherwise, there was nothing but bread and coarse mutton for their families to eat.

Nor did their patients wait for the doctors' return with any particular sense of urgency; they've long been accustomed to waiting, as the system cannot begin to meet their needs at any rate. What few medical supplies that are budgeted for in January are depleted by March. By way of example, should a patient outside the capital city have an aneurysm that requires clipping, the operation better be done within the first three months of the year; beyond that time, there are no clips left to do the surgery! The fateful alternative is an inevitable rebleed, leading to stroke or death.

Russia's women fared even worse during the 1990s, victims of what was caustically referred to as the "illness of Perestroika." Alcoholism reached epidemic proportions among females in particular. Truly dispossessed by the system in every sense of the word, prostitution became the only way for most to survive. Any pain, guilt, or loneliness this may have engendered was assuaged with vodka. What's more, the Russian preoccupation with sex and pornography that sustains this cancer to the present day was fed by X-rated films inundating the airways.

I had the occasion one evening to ask my interpreter, Sasha, whether he preferred the "new" system or the old before the fall of communism in 1990. His answer came as a shock, and spoke to the spiritual emptiness that pervades the former Soviet Union. "As a child [in the old system], I had a greater sense of security and hope for the future than I do now. Though we can only dream of what capitalism might someday afford, we miss the political stability that communism at one time gave us."

Sasha then conjured up an old Russian saying to make his point, whether applied to the impotent leadership that ruled in name only, or the Mafia that really greased the wheel: "It's always the head of the fish that stinks first." Those were harsh (and ironic) words for a fledgling Christian missionary who was weaned on the assumption that I had been chosen to be "a fisher of men!" Unintentionally, Sasha was ripping huge holes in my net. No matter which side of the boat I cast it, the catch seemed so despoiled that one had to sublimate the temptation to stay safely in port.

Lost children of God—from cradle to grave, the former Soviet Union literally teems with them. Having no living God to turn to, the Russian Orthodox Church (which has always served as an instrument of the state and maintains a tenuous grasp on the theological "establishment" even now) represents little more than an iconographic substitute. Hence the lingering perception that remains in this dark corner of the world: though the workers may be few, the harvest seems almost nonexistent. And yet, by His very nature, God's thoughts are not man's thoughts; nor are man's ways God's ways. Which is His way of reminding us that the medical missionary can only plant seeds and trust in the Lord to cultivate them in His own time.

For all the pessimism these reflections suggest concerning the impact (or lack thereof) of short-term missions, by the end of our brief stay in Siberia a few sprouts seemed to have poked through this rocky path lined with thistles. To nurture their growth is what brings God's workers back: seedlings such as a closed Bible (courtesy of the Gideons) that mysteriously appeared on top of the chief of neurosurgery's radiology view box on the third day of my visit— which had been pointedly left open to the Beatitudes in Matthew by the sixth; or the appearance of a small crucifix around Sasha's neck by the end of the week that had supplanted the stone amulet he was wearing when I first arrived.

Rice-bowl Christians? Perhaps. I have no way of knowing whether the Lord's seed will ever take root in such darkness; whether the tenuous sprouts I had noticed have grown—or simply wilted—in the chilling environs of this last outpost of Mother Russia. Maybe that's all the missionary has a right to expect for his or her efforts in such a place. Whether its people will ever experience the blessing of being called "sons of God" is His call to make.

POSTSCRIPT

Those had been my reflections after returning from Siberia in 1999. The recent tapping of its immense oil and mineral reserves notwithstanding, little has changed in this remote part of the world. The same can no longer be said for Russia as a whole, as anyone familiar with Alexander Putin's thinly veiled attempts to resurrect the former Soviet Union on the backs of Big Oil, a state-controlled media, and his cynical alliance with the Russian Orthodox Church will attest. The irony being—as self-serving as Putin's "spiritual revival" has proved to be—Russia is returning to its pre-communist roots when the Czars used the church to bolster their sagging popular support.

For those few who still brave venturing to Russia as Christian missionaries (evangelical Protestants in particular), that has had disturbing consequences. Never has freedom of spiritual expression been more threatened there than it is today—and with that, any genuine reflection of the Christlight. Need it be said that Russia is one venue I probably won't be asked to return to anytime soon? Though communism as a "religion" ultimately failed to find its way in the light of day, the friends and colleagues I left behind in this land of the midnight sun are in the midst of an even longer day's journey into night. The script remains the same; only the characters change. Once more they must "wait on the Lord." Which is why intercessory prayer on their behalf has never been more important. For the moment at least, that's all the missionary-in-absentia can do.

Theirs Is the Kingdom:
REPRISED

From the moment I first set foot on Vietnamese soil during the summer of 2001, Dr. Le Gnoc Gzung not only greeted me with open arms, but spoke thereafter in private (as discretely as he felt it safe to do) of the merits of Christianity—its righteousness most of all, for which he hungered. A Catholic by upbringing, Le had cautiously resumed his spiritual search long after having been forced to renounce that faith during his own wilderness years following Vietnam's reunification. This is his story—and that of its people—from God's perspective.

As a South Vietnamese medical officer during the war, he had been trained by two American neurosurgeons at the airbase hospital in Da Nang. When the country was overrun by the communist advance from 1973 to 1975, virtually all of his colleagues fled the city for points south and beyond. Le, however, stayed on; indeed, he never considered doing anything else. "These were my people," my friend later explained with a resigned shrug of his shoulders, "and I was their doctor."

Such a self-effacing life's view was rewarded with three long years in a "reeducation facility," the Politburo's euphemism for a concentration camp. If that had not been shortsighted enough, they relegated their country's *only* neurosurgeon to the unenviable task of defusing land mines during his internment! The sole mitigating circumstance that rescued Le from professional purgatory and almost certain death was the fact that he had treated many North Vietnamese prisoners during the war, some of whom were highly placed officers. Once a few of these former patients became aware of their surgeon's perilous plight, they petitioned the powers-that-be in Hanoi for his release. Never one to rock the boat, Le quietly returned to his practice among the people he loved in Da Nang.

Now, a quarter of a century later, he would gingerly embark upon a journey toward an even higher calling, despite being an obligate representative of the communist government for which he worked. Intimations of that were spelled out in bold relief shortly after my arrival. As my friend conveyed to me in his humble way: "I believe that you have been sent by God as an angel to light the way for our people." Emblematic of the power of the Holy Spirit in lighting my own path there, the Lord had obviously preceded me from the very beginning—and each and every visit thereafter. At the end of yet another of our conversations in his home some seven years further removed, Le suddenly exclaimed with a passion that belied his soft-spoken demeanor: "You have opened the *eyes of my heart* to the truth in what you have said!"

To the Lord's providence goes all the credit for such a propitious, if uncharacteristic, outburst. That very week before I left for my fifth visit to Vietnam, we had been studying the letters of Paul in Bible Study Fellowship. Ephesians 1:18 caught my own eye, and I committed it to memory. Unbeknownst to me (but not the Lord!), it could not have prepared the soil for Le's eventual blossoming as a believer any better: "I pray also that the *eyes of your heart* [emphasis mine] may be enlightened…that you may know the hope to which he has called you, the riches of his glorious inheritance…" That seed had been conceived by Paul some two thousand years ago. Now, in a tiny interior garden in the middle of bustling Da Nang it was finally beginning to bear fruit.

Not that this particular row to hoe yielded readily to the plow. Following my second visit in 2003, I had discretely mailed a Vietnamese Bible to Le, hidden beneath the false bottom of a box filled with medical supplies. Sadly, my friend later informed me that his Bible had been confiscated. "But how did the authorities find it?" I asked in exasperation. To which he replied: "You must understand that anytime a package arrives from a foreign country, we are required by law to go to the post office and open it in front of a customs official. They found the Bible, and I've been under surveillance ever since."

∞

Other such sordid tales I'd heard during my first three mission trips to Vietnam continued to test my obliged humility as an "honored guest" of the government. Though the "the times [may be] a changin'" as Dylan the troubadour once prophesied in song, the problem in Vietnam, perversely, is toward which *direction* is forever "blowin' in the wind." Or so it appeared as late as 2006. Up until then, pastors' sermons were rigorously scrutinized and edited by the authorities in the best of times; in the worst, scores of clergy disappeared overnight. Not through a formal inquisition as such. That would have cast a shadow over a country seeking legitimacy within the global economic fraternity it has only recently entered and fervently desires to remain.

Rather, wily communist officials, feigning personal interest in the emergence of yet another "unapproved" church, would often seek out one of its gullible members and engage him or her in conversation. "Such a fine pastor you seem to have," the exchange invariably began. "What is his name? I'd like to meet him." Which, more often than not, bought their shepherd a one-way ticket to Hanoi for "retraining." Those who succumbed to the party's dictates were allowed to resume preaching; the few who refused simply did not return. One such pastor, a "Mr. Kim," had been imprisoned so many times since 1975 that his incarceration eventually became an economic burden on the state. Although he faithfully personified the mantra of Peter and John in Acts (he could not help but speak of what he had seen and heard), Kim himself has not been heard from since.

Until very recently, such harsh methods of snuffing out the Christ-light were legion in Vietnam. Spiritual warfare was the order of the day—and that from party headquarters. Plus, there were always more than enough lackeys on the government's dole-for-dong to serve as acolytes-turned-spies in its "church." Like the idolatrous Canaanites of old, the communists of today have their own god to worship. His name is Ho Chi Minh, whose chosen *nom de guerre* ironically translated means "Bringer of Light." Those in the West who are naïve enough to believe that hero worship is not alive and well in Vietnam only need stumble across one of many sacred shrines erected in his honor.

That's what my wife, Vicki, accidentally discovered in 2001 while working as a nurse practitioner at a school just outside Da Nang. As if to set the stage for what transpired, the examination booths had been set up in the gymnasium, at the end of which was an elevated platform with a closed red curtain. Though the authorities had gone great lengths to advertise this as a "free" clinic, it proved to be in name alone. Not only had our team's Vietnamese interpreters (and patients) been handpicked and subsequently monitored; any American there was expressly forbidden to venture behind the closed curtain for reasons that were never explained.

Enter a phenomenon with which every child psychologist (and the author of Genesis) is familiar: telling someone they can't partake of the forbidden fruit becomes an open-ended invitation to do so. Which my wife ultimately did, more out of fatigue and curiosity than anything once she felt compelled to take a five-minute break from the cast of hundreds the team was treating in suffocating humidity and one-hundred-degree heat.

The first thing Vicki noticed once she stepped behind the stage curtain was a dramatic drop in the ambient temperature. That seemed a welcome respite for the moment. Yet the longer she stood there adjusting her eyes to the surroundings, the more intense—if not oppressive—the coolness became. For Vicki was not alone. In the corner was a huge gold bust of Ho Chi Minh, garnished with flowers, shrouded in incense, and surrounded by candles casting an eerie glow throughout this enclosed shrine disguised as a stage.

As she stared at the bust, an irrepressible sense of Satan's very presence swept over her. Turning tail, Vicki quickly exited the enclosure and sought out a fellow team member who was functioning in the role as clergy to pray with her for an exorcism of sorts. Now my wife is not the kind of person to put much stock in the occult. Still, she remains convinced to this day of an evil spirit emanating from that cold piece of metal—an apparition's "bad karma" she could not explain apart from the work being done at its feet down below for the Lord and God of all. By her own admission, that was as close to a satanic shrine as she had ever ventured.

The aftershock of this negatively charged encounter would shortly be felt by her translator once Vicki resumed working in the clinic. Up until then, no one except my wife had taken much notice of this elderly nun with the gentlest of hearts—a Vietnamese remake of Mother Teresa. The comfort she dispensed to my wife's patients was unlike that of the other interpreters. And

Vicki should know, having been assigned any number of them over the previous three days. Nevertheless, within five minutes of her doctor's return from this forbidden foray on stage, the kindly nun was escorted out the door for questioning by uniformed authorities. She never returned to work during the remaining two weeks the team labored there.

That was a sobering reminder of the care with which a missionary disguised as a primary-care provider must go about the Lord's work in Vietnam. Just as we had discovered in China, our own safety was never threatened as an "honored" (and hence protected) visitor of the state. The real threat falls on those whom we befriend, long after we leave—or, in this sad instance, what may befall them while we are still there.[1]

A few whom we as Americans hardly befriended in the past bring poignant meaning to the phrase "trial by fire" in its most literal sense. One in particular is familiar to virtually all of us who witnessed the brutalities of the Vietnam War harshly intruding into the comfort of our living rooms on the evening news. I'm referring to the horrific Pulitzer prize-winning image of nine-year-old Kim Phuc running down Highway One in 1972, screaming in agony, with seared flesh dripping from her naked body after being engulfed by napalm. Some may recall that she subsequently underwent dozens of debridements and skin graftings by magnanimous plastic surgeons in the United States to repair her physically. What you probably don't know is this: It was only the balm of Jesus' living water that healed Kim's *soul* once she came face-to-scarred-face with the real Physician.

But not before suffering further trials at the hand of her own government. I became aware of this only after listening to a National Public Radio broadcast to which she contributed an essay entitled "This I Believe." Her interminable interfacing with the medical profession that had nursed her back from the flames of hell lit a fire of its own in Kim's heart to become a doctor. The "heads" of the powers-that-be, however, demanded she remain something else: a propaganda symbol for the state to fan the charred cinders of its Cold War diatribe.

Kim eventually made her way to the very country she had been enlisted to decry, and eventually married there. Forgiving what the governments of both America and Vietnam did to wreck her life, however, was an understandably tough sell. It wasn't until she stumbled upon the Bible during a literary odyssey spanning years, in an attempt to reconcile her past, that she finally found the answers she sought. The Gospel became her counselor and comforter—a refining fire to light her way toward reconciliation with the only power that mattered—and that, not of this world. Kim's poignant testimony for others? "This I Believe: in Jesus Christ my Lord and Savior, who taught me to forgive. If the girl in that picture can do it, so can you."

So it would appear the majority of Vietnamese back home have done—if rarely in the name of Jesus. Still, I'm convinced this remarkable story was brought to my attention from above for a specific purpose immediately preceding my most recent mission to Vietnam in August 2008: to affirm that the work I was doing there had not been for naught. As pertains to the belated arrival of God's Kingdom in Southeast Asia, the winds of change are blowing in a decidedly favorable direction.

Granted, that probably has more to do with Vietnam's wholesale embrace of Western values in general (and capitalism in particular) than any promised reward for persecution on account of righteousness. Its people have seen far too much of martyrdom's futility in the name of "sacred" causes during the twentieth century to believe otherwise. While the Communist Party still has its watchdogs (a pack of whom from Hanoi had been sitting at a table next to Dr. Le and myself one evening at dinner, as he forthrightly informed me), the bark of its ideology no longer elicits the cowering, kowtow responses it did some five short years ago. For those intent on climbing the party ladder, of course, continuing to toe the party line is merely their way of "taking care of business." Yet for the overwhelming majority of Vietnamese now reaping the benefits a free-market economy affords, Marxism's Midas mirage evaporated long ago.

That underscores the tragic irony of the Vietnam debacle and its aftermath when viewed through the classic economic lens of "guns vs. butter." Though the North may have won the "battle" militarily in 1975, the South eventually won the *war* for men's minds. Not only has the man-on-the-street jettisoned any allegiance to a so-called "managed economy;" the unbridled opportunism of its men-on-the-make eventually infected the party leadership in Hanoi.[2] Stated more pragmatically, communist dogma fell victim to capitalist dollars. And with that fall has come an openness to new realities and fresh ideas—among them the recognition that goodness cannot be imposed externally from the top down; it must grow internally from the bottom up. More encouraging still, an increasing number of Vietnamese are re-embracing the concept that, just perhaps, some "higher power" other than the Communist Party might be in control of their daily lives.

Setting spiritual concerns aside for the moment, apart from China and perhaps India, no country has sustained an eight-to-nine-percent annual growth in its gross domestic product as Vietnam has done over the last five years—the current worldwide recession notwithstanding. That, coupled with huge capital outlays from Japan for new equipment at Da Nang General Hospital, universal health insurance at a nominal cost of twenty dollars annually per family, and government supplementation for the cost of MRI scans that at last makes neurosurgical diagnoses affordable for virtually all, has enabled central Vietnam to match the quality of medical care heretofore restricted to the westernized enclave of Ho Chi Minh City. Moreover, since having purchased an operating microscope for my Vietnamese colleagues in 2003 and training them in its use—in conjunction with instrumentation to treat spinal trauma expeditiously—they have, in effect, upgraded their neurosurgical skills some thirty years beyond the "prescope, pre-instrumentation" era I encountered there during my first visit in 2001.

To be sure, that's but a minor shift in the gale-force winds of change sweeping over the country—and, from the Lord's perspective, ultimately less redemptive than what inroads the Holy Spirit has made in such a brief period of time. Indeed, during my first two visits to Vietnam at the turn of the millennium, few environments reeked more of satanic warfare in an effort to subvert what we were struggling to accomplish. My, how times have changed! Though the majority of Vietnamese still cling to Buddhist traditions and ancestor reverence, it now seems apparent that freedom of worship among Christians has become a *fait accompli*.

Consider but one worship service I attended in 2008, having had the privilege of returning to the same church (Ten Lanh) our team had been invited to visit in 2001. It being a humid summer morning, the openness of the service was mirrored by the sanctuary's wide-open windows, allowing more than a few curious onlookers leaning through them to catch a whiff of the Spirit's presence. The enthusiasm of the congregation (now numbering around five hundred, as opposed to the handful of attendees who always seemed to have been looking over their shoulders back in 2001) was infectious. Whether exemplified during the responsive reading by a chorus of voices literally shouting the refrains as their pastor read from Psalms; passing wooden offering boxes to which *every* member donated amid strains of "I Surrender All" being sung by an enthusiastic choir some fifty members strong; or the rapt attention paid to the sermon in which Christ's name was invoked no less than twenty times—the Holy Spirit had irrevocably found a home.

As for the remaining members of the neurosurgical team in Da Nang, they have become as one in at least paying homage to where I'm coming from and why I'm there. That includes the new department chairman, Dr. Ngoc Ba Nguyen, who happens to be a card-carrying communist. Despite what someday becoming a Christian might adversely imply for his standing in the department, as yet Ba has not completely closed the door. Witnesses one occasion when, without prompting, he asked me to write down for him "something that best defined Christianity."

The Good News, I began, was that God has provided for the eternal salvation of all who believe in the life, death, and resurrection of His Son, Jesus Christ. I then turned to Scripture, with John 3:16 obviously heading the list. What really resonated with Ba, however, was my old tried-and-true explanation of grace as an acrostic; i.e. G-R-A-C-E: **G**od's **R**iches **A**t **C**hrist's **E**xpense. That literally propelled my friend from his chair. He scurried over to a locked cabinet and brought back the power bracelet I had impulsively placed on his wrist just before leaving Da Nang on my previous visit. "Tell me again about these beads and what they mean," he sheepishly inquired. "My son would like to understand them better."

More germane from Ba's perspective as a communist party member, he then questioned how one could have had such allegiance to Christ without having courted trouble with the secular authorities of His day. Just as Jesus had done with the Pharisees, I drew upon the example of the denarius,[3] comparing that to the Vietnamese dong with its face of Ho Chi Minh stamped in bold relief. "Christians in Vietnam must render to Ho what is Ho's," I explained, "and to God what is God's. In that way, you see, the established political order is not necessarily threatened by one's spiritual allegiance to a living God who *Himself* exercised such discernment."

Somewhat to my surprise, Ba was not at all threatened by what he heard. I'd like to think it was no coincidence his parting gift to me four days following this exchange was a scroll of rice paper bearing the words "God is my Fortress" in Vietnamese calligraphy, appended to which was a medallion of Christ praying in the Garden of Gethsemane. Or that he saw fit to wear the power bracelet to the airport the evening I left for home. Merely thoughtful gestures? Perhaps....

Yet one other gesture on his behalf long before I even arrived convinced me that though my friend does not know Jesus, he is still a reflection of our God who created him. For Ba possessed the empathy and foresight to alert me through e-mail that the bronze plaque on the operating microscope I had purchased for them in honor of Dwight Lohrenz had disappeared. "Maybe it had fallen off during our move to the new operating theatre," he mused— but conceded if that were so, it had still not been found. Maybe....

My own sense, however, is that the inscription I had put on the plaque of Dwight having served as a helicopter pilot during the "Vietnam conflict" may have offended a single hospital worker—or, more likely, had been viewed unfavorably by the hospital administrator who, of course, is a communist.[4] Now our relationship is such that I risked positing the latter possibility with Ba, acknowledging that had I used the phrase "War of Liberation" instead, this might have been more palatable. Though Ba did not refute that, his only concern was to have the plaque remade at his own expense to honor my friend. "I promise you it will be there the next time you come to visit," was all he said. Which was the only assurance I needed; in my own experience, Ba's word has never returned to him "empty".

No doubt these kind gestures were his way of honoring my motivations for continuing to come to Vietnam to help its people. Not that Ba is a personification of the so-called "rice-bowl mentality" we usually encounter in communist countries; rather, I have the distinct impression that somewhere in his subconscious a seed has been planted. Where such sentiments might one day lead my friend is for the Lord to decide. It does bear emphasizing, however, that my new brother in Christ, Dr. Le, had asked many of the same questions when we first met back in 2001.

True, the cultural restrictions remain the same. Embracing Christianity, with its emphasis on individual salvation, risks eroding the very foundations of Vietnamese society, what with its Confucian ethic of collective reverence for authority. Add some godless party dogma to the mix, and the recipe for a quarter-century of Christian repression is readily understood. That's why my communist (and Buddhist) colleague, who has so much to lose by gaining Christ, will probably be the last of the team to take the plunge—if at all.

In one revealing sense, though, Ba's understudies in the department have forged ahead of their chief, if everyone's insistence on beginning each operation with prayer during my last working visit in 2008 is any indication. Only Drs. Choung and Bao had appreciated its worth as late as 2006. Now, every member of the team has logged on—particularly so once they grasped the concept of Jesus as their patients' Intercessor through whom they should be praying—rather than having their meditations disappear somewhere into space amidst the incense to which their traditions had accustomed them. As one of the team volunteered, proudly displaying his "command" of western simile (or was that metaphor?): "The proof tastes [sic] like pudding."

Not that another of the junior residents didn't have some lingering doubts. As Dr. Fu put it to me: "It's only your experience that matters. That's the real answer why you're 'Number One' as a neurosurgeon with us. After all, not every patient our team operates on when you're gone has the outcome we as physicians would like. And your god can't change that."

To which I responded: "Jesus doesn't always promise to heal, Fu. Yet He *does* promise to bear our patients' infirmities, and invariably finds a way to make something good out of the bad. But only if we first ask—and then acknowledge Him when that happens."

Though I sensed Fu may not have been convinced at the time, his parting comment to me at the airport the day I left for home prompted me to reconsider. "I will always remember what you told me," he whispered while grasping my hand, "about God making something good out of the bad."

That having been said (for which I am humbly grateful), the greatest obstacle confronting Christianity today in Southeast Asia—as virtually everyone made clear to me—is not the fear of overt retribution such as constrains many Muslims from turning to Christ, but lingering concerns of offending one's ancestors. To my way of thinking, which I made clear to them in kind, God does not require them to relinquish their traditional reverence for the dead. All He seeks is a *living* relationship through Christ with those in the here and now.

With all due respect, whether a mission board would accept that notion, I sincerely believe, is immaterial to Jesus. Isn't that what His disciple, Peter, was implying as well when cautioning others to be prepared to give an answer to anyone who asks for the reason you believe in the hope that you have—but always "*with gentleness and respect*"?[5] Such respect logically extends to the petitioner's customs and traditions. Not only is there scriptural precedent to defend my position on this delicate issue; that's what more than a decade of mission work in Vietnam and elsewhere has taught me. Hence my belief that Jesus will have seen things the same way when I stand fact to face with Him at His judgment seat.

After a number of false starts, my dear friend Dr. Le finally managed to find his own way home in the Lord's embrace. Had it not been for his unexpected visit the evening before I was scheduled to return to the States in August 2008, however, Le's homecoming might well have been missed. That's when I received a call from the front desk informing me of his presence down in the hotel lobby. Ostensibly there to return a cervical plating system I had brought him to use, Le had decided that learning such a new procedure so late in his career might jeopardize his practice and, ultimately, his tenuous financial security.[6]

In truth, that was but a pretense for what was really on his mind: reconsidering his decision to convert to Christianity. It was an all too familiar refrain. "I don't want to hurt my family and ancestors," he explained. "Our traditions go back thousands of years. You see, Buddhism is a cherished philosophy that has served us well through the generations, whereas Christianity is just another religion imported from the West."

Far removed from Jesus having any use for the cervical plates I had to offer Le as a parting gesture of good will, what the Lord really needed at that moment from me was to speak boldly lest my friend close the door left open for him. "Le, Christianity is not a religion," I blurted out. "It's a *relationship*! And you don't have to leave your traditions behind to nurture that with Christ, which is all that ultimately matters."

"That's interesting," Le conceded, "because my daughter who now lives in the States has been told the very same thing. She goes to church every Sunday, and I'm so proud of her."

"You have every right to be," I affirmed. "But Jesus is just as concerned about *you*, my friend. We come to Him one person at a time—and on our own, not through another family member's profession of faith."

Le nodded in understanding and then brightened. "I promise to live and believe as you have taught me. It's the very least I can do for you, Dr. Bert."

To which I countered: "But Le, it's not about me; it's *for* Him! Consider the price He paid for your very soul."

Whereupon he grasped my hand and asked, "What must I do, then, to profess my thanks to Him?"

"Well, you can begin by acknowledging your sins, know that they've all been forgiven by His finished work on the cross, and accept Jesus as your Lord and Savior."

Which Le did, in full view of a lobby-full of hotel guests—after which he hugged me with tears in his eyes and then disappeared into the night to resume serving as a lighthouse for his people, beckoning them toward the Kingdom of Heaven.

No, darkness cannot abide the Christ-light. And in this port city where U.S. Marines first waded ashore in 1965, a handful of candles on a lamp stand still shines to cut through the Kafkaesque nightmare of our long day's journey into night in Vietnam. Under the Lord's aegis, Americans are finally returning to Southeast Asia to finish a conflict that never really ended—yet by this generation's reckoning, a conflict of eternal consequences fought by Christian soldiers bearing not M-16s, but John 3:16.

Theirs Is the Kingdom:
REAPPRAISED

Blessed are you when people insult you, persecute you and
falsely say all kinds of evil against you because of me.

MATTHEW 5:11

For we are God's workmanship, created in Christ Jesus to do good works,
[wherever] God prepared in advance for us to do [them].

EPHESIANS 2:10

I once read a story of a man and his son who returned to an abandoned well the father had used as a child. Knowing the well had been capped long before, he asked the boy to lift up its cover and tell him what he saw. To his son's surprise, the well was dry! That, the father explained, is what happens to wells when we quit using them. No longer sustained through the physical law known as "capillary attraction"[1] by drawing water upward from its underlying source, they eventually die of thirst.

Accessing the Holy Spirit is much like drawing water from a common well.[2] Having bequeathed the Spirit to all believers until His return, Jesus remains our sole conduit through which to draw from the Father's water table.[3] Being of supernatural origin, of course, this living water can hardly be described as "common." If tapped daily, it's never-ending. Yet cease to invoke the Spirit's direction (or refuse to follow His lead once given), and one's *soul* connection to God dries up. That's what befalls any relationship if it's neglected by either party. Just as water always seeks the path of least resistance, the

Spirit—being the third Person of the Holy Trinity—will take His fellowship elsewhere. Not that Jesus is ever to blame; He's always there to be drawn upon.

The above analogy has particular relevance to my "recall" as a missionary back to the States in 2005, if only to have drawn me nearer to God's *specific* purpose at a *particular* time. Though the wells we had already dug together were flush with living water, His call as to where to dig another seemed to have been "put on hold." While seeking direction for my future, I found myself vacillating between Jesus' voicemail counseling patience and a party line abuzz with conflicting advice! At length the Holy Spirit broke through and reconnected me to Scripture—specifically Genesis 26. There I found affirmation for my past and an answer, at least for the present, through what God's servant Isaac had encountered in the valley of Gerar among the Philistines. To my astonishment, his travails in general (and the significance of *wells* in particular) recapitulated my own experience chapter and verse.

Much as Isaac's ongoing disputes with the herdsmen of Gerar over land and wells spoke volumes to me, I'll spare the reader a detailed recap of my struggles over a field of springs [read: Springfield] among nominal (if skeptical) Christians of my own profession. You've heard enough about that— and me—already. Suffice it to summarize, as Isaac's prosperity increased with each new well he dug, Abimelech and his clan of infidels became more envious and threatening—to the point that their nemesis finally left the valley altogether at God's direction, ostensibly to preserve the peace. Yet Isaac was blessed immeasurably in so doing, because the more wells he dug in different locales thereafter extended the long arm of the Lord's reach exponentially.

The end result? Seemingly at Isaac's expense (hardly to be construed as costly; he continued to prosper, as did I), all of his father's offspring were blessed—and that for eternity! As but one such beneficiary some four millennia removed, it was as if the author of Genesis had chronicled Isaac's spiritual journey with *me* in mind. Not that other believers would be surprised; as all have discovered at one time or another, that's how the Holy Spirit uses Scripture to counsel and ultimately comfort Jesus' disciples.

His counsel being, the type of "well" my former associates valued was far different than what I had been enlisted to dig. Theirs were, and remain, material wells; mine, spiritual. Only after we went our separate ways ("Now the LORD had given us room and we will flourish in the land" Genesis 26:22) were our respective wants (or were those *needs?*) finally met. That's when the Spirit's comfort washed over me; for such is the way He meant things to be. Whereas my adversaries took what they wanted through stealth, I received what I *needed* by grace.

What some might perceive as "washing my dirty laundry" in public at a well of the Lord's choosing had one other potentially redeeming offshoot before leaving Springfield in 2001 for full-time missions abroad: planting a seed there that might be watered by the runoff. Though only God can make the one grow, there's enough of the other left over to sustain the most parched of spirits while washing the worst of sinners clean. That's why Jesus referred to it as "*living* water." And that's of far more eternal value than water drawn from a well for no other function than quenching the materialists' thirst. Theirs can never be satisfied; nor, like manna in the desert, can they store such water for later use. Camels we're not! To drive the point home using another "beast of burden" with which Americans are more familiar, "You'll never see a U-Haul hitched to a hearse."

Now *there's* a word picture that speaks graphically to Christ's first indictment of any would-be disciple: "Insofar as *My* well was meant to be used, how could *you* have done anything less for Me?" Consider the price Jesus paid for us to "dig" our own wells in the very valley *He* created—not to mention those costly Beatitudes Jesus was willing to die for to seal the deal! Dying to self in kind (and onsite) is one decree offering the professed well-digger down in its depths no wiggle room for an appeal.

Facing the life-after-"death" sentence that follows, on the other hand, depends on one's life view—and devotees of spiritual "wellness," no doubt, will continue to constitute the minority. Yet it's much more than just a matter of opinion; it's being *proactive* in the life choices we make that will determine the yield of whichever type of well we've dug and continue to draw from. To switch metaphors in "mid-pull," as it were, the type of foundation one builds is the key to which Paul was alluding when he said: "Fire will test the quality of each man's work" (1 Corinthians 3:13). Whether digging a well to access the Spirit, or building an altar to acknowledge His presence, that's precisely what trials *by* fire do.[4]

As pertains to believers and their wells in particular, that's also what spiritual gifts afford: manifestations of God's grace to contain those fires meant to refine when they threaten to consume. As "containers" in yet another sense, spiritual gifts serve as buckets that draw from the same wellspring of grace so that others might partake and ultimately avoid the fiery lake on Judgment Day.

This "draws" us to Jesus' second indictment as relates to what each of us has done for God's kingdom using those gifts. That's nothing if not an individual *act of worship* from His perspective. Remember Christ's encounter with the Samaritan woman—where else but at a well? When challenged there about worship practices and places, Jesus bluntly replied that neither the form of worship nor its place mattered so much to God as one's heart and commitment. This was His way of telling you and me today what He really desires—not mindless observances of meaningless rituals that placate us, but tireless use of spiritual gifts that glorify Him.

Acts of service to others, then, become acts of worship for God—*wherever* those take place. That's what my own recall in 2005 from full- to part-time missions has affirmed in no uncertain terms: At least for now—I'm precisely where Jesus wants me to be. Thanks to a handful of "surprise" witnesses in Kansas City where I now practice between trips overseas, I have His assurance (and theirs) this is one well that should not be capped anytime soon. To defend what might seem a "compromised verdict," let me briefly recount their testimonies.

"Take it to the Lord in prayer." That's an invitation the hospital chaplain often invokes when counseling those who mourn in America's emergency rooms and intensive care units. Yet just how far prayer can *take the caregiver* is rarely disclosed. In one instance in particular, a single in-filled prayer warrior took me to a place where, as a neurosurgeon, I strongly resisted going. Her husband had been admitted with a massive intracranial hemorrhage from what I suspected to be an aneurysm that had ruptured—leaving him, for all intents and purposes, dead on arrival.

At least clinically he met all the criteria for "brain death" apart from a few agonal respirations when briefly taken off the respirator as a trial: no response to painful stimuli, unreactive pupils, absent brainstem reflexes—indicating imminent death. No mistaking the reason why. His fluid-filled spaces within the brain, known as ventricles, were filled with blood—whose mass effect was so great that the brainstem had already herniated through the small aperture at the base of his skull. I advised his wife as such, and sadly confessed there was nothing that could be done to save him—"only prayer for the salvation of his soul."

To my initial chagrin, that very phrase (as sincerely as it had been uttered) was all she needed to hear. "But Terry's *not* saved," she exclaimed in exasperation, "and you as a Christian are obligated to give him every chance to make that choice for himself. We can't do that for him. It's left for Jesus to know whether his opportunity has already passed—but you and I have no way of knowing this ourselves. Being a man of God," she concluded resolutely, "I trust you appreciate where I'm coming from."

The problem, I countered, was that doing anything at all ran the huge risk of leaving her husband in a persistent vegetative state. I'd already "been there" far too many times during my thirty-five years as a neurosurgeon, bearing witnesses to what catastrophic illness does to families left to linger in this purgatory between life and death.[5] That was a valley I fervently desired not to revisit, and could assure them they didn't want to go down there with me.

"Ah, but it's down in the valley where the lilies grow," she brightened in reply, "and I'm willing to follow you there for the sake of any chance at all that Terry might one day make the decision for Christ on his own. In all honesty, I don't think He's done with my husband yet. You're a Christian doctor—and I hope a good one—but can *you* know the mind of the Lord?"

Despite my reservations, her abiding faith in what the Divine Physician *might* do (not to mention what He had wanted Terry to do long before) won me over. But only after insisting we collectively seek the Holy Spirit's guidance. No doubt the skeptic would suggest that, based largely upon how the physician presents his case, any Divine Surrogate's decision in such matters would come across as some form of manipulated groupthink. Speaking from some twelve years' experience with the value Jesus places on intercessory prayer, however, has proven to me time and again that if carer and sufferer together sincerely seek the Spirit's guidance, His answer *will* come. To be sure, it's usually not what they want to hear. Most, therefore, surrender and choose to let nature run its course.

Yet Terry's predicament from the spiritual perspective alone was a "special" case. As such, the Lord's decision to push on was universally shared by all who participated in that hastily arranged prayer vigil in the ER consultation room. Ours was to do what we could at that moment; His would be the call thereafter when to stop. That, in a nutshell, is what the Holy Spirit said to each of us.

Immediately I notified the operating room of the impending emergency surgery to remove the massive clot and attempt to clip what I believed—though did not know, as we had no other studies but a CT—to be a ruptured aneurysm. But first I had to perform an emergency ventriculostomy (placing a drain in the center of the brain) at the bedside in an attempt to temporarily decrease the massive pressure buildup. Within thirty minutes of so doing we were in the OR, where I encountered a giant aneurysm arising from the internal carotid bifurcation. In the best of circumstances I "knew" its location was such that, even if Terry were to miraculously regain consciousness, he would be paralyzed on his left side—having clipped the aneurysm in the presence of some small, but critical, perforating arteries adhered to the back of its neck.

Fast forward some six months later when Terry *walked* into my office with a huge smile on his face for his follow-up visit. Not only had he no residual paralysis that I could detect; his speech was fluent and his cognitive abilities virtually normal. Suffice it to say, what we went through together to bring him there following my "Hail Mary pass" was far too convoluted to relate here. Yet three points do bear emphasizing. First, whenever I visited Terry in the ICU thereafter his wife was sitting at the bedside reading the Bible to him. Second, once emerging from his coma, Terry made his profession to Jesus as his Lord and Savior. And third, had it not been for her steadfast faith and persistence, I would never have taken the risk of going down into such a dark valley on their behalf.

Yet that had been Jesus' point for us all from the very beginning: Had I chosen instead to commit to fulltime mission work elsewhere, the end result would have been different. For I've seen too many virtually identical cases to know that, absent having taken this matter to prayer in Kansas City that memorable evening, neither Terry nor his family would be sharing the fruit of the Spirit in the Lord's presence today.

∞

To affirm Jesus' faithfulness for those who actively seek His guidance when Satan's worm turns in the apple and their world sours overnight, as of this writing I'm currently six months into a reprise of yet another amazing triumph on the Lord's behalf. In Gerald's case, however, the cards were stacked even more unfavorably against him. After all, he had already been unofficially declared "brain dead" from a massive blood clot at the base of his hindbrain (i.e. cerebellum) by his attending physician, who happened to be my associate, Dr. Velez. All that could be done at the time of the initial emergency surgery, as futile as he had warned the family it would be, proved unavailing. Gerald never regained consciousness, and for seven days thereafter was being "artificially supported" on a respirator, with no detectable brainstem reflexes.

Yet, a problem had arisen on the way to Gerald's anticipated funeral that mandated my involvement. This happened on the evening of the eighth day "by special invitation only" in the form of a requested second opinion. It seems someone had ordered a postoperative scan, for reasons that defied common sense. The poor man had already passed on—or so it appeared to some of the "best" medical minds in the business. Maddening to relate, the huge clot had *re-accumulated* at the operative site, and the patient's wife (notwithstanding the objections of every other family member, eight in all) wanted to have it removed. I just happened to be on call that evening, and it was left for me to second my associate's opinion that subjecting Gerald to further surgery would be for naught. Or so I had been entrusted.

As providence would have it, after introducing myself I made what seemed at first a tactical error in requesting we all take a moment to seek the Lord's guidance. *Perhaps some of those involved might later be comforted during their daunting trial by fire that lies ahead*, I mused self-righteously (and assuredly), *once the time comes to "pull the plug" and let their loved one go*. Never mind that I knew nothing of their spiritual backgrounds. Possessing a politically incorrect (tactless?) streak, I rarely hesitate to impose prayer on others— if for no other justification than to at least acknowledge God's presence in such life-and-death decisions and, per chance, that one or a few "subjected" to my life's-view-put-into-action might climb on board for the long haul.

In this particular instance, Gerald's wife had already booked passage. And before the evening was over, by Jesus' persistence alone, all other heretofore skeptical family members were at least willing to hear her (and His) perspective. Although I was not refusing to do the operation, going back to surgery was hardly my recommendation. Yet Gerald's wife could not be dissuaded. Seeking the counsel of the Holy Spirit as Mediator, therefore, was our only option. For one whole hour after presenting my case, through the Plexiglas sliding door I watched this family of ten huddled around Gerald's bedside in intercessory prayer. Sensing the pessimism of everyone but his wife before retreating from the room, I fully anticipated they would make the usual decision to go no further.[6]

To my surprise (and admitted mortification), they emerged from Gerald's room after the hour had passed and asked me to take him back to surgery. The wholly (holy?) unexpected upshot of their decision was that he inexplicably began to *improve* slowly but steadily thereafter. This was roughly ten percent of the lives-changing miracle Jesus had in store. For eight other family members who had never before considered asking the Lord to become involved in their daily travails, it was a wonder to see the transformation this blind leap of faith had wrought. Gerald's room became a chapel of worship. Toward the end of his stay, he too was beginning to participate. That brought the "attendance"—and Christ's miracle—up to one hundred percent!

Some three weeks later Gerald was transferred to a rehab facility. Given his long and arduous journey ahead, I have no way of knowing how far the Lord intends to carry His reborn lamb. Yet every step of that journey thus far has been affirmation of the highest order. Not through anything I had done; rather, simply because another of God's children had stood on the Lord's promise and insisted we take the walk together despite medicine's "best evidence" counseling otherwise.

Just another walk around the desert for this "resounding gong and clanging cymbal" of a missionary in America, who so many times before had seen but one set of footprints in the sand long after I grew tired. Toting a single believer on His back at such times is surely a formidable task—particularly so, considering the dead weight I often bring to bear on the work at hand. Adding ten others and their burdens at the same time, however, is a load only the risen Christ can sustain. Okay, so He's had a lot of practice, having borne the weight of the whole world on His shoulders for over two thousand years! I can't help, then, but wonder: When the Divine Physician promises to bear our infirmities, why depend upon anyone else? Much less a fallible neurosurgeon who just "happened" to be there as nothing but His witnesses when some very frightened sheep needed Jesus the most.

∞

Viewed from outside the Lord's gated enclosure, this matter of an unrequited *need* seems to be a recurring theme. And by her own (belated) admission, a single soul once found—but now lost— desperately needed His embrace. Not that Valerie Jean appreciated this at the time; nor did she wish to be cuddled by anyone or anything associated with "organized religion." Long ago the church had shown its true colors by holding her at arm's length on account of a single "unfortunate but unforgivable" life's choice she made. Those had been the harsh words of her pastor. Yet the hushed whispers and averted eyes of countless "saints" within the body of Christ spoke volumes to this loving family of three. Theirs would have to be nurtured outside its walls.

No doubt Val's past fall from grace was the last thing on her mind when we first met in the Medical Center of Independence emergency room. Over a six-month period she had suffered from intractable vomiting and motion sickness for which no cause could be found. Following the obligate "million dollar" gastrointestinal and ear, nose, and throat workups, only in hindsight did someone order a CT scan of her brain, when a thirty-dollar eye examination revealing florid "papilledema" (pressure on the optic nerves from the brain) would have sufficed to explain her symptoms. Sadly, the scan revealed a rare but virulent cancer of the brainstem, known as an "ependymoma,"

Recognizing the urgency of the situation, Val agreed to have her surgery scheduled the following morning. But not before spending some unaccustomed time in prayer with her surgeon. Though a cynical few might perceive this as an imposition on my part, it's been my experience that the overwhelming majority of sufferers—with or without a faith-based life's view— respond gratefully when prayer is introduced into the dynamic of the patient-physician relationship, which I invariably do.

No mystery there; they have a compelling *need* at that particular moment. If sharing a word with the Lord does nothing more than put them at ease before surgery, well enough. Quite often, however, I've found that a single prayer in the beginning opens doors later to an in-depth discussion of what really matters. If done with gentleness and respect, it's occasionally a short step thereafter from bedside "evangelism," if you will, to Christ-led discipleship. As such, that's not a self-serving imposition but an open-ended invitation. God does the calling when He chooses; those who answer simply recognize now is their time to respond.

Need it be said that Val's needs, both physically and spiritually, were huge? After all, resecting an invasive tumor that had no defined borders within this central-clearing-station between the brain and spinal cord was sure to induce some distressing neurologic deficits she as yet did not have. Dysfunctions such as double vision, trouble swallowing, and perhaps even facial paralysis—the latter no small matter for an attractive, middle-aged female. That was the price she would likely pay for initiating her treatment—only to be followed by radiation and chemotherapy, each with their own anticipated setbacks.

Predictably, Val sustained two out of the three residual deficits in the course of undergoing four separate surgeries. Distressingly, other complications followed that prolonged her convalescence. Amazingly, she took all of this in stride with a gutty resourcefulness and witty sense of humor that belied the ultimately fatal hand she had been dealt. Among many other qualities, that's what made Val so special: it's what she *did* with the time she had.

Emblematic of that, none of these physical trials diverted her attention from the one concern that consumed my patient, who by now had become a dear friend: Would her daughter, Ruthi, find the spiritual underpinnings for her own future that Val thought she had lost herself? Here was a nine-year old cherub who was the "spittin' image" of her very special mother (their words, not mine). Moreover, Ruthi's intelligence and emotional maturity mirrored that of someone twice her age. Need I add her capacity to love and make others simply feel good? All were testimonies to the nurturing she had received from two very devoted parents long before I ever became involved in their lives. Ruthi glowed like a wraith in the Christ-light she reflected, but as yet did not know she possessed.

And that was the problem, at least as Val perceived it. Ruthi was at a pivotal point in her own life spiritually, which only added to the pathos of her mother's plight. Not that anyone was privy to my patient-turned-soul-sister's angst (apart from her shared confessions with me); indeed, she was so busy glowing herself that the darkness of her purgatory within never saw the light of day! And what, for Val, was that dark recess where she wrestled daily? Hardly her physical trials, two steps forward and one backward; rather, the haunting thought that "before she left" Ruthi might not have entered into the Lord's pasture to which her mother seemingly had been denied. Or so Val thought. Yet, unbeknownst to her, Jesus had a very special reception to orchestrate in her honor, of which the entire family would become spiritual beneficiaries as three children of God.

Space does not allow for a rehash of all we went through together during those first three months of Valerie's convalescence. Nor would doing so have the same impact as allowing Val herself to summarize what she really prized when all was said and done. That came in a letter she had written, which I received from her spouse, Laurie Ann, long after my gentle lamb ultimately surrendered her life here on earth to the Good Shepherd:

Dear Bert,

Thank you so much for coming to Ruthi's baptism today. I know you don't like to take credit for doing the Lord's work, but I truly feel His name is glorified when we acknowledge the work He does through us. And you, my friend, have brought the Holy Spirit into my life in so many ways.

I think back to the night I first met you when, brain tumors aside(!)...I was a fallen shell of a person. If it could only have been that I was a skeptic or even a nonbeliever, I wouldn't feel such shame now. But I had completely turned my back on the Lord and lived to shut out His presence in our lives [as a family].

Yet now I'm so thankful that He put you on my path to gently nudge me back into the pasture where I belong. It scares me to think of how lost I was, mostly because I had nothing spiritual to give to Ruthi...That's why I'm so very thankful our Lord blessed me with a friend like you, Bert. Yes, it was a blessing to have my tumor removed—but the more precious gift was having my spirit restored! The most wonderful blessing of all, however, is that my family is now reaping the benefit....

In His debt,
Val

What a family it was—and, in an eternal sense, remains! Never have I encountered a daughter so young who reflected such an intense Christ-light by virtue of the love her parents showered upon her. Sure, Ruthi's home life might be described as somewhat "different" than most of the kids in her class, and undoubtedly she suffered ridicule and persecution because of it—to the point that home-schooling became the only alternative during her late grade school and early junior high years. That did nothing to sublimate Ruthi's social skills, however, nor the two sources from which they came.

Being a silent observer as a fly on the wall, what a joy it was to watch the three of them horsing around and teasing one another during Val's return appointments to the office! Or to have the privilege of sharing worship in their church where Ruthi was baptized. It had never been too late for them to journey up the mountaintop together to sing His praises—though far too early to be led back down once my dear friend's tumor recurred.

And that's the strange thing: I've lingered with other families in the twilight of death's valley so many times before. Yet for these three "candles in the wind" who ultimately found themselves there in the presence of the Holy Spirit, rarely had the *Son* shone so brightly! That's all Val ever wanted for her family. And that's precisely what Laurie Ann and Ruthi inherited and reflect to this very day. Rest well in His arms, then, Valerie Jean: Your candle burned out long before its due, but your *legacy* never will.

More than a few lost sheep of the pasture don't share that desire and actively resist being ushered through the narrow gate in search of restitution. All they wish to do is make it through another bone-chilling day—heads bowed, gnawing at the frozen tundra, totally deaf to the Shepherd's call. For the most recalcitrant He uses the staff to grab their attention with a sharp rap across the nape of the neck. That's what happened to Mike, who bore the brunt of the blow with his very soul hanging in the balance.

By all appearances this burly lamb was a rebellious sort of fellow who reveled in living life on the edge. His own had been hewn from the ripsaw of a construction-worker's lot: across the grain and not without chips, which he bore stubbornly on his shoulders. Yet the *eyes* of this defiantly independent soul who now lay in the hospital bed before me betrayed something else: fear! Any why not? Shortly after undergoing a chiropractic manipulation for intractable headaches and shoulder pain, he had become paralyzed from the neck down.

The onset of Mike's paralysis was something of a mystery to me; more so once I reviewed his MRI scan. To my surprise, there was nothing compressing the nerve sac in the high cervical area. Apart from initiating an intravenous steroid protocol usually reserved for high-speed-impact spinal-cord injuries, no surgery could be offered that might reverse this inexplicable tragedy besetting a middle-aged man who, to that point, had been the picture of health. Notwithstanding his recurring neck and shoulder discomfort, which Mike self-medicated more often than not with a six-pack of beer on evenings after work.

Instinctively (and without first asking permission to do so), I offered a prayer over my patient at the bedside, hardly taking the time to introduce myself as the spine-consultant called in to make him walk again. Judged by his response, "witchdoctor" would have seemed more appropriate: "A nice touch," he retorted as I finished praying, "but where's the *real* surgeon who's going to get me out of this?"

Mike's wife reacted altogether differently. Weeping gently during my prayer, she politely asked to speak with me afterwards outside the room. "What a comfort for me to know we have a Christian doctor!" she said, and then made a point of apologizing in advance for her husband's apparent ingratitude. "Any prayers at this particular time are likely to fall on deaf ears. You see, Mike's been wounded in the past by the legalism, hypocrisy, and false hopes of what he calls 'Bible thumpers,' and wants no part of what you and I share."

That's an indictment I'd heard all too often before in, of all places, the Bible Belt of America's heartland. Though our conversation ended that first day with this sad admission, it hardly kept me from praying every day thereafter for discernment as to what I might do as a doctor to meet the understandable "demands" of my downtrodden patient. Nor did I ever doubt his wife was doing the same.

As matters turned out, I for one initially misjudged what my intercessory prayers were intended to do *for God* as much as for Mike. That proved a timely reminder of what the Lord had already taught me so often before in the mission field: Christ-centered prayer is less an end to meet our earthly needs than it is His *means* of aligning our thoughts and actions with God's will. And in this particular instance Jesus had something more in mind than the sole restoration of a paralytic's body; what He wanted all along was Mike's soul fellowship in the body of Christ.

So as for my charge not to miss out on this opportunity, Mike mercifully (and inexplicably) began to improve, despite nothing I was doing apart from the "shot-in-the dark" steroid approach prescribed. Nothing, that is, except praying—which, I *did* do, day after day. Each morning on rounds, accordingly, brought new hope for Mike (and more affirmation for myself) as I watched him slowly but surely regain his strength. By the third week, to everyone's amazement, our previously paralyzed patient was walking again! Not that this agnostic was willing even then to give the Lord any credit. Which serves as a prelude to Jesus' final curtain call that all three of us nearly missed…

The day of Mike's planned discharge I received a call in my office asking whether I needed to see the two of them before they left. "That's probably not necessary," I remember relaying to the nurse who called. "He's no longer on any medication that I need to prescribe. Have them make a follow-up appointment with me in one month." Yet Jesus had other plans. Once I hung up the phone, the Holy Spirit tapped me on the shoulder, nudged me into my car, and sent me to the hospital.

On the way I mulled over any number of stories or parables from Christ's ministry that I might use to break through Mike's resistant spirit. For reasons I could not decipher at the time, I settled on the same account I had related in Siberia to Ludmilla and her merciful attendants concerning the four stretcher-bearers who had climbed up on the roof in Capernaum with their paralyzed friend in tow so that Jesus might heal him. To my way of thinking, any number of examples of His miraculous healings might have sufficed. Not so for the Holy Spirit within, who had escorted me to the hospital and led us both to where we needed to be.

Upon our arrival Mike was getting dressed. Handing him his shirt (which he buttoned with a dexterity totally foreign to him just three short weeks ago), I recounted the story. Emphasizing in particular that his wife deserved the same credit as the stretcher-bearers in Jesus' day, she suddenly let out a gasp and fell to the floor sobbing uncontrollably. *What in the world have I done?"* I wondered. *I was only trying to open Mike's eyes to the wonder of the Lord's mercy shown His loved ones, faithfully bearing our burdens in time of need. Now it seems I'm only adding to them!*

At which point his wife proceeded to pick herself off the floor and in a quavering voice asked me: "Dr. Park, do you know how Mike got to this hospital and to you—if not the Lord?"

"No," I sheepishly confessed. "As the neurosurgeon on call that day, I had simply received a page from the ER announcing his arrival."

To which she replied: "But what about this beautiful story you just told us? I assumed you simply must have known since you chose that particular miracle."

Perplexed, I asked her to explain—and her fact-is-stranger-than-fiction account was more than enough to blow me to Kingdom come. Which was precisely Jesus' intent for us all.

"At the chiropractor's office, Mike had been left in the treatment room alone following his manipulation," she began. "Shortly after he closed the door to redress, we heard his cry: 'I can't move!' We tried to open the door, but for reasons I still don't understand it was locked. Frantically I called his best friend on my cell. In no time at all, he, along with three others, came over to the office and [presumably with the chiropractor's permission] broke down the door." Whereupon she brought the whole house down with her final revelation: "As you know, Mike's a big man, and now he was paralyzed. So what did his friends do? They *used the door* they had broken off its hinges to carry him to the hospital!"

I was totally blown away. Modern day stretcher-bearers literally bringing their paralyzed charge and laying him at Jesus' feet for a healing that only He could—and did—perform. Of all the Gospel miracles I might have chosen to connect with Mike at this pivotal turning point in his life, the Holy Spirit had prompted me to relate the sole account that would bear fruit. He was as good as His Word. In the sterile environs of a hospital room, one very repentant sheep of the pasture surrendered his life to the Lord.

As for the broken-down door, I know a good Carpenter who has a great pair of hands and could repair that as well if He chose to do so. Yet the buzz on the street is that He's been called to be a Shepherd instead. I can certainly relate to His midlife career change; being under new management, my Boss, Jesus, taught me long ago that mending broken bodies and souls for free is far more lives-changing (theirs *and* mine) than paying the bills doing trim work. Besides, *His* Boss never asked Him to take the time out of His busy day to replace the door. *Word* has it there's a reason for that: to remind us the only way to salvation is through the narrowest of gates *left open* by this Carpenter-turned-Shepherd, who beckons His lost sheep to enter.

Great Is Your Reward in Heaven

Blessed are those who are persecuted because of righteousness…" Or for whatever reason; righteous or not, our souls cry out for an explanation as to why we are made to suffer. That's human nature. To be sure, any persecution both here and abroad that I had experienced by way of comparison was no match for what the Kosovar refugees suffered at the hands of the Serbs. Theirs was persecution of the basest and most indefensible sort—though far removed from what Jesus was referring to in the Beatitudes. After all, the eighth and ninth of Christ's blessings from Matthew's version of the Sermon on the Mount were meant to comfort those who were reviled and persecuted for *His* sake. That would scarcely apply, much less appeal, to the Muslim mindset.

As for my own at the time, the futility of our mission in Albania did have one painfully "redemptive" payback: if they were to suffer, then surely I (who had been pretentious enough to believe we could make a difference in the very name of a Christian God they understandably loathed) deserved to be dragged onboard their sinking ship with them. That's because I had my own demons to wrestle with back home. For one, before leaving for Albania I had not been reconciled to those who were persecuting me in my practice. Nor could I forgive others responsible for a far greater suffering inflicted on my father. Both of which underscore my previously expressed point that one cannot be at war with others (or self!), then drag God into it, and still expect to be an effective peacemaker on His behalf.

This brings me in a rather circuitous fashion to the Lord's unmerited grace and the affirmation I paradoxically received at His expense. Unmerited, because I ultimately disobeyed Jesus' clear command to make the best of a bad situation. Paradoxical, insofar as He remained faithful despite my refusal to follow His counsel from the start. Let me explain.

Just after my deciding at the last moment to go to Albania (and, it should be said, with no time spent in prayer seeking God's direction), my father had injured his back while attempting to pick up my stepmother from the floor following a fall. Both ended up in the emergency room that day—she with a badly bruised jaw, and Dad with a debilitating herniated disc. That was the sad culmination of a trying two years for my father, who had been attempting to care for his wife at home following her diagnosis of rapidly progressive Alzheimer's disease. The time had come to place her in a nursing home, and I knew Dad would not surrender if left to do that on his own. Yet I had already tentatively made a commitment to go to Albania. With a heavy heart, he insisted I go—assuring me he could manage until my return.

While in Albania I continued to perseverate on what I perceived as an abandonment of my father so I could do the Lord's work. And once having surmised there to be no profitable work to be done (much less any harvest to be reaped on His behalf), my guilt accelerated exponentially. By the evening of the third day I was as depressed as many of the refugees I had been futilely ministering to in the clinic! That night I couldn't sleep, torn between my commitment there and my obligations back home. Was it to be God—or family? Belatedly, I turned to the Bible for guidance.

Leafing through Matthew, I stumbled across a passage that brought fresh insight to my predicament: "… everyone who has left houses or brothers or sisters or *father* [emphasis mine]…for my sake will receive a hundred times as much and will inherit eternal life" (19:29). Oh, how I yearned to strengthen my relationship with Jesus! Practical experience, of course, had already taught me that the way one nurtures any relationship is through communication. To God, this means prayer. Now that He had me on my knees, I knew the Lord was speaking to me. How, then, was I to manifest that love in action? The New Testament is replete with verses on this very point: *one must obey…*

No doubt the timeless truth of God's Word staring back at me clearly implied I had little choice in the matter. Up until then I had sweated blood during the early morning hours—just as Christ had literally done the night before facing His greatest test. At length I found the answer for which I was searching, as had Jesus: not my will, but *God's* will be done. At 4:00 AM I turned in, fully committed to staying on.

The timing of this particular decision, however, betrays a recurring hitch in my Christian walk—one that continues to frustrate my best intentions even to this day. For you see, my quiet time with the Lord is invariably (though not always most profitably) spent late at night, largely because my physiology dictates that. I'm simply not a morning person. Consequently God's instructions always seem so much more enlightening at night before I go to bed.

The first light of day is all too often another matter. Things are paradoxically darker for me then, and His direction not quite so clear. That's a sad admission. If ever there were a time when a fallen man like myself would benefit from the Lord's guidance, it's in the early morning when I first face the day, less certain of the way forward. Now, in the overcast morning gloom of a farmhouse in Albania on the other side of the world from a man who had always been there for me, my resolve of the night before vanished. I reversed the decision made just two fitfully slept hours before and hitched a ride to the coast to catch a ferry for Italy and, ultimately, home.

My precipitate action had turned one of the underlying themes of the Bible on its head: "Remember in the darkness what you once learned in the light." Like Jesus at Gethsemane, I had sought God's direction in the *dark* and received it. Yet, just as Peter had done, I denied my Lord three times in the *light* of day by (1) ignoring His Word and clear command, (2) abandoning His search for those lost sheep among the Kosovars, and (3) placing the needs of my earthly father above my Father in Heaven. That was as low as I ever remember being in my Christian walk. Having reverted to a crawl, my hasty retreat threatened to become a rout. For I was now very much alone, with nothing but a knapsack on my back, guitar in hand, and no ticket to make my way to Rome and catch a flight to New York on standby. *Ample retribution*, I remember thinking, *for one who has denied the Lord and gone his own way!*

So I berated myself during that lonely voyage home, the first leg of which began with foolishly booking passage on a rug merchant's sloop across the Adriatic. That proved to be frightening as well once I discovered at mid-crossing that the Albanian captain with whom I could only communicate through hand signals (and American dollars) was an arms merchant in disguise! Tucked within his rugs ostensibly for sale were AK-47s and rocket launchers. Had he perceived me to be some sort of Serbian agent, my faith-based journey might just as easily have ended with baptism by immersion of a different sort—one thousand feet under and lashed to a stone, "dying to self" in the most literal sense of the phrase in the middle of the Adriatic.

Thankful to relate, Jesus provided for my safety. I survived the crossing, but not before—as a disobedient, modern-day Jonah fleeing Nineveh, where God had directed him to go—being swallowed up by a "whale" of my own making. Spiritually I was in the darkness of its belly; yet, just as happened to Jonah, some three days later the Lord "resurrected" (regurgitated?) me to resume His work.

That was but the first of many unmerited blessings Jesus would bestow. Once I arrived home, physically exhausted and an emotional wreck, He guided my steps in securing a nursing home placement for my stepmother, assuaging my father's guilt in so doing, and last—but by no means least—ministering to him physically. By now Dad's pain had become intractable and his partial paralysis progressive. He agreed to undergo surgery and asked me to perform it. With the Lord's guidance, the surgery went well, and his leg pain and weakness disappeared.

I had misread Jesus' intentions from the very beginning. No wonder! You may recall that I had spent little time in prayer seeking His will before going to Albania. This was His way of telling me now: "Just because you perceive a need, don't automatically assume you're the one to meet it. Be *called* before you act; otherwise you may miss the more important task I have for you to fulfill." What He clearly had in mind was ministering to Dad first. In characteristic self-effacing fashion, Christ gave me the opportunity to serve my father at the expense of the work I *thought* I had been called to do elsewhere for His own.

Yet that was hardly the end of the grace the Lord extended to me at a time when I least deserved it. Having fulfilled the criteria of His first beatitude, "the poor in spirit," through no fault but my own, Jesus inexplicably blessed me beyond measure—far more than being a servant to Dad as his doctor. Now He had another treasure in store for the both of us, despite my father facing a second crisis so cruel in its implications that even now I have difficulty grasping it. See if you don't agree.

When he remarried some twenty-five years ago after the respective deaths of my mother and Mimi's husband, Dad had agreed to sell our home and possessions and move into her house. That proved to be a satisfactory arrangement (not to mention an endearing relationship) for eighteen years. Some *four* days after moving Mimi into the nursing home, however, and just two days after his operation, her sons demanded he move out of "their" home and find another place to live! Still in the acute convalescent stage of his surgery and with nowhere to go, Dad agreed to move in with me until a more permanent arrangement could be made.

By both our admissions, this proved to be His richest blessing of all. Our heretofore loving (though often too distant) relationship flourished in the sharing of a home together again. We were like kids left unattended in my grandfather's bakery munching donuts as they came out of the oven, all the while trying to reconcile our good fortune! Why had we been given the chance so late in life to renew those intimate ties that all too often fray and unravel over time? How can one describe the joy of having my father greet me each morning with hot coffee and a bagel to be shared over conversation before I headed off to work? What could possibly match returning home in the early evening to sit down together and recount the day's events, share a laugh or two, and then tuck Dad into bed with soft strains of Jimmy Dorsey or Benny Goodman wafting up from the radio in his bedroom below to the landing where I studied?

That's affirmation, and through no other instrument than God's grace. Father and son—dispossessed and disciple—had met each other on the road down in the valley, only to climb the next hill together and sing His praises. Blessed indeed were we that halcyon summer; for great was our reward in God's Kingdom here on earth.

Two years after I operated on my father, followed by our joyful reunion as housemates, Dad was diagnosed with terminal cancer that had spread to his spine. By his own admission that's a painful way to die. Yet, through the lens of a steadfast faith that diffused his suffering like a prism, he endured it as a small price to pay. After all, Popo knew the trials and tribulations of this life were drawing to a close, and eternity in the presence of his Father beckoned. And that, most assuredly for my own father, was not simply a wish to be convinced of; rather, it was the Son of God's promise! Jesus had already made good on that through His own incomparable suffering, only to be resurrected to life everlasting, as Dad knew he too would be.

Not to discount the formidable armamentarium of painkillers my father received to assuage his suffering, the benefit of which Jesus did not have to lighten the burden when His own time came. This much, though, Dad and I knew we would face sooner than later: my ministrations as his physician would fail him in the end. Death, orchestrated by God's mercy at a time of His choosing, would win. And Christ, as his divine and omnipotent Physician, would be there to comfort him, just as He has done for all believers through the ages at the moment of their passing.

As befits my nature, of course—once the two of us are reunited—I fully intend to confirm that none of my father's hopes were unfounded, even toward the end when a combination of sleep deprivation and drugs clouded his vision. Consequently he had spent the very night of his passing in a quiet delirium scribbling meaningless figures in his checkbook one moment, warily eyeing the "spiders crawling all over the ceiling" the next. At length he settled back into a fitful sleep.

After a minute or two I approached his bed, leaned over, and tapped him on the chest. "Popo, there's something I need to tell you," I whispered, my voice quavering with emotion. With that, his eyes flew open—and, for the first time in hours, they shone with a resolute clarity that defied his moribund condition. "Dad, I want you to know what you've meant to all of the grateful patients you treated during your forty years as their doctor; but more important, what you've meant to my brother and me. If our lives are meant to reflect Jesus as a role model, then take my word for it: you've been the very best likeness of Him I've ever known."

With his eyes fixed squarely on mine, and in a clear, resonant voice, he replied, "Bert, that's the finest compliment a father can receive from his son."

And the greatest gift God's Son could have given me. Jesus had drawn back the curtain of impending death just long enough to bring closure to our relationship by allowing me to say what every man yearns to tell his father— and to *know* it's been received! At that moment I realized, as both physician and son, I hadn't failed him after all. Nor had Christ. For great is Dad's reward in Heaven—as mine too shall be. By His grace alone.

Closing Arguments
and Redirected Verdicts

Cross-Examination

Such a comforting benediction when espoused by nominal Christians admittedly evokes a cynical response from the Prosecution—though never so vehemently as a far more familiar refrain it has heard *ad nauseam*: "I'm a member of the church in good standing—and a pretty good person to boot. I acknowledge the Holy Trinity, even though it's sometimes difficult to 'get my mind around.' Yet this much I know for certain (or at least have been assured by my pastor!): Jesus has already paid the price for our sins. Everything's okay, because we're all guaranteed to be justified by grace through faith….So what's the problem?"

In a word, *huge*! The real issue, the Prosecution points out, is not how the church would have us behave (or believe) as a body, but what Christ expects of us *individually*. I couldn't agree more with that premise—though by way of bolstering our defense, hasn't Jesus already provided you and me as disciples a road map to follow in His Beatitudes? Doesn't His Word afford an abundance of "case studies" to be drawn upon as testimonials from those who preceded us? (See "Rebuttal for the Defense" following this chapter.) Taken together, that should make for an open-and-shut case on our behalf. Or so I thought before undergoing a soul-searching examination at the foot of the cross by Christ's star understudy, Dietrich Bonhoeffer.

His life (and subsequent martyrdom) epitomized the "road less taken" by few Christians some two generations ago, if not any of us today who would call ourselves "followers of Christ." A German by birth and a Lutheran pastor, Bonhoeffer had founded an ecumenical movement in Great Britain during the 1930s known as the "Confessional Church." Yet this heretofore armchair theologian was ultimately compelled to venture outside the safety of sanctuary walls to preserve the gracious redirection of his life (and those of future generations) for the sake of Christ alone.

For you see, Bonhoeffer's "recall"—in the literal sense of the word—echoed the tragic conflict of loyalties to which Christians in Nazi Germany were exposed: Either work for the defeat of their nation in order that all Christ stood for might survive; or accept the victory of Germany by default, thereby destroying His Church. Following the Lord's lead, in strict obedience as an *individual*, he returned to Hitler's Germany in 1939 as something of a "spiritual revolutionary" within the church underground. In contradistinction to other resistance movements appealing to nationalism or ethnicity, his was a call to and for a higher kingdom.

What Bonhoeffer discovered during his arduous ascent to the mountaintop of saints is that God's grace is inseparable from His call that necessarily follows. And by the very nature of calling oneself a "disciple," that summons can only be answered alone. Whereas denominational doctrine collectively drives,[1] grace individually draws—moving the true follower beyond the pew and into God's plan; from under the steeple and into the streets; out of the talk and into the walk.

Need it be said that imposing Jesus into "polite" civil discourse in Nazi Germany during the 1940s was hardly deemed politically correct—and for which there was a huge price to pay? How sad, then, to consider that Bonhoeffer may have paid the ultimate price for an (as yet) unrequited cause in a far less oppressive environment today here at home. After all, more than a few contemporary denominations scarcely acknowledge Christ in their services, much less His Word. If the truth be known, however, it is not Jesus who turns off the unchurched and nominal Christian alike in America; rather, it's those superimposed doctrines, traditions, and, yes, *legalisms* fostered by fallible human beings such as ourselves that rankle—"rules and regulations" on the one hand, false hopes and consolations on the other.[2]

To cite but two of the former within the fold: baptismal sprinkling vs. immersion for the initiate. (Not to mention church membership being restricted to those baptized within a specific denomination! Where in the world did Jesus—or John the Baptist—require *that* as a "right" of passage?)

Then there are those staunch fundamentalists who would assert that a glass of wine on Saturday night buys a one-way ticket to hell—as opposed to "mainstream" churchgoers just as certain they can redeem a return ticket on Sunday morning with a generous tithe.

I'm nitpicking to make a point. It was precisely such entrenched dogmatism on far weightier issues within the sixteenth century church that precipitated the Protestant Reformation: priests as intercessory confessors; restricted communion; the shameless sale of "indulgences;" a Latin liturgy that kept the masses in the dark.[3] That was the bad news, and the past tense was used for a reason. The Good News is—and will remain so—*answering Jesus' call individually* liberates us from such manmade poppycock espoused by Protestant and Catholic denominations alike.

The downside for "libertarians" like you and I? Jesus does ask for something in return: single-minded obedience; becoming *doers* of Christ's Word; sharing both the suffering and rejection of His cross. That's genuine discipleship. This alone justifies calling oneself a "Christian." Brash statements all! Not mine, but Bonhoeffer's—who had an unimpeachable source. His name is Jesus (see John 14:23–24).

"It hasn't seemed all that difficult for me thus far," you say? Well, perhaps there's a reason for that. It's called "cheap grace," which Bonhoeffer cogently identified as the gravest threat to Christ's church (and remains so today; more about this shortly).

"So what should be the *real* cost to ourselves?" you ask. "If we're truly meant to take Jesus' word so literally, wouldn't that provoke an intolerable 'disconnect' between what the world requires of us as workers and His demands on us as disciples?" Sorry, but that's little more than a plea bargain for a select few to return to monasticism—what Martin Luther ruefully recognized in his day as an individual achievement the mass of laity was not expected to emulate. Hence the fatal double standard that persists today: a maximum and minimum yardstick with which to measure Christian obedience.

More threatening still, "where in Heaven's name" will answering Jesus' call lead us? Which was precisely His point—though there was another. The first disciples had asked Him the same thing: "Lord, we don't know where you are going, so how can we know the way?" To which Jesus replied [emphasis mine]:

"*I am* the *way*…No one comes to the Father except through me" (John 14:5–6). And for good measure: "… no one *knows* who the Father is except the Son and those to whom the Son chooses to reveal him" (Luke 10:22). Knowing Him provided direct and eternal access to God. That was supposed to be enough for them. It should be enough for us—but only by *acting* upon His Word. Stated another way (and here's the hard part for the broad majority today left sitting on the fence, whether disguised as "pew-ploppers" or members of the "frozen chosen": if you truly believe, then answer His call. If you don't yet believe, then answer it all the same. Because He's asking you to do so…

That's a tough "call"—though not in the sense of being debatable for any would-be disciple. And again, certainly not my call to make, but Christ's. The quest to truly *know* Jesus, and know He knows you, begins and ends in the pure words of the Lord Himself.[4] Consider the first and last words Jesus spoke to Peter: "Follow me!" (Compare Mark 1:17 with John 21:22.) Between those identical commands lies an entire lifetime of discipleship with no guarantees—at least that the temporal world can offer. This should serve as a cautionary tale: Like Peter, we need to be reminded time and again of the true cost of discipleship.

No one understood this better than Dietrich Bonhoeffer (which not only accounts for the title of his seminal work, *The Cost of Discipleship*, but my choice as a spokesman for the Prosecution). One man's obedience *can* make a difference. That's precisely the legacy both Christ and Bonhoeffer left for us to emulate: answering the call; reflecting God's grace; recreating ourselves for all to see in what little time remains. The first step in this transformation is an act that radically intrudes on one's present station in life. Only by "dying to self"—turning away from our own concerns—can we focus on Christ and His call. Which is His way of reminding us, "You can't stay where you are and go with *Me* at the same time."

Yet this break with the past may still be just an "external work" of good intentions— unless it's *Jesus'* command to which we are responding. So where does one begin? By focusing not on the work we're doing (simply being a "good doctor" comes to mind!), but on the *Word* with which Christ calls us to do it. That's why the Holy Spirit's discernment is so important; He sees things through God's eyes and responds with Jesus' heart.[5] That's what Paul was driving at with his intercessory prayer: "I pray…the *eyes of your heart* may be enlightened…" (Ephesians 1:18; emphasis mine). That's how, in an elemental sense, we become "as one" with the Holy Trinity and know we're heading in the right direction—under His.

Despite such exemplary instruction, at certain points in my ministry I found myself becoming not "as one with," but *at odds with* God. In fact, the Holy Spirit convicted me twice on that account. The first was in 1998 in Albania when I was called there by an organization—not by Christ—with little time spent in prayer beforehand to discern His will. That was but one lesson the Lord taught me in retrospect, and which bears repeating: Just because you think you *might* have been called is not a reason to go; He may have something more important for you to do right where you are.

A second and more pervasive failing, oddly enough, manifested itself during my four-year hiatus from private practice to do fulltime missions abroad before returning to the States in 2005. No mystery as to why—some very exposed loose cannons on my deck that Jesus wished to secure ("control" would not fit His nature), I was still priming for battle! Rusting weapons of self-defense like finding scope for my own ambitions; animosities over past slights; and, yes, even family responsibilities both past and present.

As for the first self-serving notion, that reverberating shot across my bow still makes me hunker down at Jesus' feet. My ambition? Or His call? Having exposed the flanks of my conviction to snipers from Satan's parapets, I now had to endure a more sustained enfilade—and perhaps justifiably: not perceiving the Holy Spirit's direction like I used to; sensing that daily prayer had become more of a ritual than the mutual exchange He intended it to be; discovering what few genuine prayers I prayed seemed to have gone unanswered. Hence, the "wilderness" years at sea from 2001 through 2004, cast adrift in the throes of spiritual warfare.

If there's one redeeming truth I've taken away from that conflict, however, it is this: Genuine discipleship is the exclusive attachment to a Person (not a church, an organization, or a missions board)—One who happens not to be just a "good teacher" (Luke 18:18) but the living Son of God! This exclusivity places the disciple in an irreversible situation, where venturing forth in faith becomes the only alternative. There's nothing left to do but sail through the firestorm under the Holy Spirit's direction. Once embarking on the voyage, one comes to know the Lord *personally* and recognizes His voice when He calls. That's what my wilderness years, aided and abetted by the perspective of Dietrich Bonhoeffer, taught me—albeit only in retrospect.

You see, graduating from Discipleship 1 and 2, attending Bible Study Fellowship on Monday nights for eight years, or merely assuming the label of an "earnest" disciple by embarking on fulltime missions abroad was just a beginning. Having failed thereafter as often as did Peter, I had fallen woefully short in my understanding of grace and the true cost of discipleship. Whether one chooses on his or her own accord to stay on this side of the ocean or go abroad, Jesus will not be fooled. Because He knows the heart. That's Christ's *acid test*, etched in stone from His own, as expressed in the Beatitudes.

The implications for ourselves? Apart from truly answering Jesus' call (and no other), we risk falling into the trap of what Bonhoeffer has aptly termed "cheap grace," which he defines as "the *very denial of the Word of God*." Now that's a serious charge! So just what is cheap grace? Try these indictments on for size, and judge for yourselves whether they might not fit:

1. Cheap grace is a mere confession of faith—an assent to an ideal.

2. Cheap grace is forgiveness of sins that's proclaimed from the pulpit as a generalized truth on behalf of a loving "Christian" God, as opposed to the "vengeful" God of the Old Testament. It's preaching forgiveness without repentance, communion without introspection, discipleship without the cross.

3. Cheap grace costs us nothing. "Everything has been paid for in advance," we say, "so everything can remain as before" (including, of course, ourselves). After all, what is grace if it's not given freely? That's the pervasive, feel-good, "I'm okay; You're okay" mindset threatening our very sanctification.

4. Cheap grace is an interest-free bailout we bestow on ourselves: a minimum standard of obedience, leaving the maximum to those in the ministry, monasteries, and, yes, missions. Bonhoeffer grasped the paradox: If anything, the Reformation of Luther hardened us over time into neglectful disobedience, as if we have been given some sort of dispensation from truly following Christ—like the indulgences Catholics used to purchase in the Middle (or was that the Dark?) Ages.

5. Cheap grace is fixing our eyes on the work we do rather than on the Word that calls us to do it—and as I've already implied, perhaps no one has been more guilty of that than myself.

6. Cheap grace stems from the very revival mentality we seek. Consider the life's blood of today's megachurch: those praise and worship "performances," what with their heady impact on our youth that belies the true heart of worship—"When the music fades, and all has slipped away…"

7. Cheap grace is a bastardized refrain of the old Reformation battle cry, "Not by works, but by grace and faith alone!" That remains for some a justification for doing no works at all.

8. Cheap grace is "partnering" with one's checkbook so that someone else goes on mission "for" us.

9. Cheap grace is akin to a vaccination; we've gotten just enough of Jesus to prevent us from catching the real thing—what C. S. Lewis calls "the good infection." We leave the world behind for two hours on a Sunday, basking in the assurance that our sins, as good Christians, have been forgiven. Have we not been justified to God by faith and grace alone? Yet that's a perversion of the real Pauline formula: "justified freely by His grace…through [our] faith." (Look it up!)[6]

GRACE: **G**od's **R**iches **A**t **C**hrist's **E**xpense. What's been said before bears repeating. That which cost Him so much should cost us who call ourselves disciples no less. It's called "dying to self." This hopefully brings some readers to the distressing realization of what Bonhoeffer's life and death highlighted in bold relief: The church has made grace available at too low a cost. We've given away the Word and sacraments wholesale—baptized, absolved, and confirmed without condition. (After all, only the *numbers* matter, and they become a cheap justification for the missionary's "harvest" as much as a church's very existence.) What the Prosecution is underscoring is the huge difference between *believing* in Jesus and *following* Him.

That gives us an inkling of what real grace—*costly grace*—is: at once both faith in the words of Christ and a calling of ourselves. Then what does the Word say? First, "Follow me!"— no questions asked. "I call thee, and that is all." Didn't Jesus tell Paul [Saul] the same thing in so many words at the moment of his conversion experience? "Now get up and go into the city, and you will be *told* what you must do." Lest Paul miss His point, the Lord then confided to his benefactor of sight-regained, Ananias: "I will show him how much he must suffer for my name" (Acts 9:6, 16; emphasis mine). Just as Paul subsequently discovered, that's *costly* because it compels us to break from our prior attachments to the secular world. Yet it's also *grace*, as in both a treasure and a promise: a treasure hidden in a field; a pearl of great price for which a man will sell everything to possess; and a promised inheritance of everlasting life as adopted sons and daughters whom Christ knows!

Such blessed assurance stems from a logical progression:

It's costly because it calls us to *follow*; it's grace because it calls us to follow *Jesus*.

It's costly because it compels us to *submit*; it's grace because His yoke is *easy* and His burden *light*.

It's costly because it costs a disciple his or her *ephemeral* life; it's grace because it gives *eternal* life in return.

Above all, it's costly because it cost God the life of *His* Son; it's grace because God did not reckon that too dear a price to pay for *our* lives.

Now, I know what you're thinking; you've said it before: "Jesus is asking *me* to make a clean break from my prior existence and attachments? And this stuff about the Beatitudes! He 'ups the ante' on something we can't fulfill to begin with (the Ten Commandments), and then bids us do it anyway. That's too great a price to pay—if not impossible!" Peter recognized that himself, absent Christ in his own life. Seeing the Lord on the shores of Galilee, he dare not climb out of the boat on his own strength. And so he cries: "Lord, bid me come to you across the waters!" And Jesus simply says: "Come." You see, Peter had enough faith in the *word* of the Lord to ask for more, because he finally tumbled to the realization that Christ asks nothing without giving each of us the strength to do as He asks.

So how do we know when we're truly being called, instead of just doing works of good intentions? Some, like Paul, seemingly had no choice in the matter. For those like ourselves who do, Peter answers for us: He *asked* to be called…because the Holy Spirit will be given to those who ask Him (Luke

11:13). The first disciples saw the risen Christ and believed; today we hear the Word and should believe—because Jesus is as alive now as He was then. "In the beginning was the Word, and the Word was with God, and the Word [is] God" (John 1:1). Hear the Word; hear Jesus Himself; and you will hear the Call.

Accepting Christ as whom He claimed to be (and His words to be inerrant), we would also do well to take seriously what He had to say of the future—and Matthew 24:14 above all: "This gospel of the kingdom will be preached in the whole world…and then the end will come." Perhaps the time has come (and there's not much of that left!) to apply Dietrich Bonhoeffer's testimony to our own lives. Are we hearing and doing the Word, or are you and I going deaf just "listening to the music" while talking the walk? Make no mistake: If you don't answer the Call, you'll never *learn* to truly believe, your faith and sanctification will not grow, and the fruit of your salvation with and through Jesus risks being lost. This separates us from God, which is the real definition of hell…

With that sobering witnesses and closing argument, the Prosecution rests its case—signed, sealed, and delivered.

Rebuttal for the Defense

You've heard it all before: "We are justified by grace through faith. Good works have nothing to do with our salvation; Jesus has already done the work for us." That's bread-and-butter Christian theology—although far too generously sliced and slathered. To fully digest its implications, perhaps we'd do well to remember that there *is* a Recorder of Deeds to whom the Prosecution refers as worthy standards of conduct befitting a wannabe disciple. These are contained in the Book of Life, appended to names inscribed there for eternity.

Surrounded as we are today by such a great cloud of witnesses, these are saints we were meant to emulate. Need we be reminded, however, that for now this is "privileged information" immune from the process of discovery? That presents a problem for the Defense—mine in particular. Without some affirmation that there is a God who knows us personally, I hadn't a leg to stand on, much less living water to sustain the spiritual homestead I'd built on Jesus' foundation.

Are we co-inheritors of the sacred claim—or squatters professed more in word than deed? How do we know we are being truly led by Jesus as disciples, whether we call ourselves "servants," "missionaries," or, yes, even "prophets"? I'll be the first to admit the Lord has never spoken to me directly; yet I *do* listen to the Holy Spirit, who often speaks unambiguously through His Word. And that's where the Prosecution drove me: back into Scripture to ferret out those role models who had been spoken to (and directed) by God personally.

The long version, of course, can be found in the so-called "roll call of faith" in Hebrews 11. Yet these heroes of the faith were confined to the pre-Christian era. And insofar as neither qualifier applied to me, I sought affirmation instead from those whom God had literally *befriended,* whether B.C. or A.D. Trusting you too might find the same comfort in knowing such divine relationships exist, consider the following "short list" in chronological order upon which we might yet base our defense as workers for, and inheritors of, His Kingdom.[1]

Following His heart-breaking encounter with Adam and Eve in the Garden, God refused thereafter to communicate with mankind personally until enlisting a mediator at Mt. Sinai to do that for Him—Abraham and the patriarchs arguably aside, though *Yahweh* "did not make [Himself] known to them" by that name (Exodus 6:2–3), which bespeaks a *personal* relationship. Not only did Moses have the unique privilege to see the invisible God (Hebrews 11:27); he also conversed with Him while in the wilderness "as a man speaks with his friend." Having been assured the Lord knew his name and viewed him with favor (Exodus 33:11–14), on a few occasions this stuttering sheepherder even bargained with God for the benefit of His chosen people. Obviously this had been a one-of-kind relationship. Yet a precedent had been set for other disciples to follow—to do the Lord's work and fulfill His will through benefit of hands-on, heart-to-heart instruction.

The next to catch my eye in specifically addressing this notion of a personal relationship, not surprisingly, was one seeking after God's own heart some four hundred years later. Whereas Moses' predecessors had to take it on faith that an all-knowing God was directing their steps, David immersed himself in one-on-one encounters throughout the Psalms with a God who was always there to listen and, on occasion, to speak. "Oh LORD, you have searched me and you know me....you created my inmost being;...I am fearfully and wonderfully made;...All the days ordained for me were written in your book before one of them came to be" (Psalm 139:1, 13, 14, 16). David, then, was speaking to God "up close and personally."

Isaiah thereafter, in the seventh century B.C., staked his own claim to God's personal presence in his life: "Before I was born the LORD called me; from my birth he has made mention of my name....in the shadow of his hand he hid me;..." (Isaiah 49:1–2). But for what purpose? And to what does this "call" refer? For answers I turned to a near contemporary of the sixth century B.C., the prophet Jeremiah. Of singular interest to me is that the Lord was now speaking *to* Jeremiah by way of affirming his predecessor's "audacious" assertions: "Before I formed you in the womb I *knew* you, before you were born I set you apart;…as a prophet to the nations" (Jeremiah 1:5).

Therein lay the genesis of this divine relationship for us today, as much as for David, Isaiah, and Jeremiah: God knows us before we have any knowledge of Him, and has a plan for us in what we are called to do. But aren't we just speaking of prophets here—not you and I? Hardly! For anyone who "calls" himself a disciple is being *called* by God to perform a specific task for His people with his or her particular skills in mind. We therefore can return to Isaiah with fresh new insights regarding that call and its purpose. Specifically, Isaiah 49:5–6, where the Lord who called Isaiah to be His servant says: "I will also make you a light to the Gentiles, that you may bring my salvation to the ends of the earth."

In the aftershock of that cultural bombshell of a commission, the long arm of the Lord was being extended to the Christian era.[2] This bridge of faith, however, had to be crossed by someone who had been on both sides and had everything to lose. That's what Jesus was telling an "infidel" named Saul on the road to Damascus, the next chronological reference revealed through my search: "I have appeared to you to appoint you as a servant and as a witness of what you have seen of me and what I will show you" (Acts 26:16).[3]

With reference to this most personal (and undoubtedly chastening) of calls, what was Saul's [Paul's] response? "But when God, who set me apart from birth and called me by his grace…I went *immediately*…" (Galatians 1:15, 17). Sound familiar? Shades of Isaiah and Jeremiah—and foreshadowings for us all! We are set apart from birth to do God's bidding (though some deny the call until middle age, as did I), but only through His grace.

Paul then goes on to develop a logical progression in Ephesians 1:4–5: "[God] chose us in him before the creation of the world.…In love, he predestined us to be adopted as his sons through Jesus Christ." Listen to what Paul is saying. Christ alone is the Mediator. Lacking a personal relationship with Him (for what else could being "adopted" imply?), we have no inheritance—much less any reason for being. Rather, *His* reason being: "For we are God's workmanship, created in Christ Jesus to do good works, which God prepared in advance for us to do" (Ephesians 2:10).

That progression unfolds succinctly in Romans 8:29–30 to Paul's conclusion: "For those God foreknew he also predestined to be conformed to the likeness of his Son,...And those He predestined he also called; those he called he also justified; those he justified he also glorified." You see, God either *chose* some by His grace beforehand (and hardened others for His purpose; see Romans 9:15–18)—or He *knows* those whom, by faith, would become His people. Either way, He alone is sovereign: "Does not the potter have the right to make out of the same lump of clay some pottery for noble purposes and some for common use?" (Romans 9:21).

Now it's not my intent to resurrect the age-old debate on this so-called "doctrine of election," but to make a point. Yet don't listen to me, or even Paul; listen to Jesus, who makes it for us in John 15:16: "You did not choose me, but I chose you and appointed you to bear fruit—fruit that will last." And should you feel you lack the wherewithal to pull that one off, take comfort in John 14:16, 15:26–27, and 16:7 to affirm Christ's personal gift of the Holy Spirit who makes this all possible.

With the preceding "short list" of examples in mind, let's now revisit some basic tenets of the Christian faith from your own perspective. Do you believe in the Holy Trinity (i.e. one God manifested in three Persons)? If so, did God not choose you before the world began? Has He not called you for a purpose? Did He not leave a part of Himself within you? God, then, knows you! And His grace, in the words of the Prosecution, "defines the relationship" you have with Him through Christ.

This relationship is nurtured by His indwelling and abiding Spirit. Here's how it works. God's grace may be defined as "the work of the Holy Spirit from conception to death in the life of a Christian." It all begins with something called "prevenient grace," which manifests itself in three stages: (1) the presence of God's Spirit even *before* we are conceived; (2) His initiative in rescuing us *at birth* from the inherited impact of original sin; and (3) the promise of a loving Father who then "courts" us *between* conception and conversion, such that we at least have the freedom to say "yes" when He calls our names. That's convincing (convicting?) grace (hence the significance of Isaiah 49:1–3 and Jeremiah 1:5–7). In other words, prevenient grace keeps us from falling too far away (through actual as opposed to original sin) from the relationship to which we have been called from the beginning before reaching the age of accountability.

Now once we've been either convinced or convicted and allow grace to take control of our lives at conversion, the Holy Spirit gives the believer something he or she never had before: both the *inclination* and the *power* to obey Him! We simply can't have the one, or exercise the other, on our own accord. By appropriating that unmerited gift for ourselves as Jesus would have us do, something called "sanctifying grace" grows (and ultimately prevails for those who persevere) between the point of conversion and physical death (see Psalm 139; Romans 8:29).

That, in summary, was John Wesley's take on the presence of grace in a Christian's life from cradle to grave.[4] Denominational doctrine aside, it makes a lot of sense to me as part of the framework upon which we might defend both the reality of a personal God in our lives and through our own calling. Yet there *is* a caveat: Though one's salvation is an integral part of God's plan, it's just a beginning. Jesus takes the Father's intent another step further as a means to His end. For the sobering truth of the matter is (respectfully submitted), perhaps God doesn't care so much about our salvation as He does our *sanctification*! Why? Because what "sanctification" other people see in us more appropriately turns our reflection of Christ's light back upon the *Father*— that they might know He is God.[5]

To bring our share of that harvest to fruition, however, we must first identify our individual spiritual gifts and then put them to work (refer to 1 Corinthians 12, Romans 12, 1 Peter 4, and Ephesians 4 for a representative list of those). Such gifts (1) are of supernatural origin; (2) always accompany obedience to a God-given impulse; (3) become manifest within a Christian's individual "sphere of influence;" and (4) prepare others for his or her particular ministry (Isaiah 49: 5–6; Acts 26:16; Ephesians 1:4–11, 2:10). That, in a sacred jar full of blessings, is what God has in mind for each of us—and what is implied by His grace "defining the relationship." Most assuredly, therefore, Scripture is not just referring to prophets—but to *you* and *I*!

Yet, here's the strange thing: Despite being cracked jars of clay ourselves, Jesus not only fills us with His "fruit of the vine" [read: works of the Spirit] for others' sustenance; He follows a divine recipe—His Beatitudes—to "ferment" our own progressive sanctification, come what may. And should that threaten to peak prematurely (or long past its prime), He adds a dash of blessed assurance only the Head Vintner can provide: "Rejoice and be glad, because great is your reward in Heaven, for in the same way, they persecuted the prophets who were before you" (Matthew 5:12).

Mark that well. Christ Himself is identifying all those who would call themselves His disciples today with the prophets of old. And what were Jesus' last words to them (and us) concerning the specific task to be performed on behalf of His people? "Therefore go and make disciples of all nations, baptizing them in the name of the Father and of the Son and of the Holy Spirit,…And surely I am with you always, to the very end of the age" (Matthew 28:19–20).

Which leads to at least two further points to consider in our defense. The first is that Christ has brought us full circle back to Isaiah: The Lord has called us to be His servants…that we might bring His salvation to the ends of the earth.

But surely you ask: "All *nations*? Ends of the earth? That leaves me out! I don't have the tools or resources, much less the inclination, to be a missionary."

Not so fast! Rest assured the risen Christ has already invested His very life in you, and has made all the necessary preparations. For one, giving us the tools/resources (read: power) and the inclination is precisely what God's grace in the form of the Holy Spirit *does* in the life of the believer. As for the seemingly daunting task of baptizing an entire "nation," obviously something has been lost in translation from the original Hebrew idea of *goy*, as in "nations." The New Testament uses the Greek word *ethnos*, meaning "people." Which is to say, you don't even have to leave your hometown to answer Jesus' call— or to "call" yourself a missionary!

But doesn't this plea bargain of sorts fly in the face of the Prosecution's charge that Jesus' fellowship is promised only to those who have left all to follow Him? Shouldn't we already be closing up shop, packing our bags, updating immunizations, and transferring what little remains of our 401(k)s to purchase airline tickets? Thankfully, in our defense, it's not where we "go" for Jesus; it's what we do *with* Him where we're at…And the fact of the matter is, there's simply too much of His work left undone here at home.

That's precisely what we are called to redress daily as Christ's followers. If one thing characterized the Son of Man throughout the Gospel accounts, it was His willingness to drop everything He was doing in His travels to fulfill a single seeker's immediate needs. Setting aside our own worldly agendas (i.e.

"leaving all") to do the same allows most of us, paradoxically, to "stay" where we are and *still* be where He is working. After all, we're not being led by Jesus in a physical sense, but by the promptings of the Holy Spirit He left as our Counselor to follow.

So much for His necessary preparations. As pertains to "following," there is also something to be said once again on our behalf for scriptural nuances. Much as *ethnos* has been transposed in modern translations from "people" to "nations," the Greek word for "follow" [*akoloutheo*] is more properly translated from the Aramaic Jesus spoke to mean "doing what He would do," as in following His *ways*.

Let's be honest. How often have you and I felt "put upon" by someone who perceived that his or her needs required interrupting our daily "devotions" at the altar of business or family? Better instead we take to heart what it must have been like for Jesus to know He was on his way to Jerusalem to be *put upon* a cross—yet He still had the heart of God to respond as if that person's concerns trumped His own. Christ never ignored a "nobody" who crossed His path. That's His lead we have been graced to follow. It's a small cross to bear along the high[er] Way.

My second point focuses more briefly though precisely on what Jesus said: "I *am* with you"—not "I *will* be with you." (Remember how God identified Himself to His people in Exodus 3:14? "I AM WHO I AM.") Jesus was identifying Himself with the Father, which He later reaffirms in John 8:58: "… before Abraham was born, *I* am!" That too was God speaking in the Person of Christ, just as He did in bequeathing us His Great Commission. And it's *ours* to follow, wherever we're at and whenever Jesus calls.

While you may not have to leave home to be a missionary, there *is* a "take-home" lesson: God wants you to know Him personally and follow His ways. He would not have created you otherwise. If you've failed in nurturing your relationship with Him thus far, take heart! That was then; this is now. And *now* is the time to stand on Christ's promise that you have already been forgiven and will be made "perfect."

We need to be reminded, however, that our hunger for sanctification is satiated only through obedience to God's will, just as Jesus had learned (and done) Himself (see Hebrews 5:8–9). Remember Christ's enigmatic reply to the disciples who had inquired as to whether He was "hungry" just after His encounter with the Samaritan women at the well? "My food…is to do the will of him who sent me and to finish his work" (John 4:34). What, then, was God's "will" to which Jesus referred? "[T]his is the *will* of him who sent me, that I shall lose none of all that he has given me, but raise them up at the last day" (John 6:39). As for His "work": "The *work* of God is this: to believe in the one he has sent" (John 6:29).

That's Jesus' clarion call to reconcile what we are and do with what He created us to be! Mind you, we don't have the luxury to first "get to know God" and then do His will; we get to know God by first *doing* His will and completing the work He has given us to do. Which is only to say that true followers must begin by choosing to enter into this proactive relationship through the narrow gate of obedience. The terms of that relationship are clear: He has called you for a purpose, a specific task—to reflect the Christ-light through your sanctification in order that others might be saved. So, as a poor imitation of your "court-appointed defender," grant me the privilege of posing the same two questions Jesus asks us all: Are you fulfilling that purpose? Will He *know* you in the end?

Bear in mind this is not a done deal. Like any relationship, it can be lost through disobedience or simple neglect. "But your salvation is assured; that can't be taken away! The *fellowship* may be broken, but not the relationship. You're still a member of the family." Or so my evangelical friends tell me. Yet, I'm not quite so sure, and here is why. Taken at "faith" value, Romans 10:9 offers us the blessed assurance we seek—and a quite simple offer at that: "If you confess with your mouth, 'Jesus is Lord,' and *believe* in your heart that God raised Him from the dead, you will be saved." But here's the catch. Without walking in faith to begin with, trusting and obeying the risen Lord completely, we will never *learn* to truly believe! And that's the very linchpin upon which our salvation ultimately depends. That's what sanctification does.

Doing anything less (remember the first of the Prosecution's concluding indictments, framed as a question) leaves us open to the charge of "abandonment." Tough words! But true. Just ask Jesus: "Many will say to me on that day [they stand before His judgment seat], 'Lord, Lord, did we not prophesy in your name, and in your name drive out demons and perform many miracles?' Then I will tell them plainly, '*I never knew you*.'…[because] only he who does the will of my Father…[will enter the kingdom of Heaven]" (Matthew

7:22–23, 21). Could the Lord be "defining the relationship" any more clearly? I think not.

Paying lip service to Christ as Lord and Savior of your life is one thing; obeying Jesus' word—answering His call—is quite another. True, the Holy Spirit dwells within all believers; yet we must surrender daily to His counsel so that sanctifying grace prevails until the Father's work is completed. The latter may not happen in our lifetime; yet we alone are responsible for what happens on our watch. True, too, we are "justified by grace through faith;" yet we are still judged by our works. Those works are the fruit of one's salvation apportioned by God's grace; yet only insofar as we allow ourselves to be drawn near to its source by following Christ's lead. Our individual sanctification is then assured (and what a blessed assurance that is!); yet apart from what this means for you and I, that makes all the difference in the *world* to Jesus—for *its* redemption.…That's what sanctifying grace is for.

To explore the implications of what authentic sanctification entails, the Prosecution introduced its no-nonsense first lieutenant during cross-examination in the person of Dietrich Bonhoeffer (see "Cross-Examination"). By way of challenging our defense to become even better disciples, through good times and bad, we best recall something of his pristine credentials. From the very beginning, Bonhoeffer had answered Jesus' call to the letter. In the end he answered it with his life—hanged by the Gestapo (without a trial) in a concentration camp in April 1945, three days before the liberation of Germany—a true disciple and *saint* in every sense of God's Word.

Now let's consider a "saint" of a different sort. Few would dispute that Mahatma Gandhi probably came as close as anyone has walked in imitation of Christ. And yet in the end he missed the point—and with that, his eternal inheritance. We certainly didn't help matters. In Gandhi's own words: "Christ I like. What I dislike about Christianity are the 'Christians'…!"[6] So Gandhi turned to an ideal instead of to people—much less to a Person, whose name is Jesus. Refusing to cast his lot with the Intercessor for his soul, he lost his otherwise rightful (and righteous) place in God's Kingdom.

That's hardly a self-righteous surmise on my behalf. No; Gandhi recognized this himself in the end, as the concluding remarks to his autobiography sadly make clear. "I worship God as Truth only. I *have not found him*, but I am *seeking* after him." So what is "truth" as Gandhi perceived it? "A perfect vision of Truth can only follow a complete realization of 'ahimsa' [which he defined as 'an absolute reverence for life']." That's a noble sentiment. Yet despite living that sentiment (doctrine?) to its fullest, consider the ultimate fruit he gleaned from it—assassination at the hand of an extremist in 1948.

No such exemplary life left more tragic irony in its wake. For one, Gandhi's ideals did not die with him—though he remains dead nonetheless, and still in ashes. For another, in Gandhi's own words written toward the end of his spiritual journey: "I have tolerance for all religions, but not a *living faith in* God." That's sadly ironic, because all Gandhi really lacked was *faith in a living God!* Yet a third bit of self-revelatory irony: "I do not seek redemption from the consequences of sin; I seek redemption from sin itself...or at least the thought of it." For all of Gandhi's legendary self-discipline as a near-perfect imitation of a Christ he emulated and yet did not *know*, that laudable goal has proved unobtainable for humankind. No man can accomplish this by himself, try as he might. And no one arguably tried harder than Mahatma Gandhi.

Sadder irony still: "As long as I have not realized this Absolute Truth, so long must I hold to the *relative* truth as *I* have conceived it..." That's an appeal to the "virtues" of relativism as a paltry and evanescent substitute for truth—as in "a god of our own understanding." Yet the tragedy comes full circle in Gandhi's final conclusion of the matter: "I have gone forward according to my light [not the Christ-light, which he subconsciously reflected but never acknowledged]. Often in my progress, I have had a faint glimpse of Absolute Truth, of God, and daily the conviction is growing in me that he alone is real and all else in unreal....But it is unbroken torture to me that I am *still so far from him*..."

In effect, Gandhi was depicting the real definition of hell—separation from God—and sadly still found himself a part of it the day he died, if not for eternity thereafter. Did Jesus, then, *know* Gandhi? He would have liked to. Christ alone is the Gate. Gandhi was so close to entering it, yet, in the end, so far. And that's forever. Time is short. Eternity is long—very long.

Note

I readily admit to some reservations about having taken Gandhi to task--a man whose works alone easily surpass what either you or I have done for mankind while "in the body". Indeed, if we are to take Jesus' words at face value, His parable of separating the sheep from the goats at the Judgment Day leaves room to argue that Gandhi might yet have "earned" his inheritance in the Kingdom. As that parable (and 1 John 3:14) make clear, Christ's basis for judgment will center upon whether the supplicant has shown *unconditional love* to God's people. And that, Gandhi most asssuredly did. To argue the point further on his behalf, can we not count on the Creator and Judge of things to make the right call, irrespective of Christ's proclamation that He alone is the gate to salvation? Moreover, simply because Gandhi found himself "still so far from God" at the end of his spiritual journey, it bears remembering that such a hallowed saint as Mother Theresa voiced the same despair in her own recently published memoirs.

Blasphemous musings? I don't think so. The point being for lesser mortals like you and I, why take that chance? Our eternal inheritance is an unmerited gift—bestowed by One who paid the ultimate price on our behalf.

Verdict

lthough the gate into Jesus' presence may seem narrow at its entrance and His pasture fallow on the surface, the Father's water table beneath runs broad and deep. How, then, to access that water once inside—and for what purpose, as a professed disciple in your own right? Will the living water from those wells *you* dig under His direction be of short-term sustenance for yourself, or have you been called to draw it for others' salvation from the eternal fount of God's grace? That's a question I had wrestled with myself during the wilderness years from 2001 to 2004—"wilderness" in the sense that I was being led from one valley to another in the Lord's service, though all the while receiving far more affirmation for my efforts than any disciple deserved.

The latter, paradoxically, presented a problem. Knowing Jesus always favors those who are "marginal" in society—the poor, the sick, the sinner—I also appreciate that, at least for the time being, I am not among them (except, of course, as regards the last!). The chastening thought that goaded me through those years and lingers still, consequently, is this: *Insofar as I'm so unworthy of such grace, could it be that I have already been given my just reward?*[1] Chalk up the delay in that particular verdict to a hung jury—until I face my own jury-of-One at His judgment seat.

No doubt I had benefited immensely by experiencing what Isaac went through—struggling over wells for the Lord's purpose, not our own. Yet once I found myself dividing time between Kansas City's own "field of springs" and the rest of His harvest field in 2005, a second question arose that demanded a verdict: *Had I been pushed from place to place? Or was I being drawn?* The life-transforming encounters related in these pages finally convinced me this potential indictment has been adjudicated in favor of His grace, whether at home or abroad. As was invoked earlier in a slightly different sense, grace *draws*; materialism *drives*. To defend that verdict, let me contrast the two using but one example with which I'm intimately familiar, having dug wells of my own on both sides of Jesus' gated enclosure.

Most surgeons I know measure their self-worth by the number of operations they do. As a bonus to their net worth, that translates to big bucks. Yet *whom* the surgeries are "done on" is prized more highly still, as word of mouth among the upper crust remains the society surgeon's "well" of sorts—in reality a "[water] wheel of fortune" that skims the surface with each revolution, dredging up only the most *visible* (and valued) sustenance.

To draw from both metaphors, catering to the "well-'wheeled'" drove my former elder herdsman of our group in Springfield to near distraction! Yet what goes around comes around; the most superficial channels (no pun intended) feeding a well—or stagnant pools on the surface—are always the first to dry up. That unspoken threat hangs like a double-edged sword over the materialist disguised as a surgeon-in-mask who happens to wield a scalpel: Slice from the upper crust unevenly (i.e. have a complication or a poor result) and "the rocks cry out," burying one's well (and wheel!) in a public-relations landslide of biblical proportions.

Such rubbish (and others' rubble) aside, here's a third and far more relevant question you will have to answer for yourself. I suspect you wouldn't be reading this book unless you have already found the allure of the material world wanting and are actively searching. For precisely *what* you may not yet know—but at least your heart and mind are open to some form of spiritual reawakening. Now, seeking implies need. Within our present context, this means finding a valley that best accommodates your spiritual gifts, where you can construct a well that will continue to fulfill. Perhaps my past experiences as a seeker of the same might shed some light on your own.

One of those "God things" that's been a recurring blessing in my own search as a Christian (and amazes me to this day!) is how often He has put certain books in my hand alongside the Bible when a specific question needed an answer. As regards tying up loose ends within this verdict summation, my question was this: Where might my trials as a would-be disciple interface with your own experience? After all, you may think we're not searching in the same valley, if identifying one another by our respective denominational or local church affiliations is any indication. What, then, is the proverbial missing link that binds us as seekers?

George Barna addresses this in his thought-provoking book *Revolution*. The answer puts us on equal footing (albeit different paths) as servants of Christ in *His* pasture. As perhaps the premier Christian marketing research firm today, the Barna Group has crunched the numbers and identified a burgeoning wellspring of believers intent on developing alternative means of serving. These, more often than not, lack the imprimatur of a denominational church, reflecting instead the universal Church Jesus has in mind. And there's life-changing affirmation in such faith-based initiatives with a capital "C," as God made clear long ago: the local church is *not* the hope of the world, nor should it be the source of our spiritual identity. Jesus is—on both counts!

Speaking for the Lord we know from Scripture, Barna would remind readers that nothing in God's Word calls us to go to a given church *per se*; rather, we are called through sacrificial love to *be* His Church. If that constitutes a "revolution" of the heart, as this grassroots movement from below is depicted, then our shared mindset as "spiritual revolutionaries" in the field becomes self-evident: Do whatever it takes to get closer to God and assist others in doing the same. As a seeker of the Way, doesn't that describe you? Or at least what you want to be—and were *meant* to become?

With all due respect, I feel comfortable presupposing your as yet undeclared identity, because my best friend and soul mate, Greg Hankins, challenged me with the very same suppositions. Being my next-door neighbor as well, it was a short step for him to bring Barna's research to my attention after reviewing the first draft of my manuscript. Having critiqued it from the perspective of a pastor (with all the red flags it might have raised for this representative of a local church), Greg readily identified me as the *revolutionary* I am—of which I was ingenuously unaware! And insofar as both men have placed my spiritual journey within just such a context, the three of us are now extending the same invitation to you who are still seeking.

Might you also have the makings of a spiritual revolutionary, and the

longing (no, *calling*) to participate in this coming decade of profound transformation in outreach for Christ's Church? When measured by the tepid
demands of the church (with a small "c") from which so many believers feel
estranged today, perhaps Barna's challenge offers an alluring cachet that
matches the identity for which you've been searching—as an authentic disciple Jesus created in His image. Parenthetically, that's what my own "war stories" from the front intended to evoke: not just a "call to arms," but a
"redeployment" of those Spirit-driven foot soldiers made to march to a different drumbeat than mainstream believers; yet at the same time made to feel
comfortable in their new identity within the Revolution—as the very followers Christ loves and knows personally.

Know this, however, before you rush to enlist and take up arms: just as
those prophets of old were unwelcome in their own hometowns, so contemporary spiritual revolutionaries are viewed with misgivings if not overt suspicion. More than a few slings and arrows are likely to come from some
surprising quarters, among them your church, close friends, and even family.
The skepticism of those who choose to lead more "conventional" spiritual
lives is a daily reminder that such boldness in His name always comes with a
price: their discomfort, and your own by extension. That's but one of the
costs—perhaps the most painful—of true discipleship.

Consider the upside, however, of throwing in your lot with this revolution that Barna has persuasively identified as the fastest growing and most
transforming phenomenon in the Church today. As for the adverse impact on
your worldly relationships, those are often reconciled in time for the disciple
who perseveres. Seeking your indulgence with yet another personal example:
Shortly after I had answered Jesus' call to the mission field, my dear father (an
entirely sincere, if "traditional," believer in his own right) exclaimed in exasperation, "Bert, you're simply too *good* to be doing this. Look at the practice
and reputation you've built. Isn't that enough?" Only to have our spiritual
sojourn together resurrected in the end and poignantly underscored by his
last words to me the night he died. With Jesus as our Mediator, Dad and I
reconnected at a point in time when we needed each other the most—he for
comfort; me for affirmation—but also for eternity in a way we never had
while he was still alive.

As for other members of our immediate family, I don't mind admitting that my brother, Bill, and sister-in-law, Judy viewed me for years as some half-cocked spiritual wannabe and do-gooder. Only to find new meaning in their Christian walks once they embarked on an in-depth study of the Word through Bible Study Fellowship, plus some (dare I say?) "revolutionary" commitments to community service. Though both acts of worship were undertaken outside the walls of their church, neither Bill nor Judy of course would (as yet!) identify themselves as "firebrands." No matter. Nothing has given my wife and I greater satisfaction than to have shared vicariously in their reawakening—Vicki's steadfast dedication to the Word being a far more influential witnesses for my sister-in-law in particular than my own work abroad. Which is only to affirm yet another of Jesus' decrees: "You are missionaries to your *family* first." As for His verdict that follows: "To have persevered along My Way is to have borne fruit of the sweetest kind that lasts."

Making reference to Bible study does evoke one ancillary indictment for which you as potential well-diggers (if not revolutionaries) must honestly reconsider. Should you enlist in His service, from what source will you receive your marching orders? That takes us back down into the valley in search of those wells, the sort fed by endless streams of living water. Sad to admit, far fewer than should will draw their sustenance and direction from God's Word, the source He intended us to use.

Not so the Vietnamese napalm victim scarred physically (and seemingly spiritually) beyond self-recognition, who found in the "valley" of a library the only water that could mollify her pain. There, with an empty heart yet open mind, Kim Phuc drew from the most important source she ever tapped: an opened Bible—just as God intended for the poor in spirit who would come to Him and drink. Hence the indictment that respectfully *requests* a verdict: How many would-be disciples leave such a well, long since capped, untapped in their own homes?

As for those Christians who occasionally dig into their Bibles, many are at least familiar with Christ's metaphorical use of "salt" and "light." Yet even the most scripturally attuned often misinterpret the gist of His message—or so my own experience in missions would suggest. Viewing the Potter's field through these respective lenses, as Jesus intended, brings to the eye a whole new perspective: focusing on the need to *build relationships* through unconditional love. That mandate as a disciple strikes to the very heart of the Lord's work—so much so that it justified placing these two conduits in the heart of this summary verdict. For without salt and light *within* the Beatitudes, its life's blood has no vessels with which to transmit His essence.

Far more effective than the sanctimonious practice of handing out pithy tracts door to door—if not beating people we hardly know over the head with a Bible—nurturing a loving relationship beforehand (and sustaining it once established) is one sure way the Good News will eventually receive the hearing it deserves. "How can one be so certain?" you ask. Well, simply because at some point in that relationship, someone whom the missionary (or the neighbor down the street) has genuinely befriended is bound to ask: "Just what is it about this person that makes his or her being here so special? Where does this goodness come from? Is that something I might tap into myself? Dare I risk going there?"

Forgive the uncouth simile, but reflecting the Christ-light is like hanging a "blue light" to which bugs are drawn inexorably out of the darkness. Yet there the parallel diverges. They are drawn not to be "zapped," but *infused*, by the very "energy" [read: Spirit] that transforms a hollow shell of clay "B.C." into a glowing vessel of grace "A.C." That's what relationship building does. It draws these "creatures of the night" near for His sake—and ultimately, their own.

To build further on diverging parallels as simile, you may recall that the three sides of a prism are "parallelograms" that refract or *disperse* light (as opposed to a lens that converges it). Using the Christ-light as a prism is akin to placing it on a stand so the entire room is suffused in its glow, dispelling the darkness. In order to ignite our prism lamp, however, one must first be invited in. That's another thing relationships do: They unlock darkened rooms, if not closed hearts and minds.

Salt, of course, serves an altogether different function—and one that many believe is even less understood in some Christian quarters, most notably among those of the so-called "evangelical culture." Indeed, a few bold if prescient observers have labeled the *privatization* of their faith as the "great heresy" of the twentieth century. And with good reason from Jesus' perspective. Speaking for Him (prophetically, I think) during the same year (2005) Barna published *Revolution*, Jim Wallis in his seminal book *God's Politics* offers a Christ-like verdict in its own right: "A personal God is *never* private." He never intended to be.

Just ask Jesus. We are charged (as was He) with intermingling among—and befriending—unbelievers in the "real" world, both to preserve what is good and refine the secular substrate we permeate. That is, after all, how salt functions. But only if we *place* ourselves there and nurture those relationships unconditionally. Otherwise, as Wallis correctly surmises, "our 'private' faith becomes [nothing more] than a cultural religion providing the assurance of righteousness for people *just like ourselves…*"

This is where, I would respectfully submit, various mission boards, mainstream churches, and their representative institutions often miss the shared meal (and mandate) Jesus has provided. Not to mention the precious gift of spiritual transformation, which is what the servant-as-salt is supposed to bring to the tables of the lost. Witnesses the unfounded fears of more than one Christian hospital I've partnered with abroad, whose governing boards remain intent on quarantining themselves from other workers outside the faith so as to not "subvert" their mission statement. Or any number of local churches of which Vicki and I have been members, whose mission teams were always commissioned by the congregation before being sent out—though our own, undertaken in Christ's name, never received the same blessing.

That's not sour grapes; I'm merely suggesting they've misread God's text. And it's not buried in fine print, as the salutation in Galatians 1:1 affirms: "Paul, an apostle—sent not from men nor by man, but by Jesus Christ…" Moreover, Barna's research suggests we're not alone in our experience—or in my thinking, for that matter. What he describes as a "disturbing trend" is the collective reaction of pastors to those congregants who indulge in such "faith adventures" outside the walls of the sanctuary. In effect, their less-than-supportive responses boil down to this: "Continue doing what you're doing if you like, but don't introduce 'foreign elements' into the local church's agenda." As one of my former pastors put it: "Bert, you'll only confuse the others and divert their attention from what we're doing here."

Jesus' response is altogether different, seeking as He does true spiritual transformation among His followers. He would remind us that living in accordance with a biblical worldview, in and of itself, becomes *transformational*—something that changes us from within, wherever that is exercised. Identifying one's spiritual gifts and then using them for His Kingdom (not theirs) is *transformational*. Ministries undertaken at the Lord's behest, with or without the local church's blessing, can be *transformational*. Indeed, connecting with others as members of a cross-denominational mission team often proves *transformational* for servant and sufferer alike. More bluntly if metaphorically stated, should our salt as Christians not prove durable enough to refine the whole (whether church or culture), then it's good for nothing and deserves to be thrown out and trampled underfoot. Those aren't Barna's words, but the Lord's! Not *my* verdict, but His.

To be sure, metaphors alone won't pass muster for the broad majority who seek instead "personal relevance" as to how their own salt and light might best be used to reflect God's glory—much less can they provide "concrete evidence" such sacred wells for them to draw from really exist. That is the intended relevance of this book: adding more channels and depth to the wellspring of testimony for a God who works personally in the lives of those in need; those who actively seek His direction; those who, once having received it, drink of it to the full—dregs of ongoing injustice, persecution, and all.[2]

Though this last caveat is often painfully relevant on a very personal level, wearing the mantle of a spiritual revolutionary is hardly so threatening as that "millstone" of a badge around our exposed jugulars might seem. For one thing, the victory is already won! All we have to do is show up and weigh in, fully vested in His armor, with the sword of the Spirit in hand. For another, Jesus' yoke is easy and His burden light. He will never give us more of a load than we can bear—or share. That's when the Holy Spirit comes to our rescue. He gives His soldiers the inclination—and then the strength—to follow Jesus down into the valley together. Which solidifies in kind our relationship with Him there, so that we might know God's eternal fount of blessings is as real as it is sustaining.

This captures the very essence of what Dietrich Bonhoeffer said, and what I discovered during my own spiritual journey as evidence cemented in stone: Without first walking by faith in total dependence, no questions asked, I could never *learn* to believe!

"Learn to believe." Now *there's* an odd phrase on the face of it. Doesn't one "believe" first, and then test the waters (i.e. the Spirit) as he or she proceeds along? Such seems to be the prevailing wisdom among Christians today. Yet I think it's significant that, of all the disciples Bonhoeffer pays homage to, only Levi [Matthew] immediately answered the call for Christ's sake alone.

Unlike the first and better known disciples, Peter [Simon], James, John, and Andrew, who had already met Jesus following His baptism at the Jordan—but did not surrender all to Him until later at the Sea of Galilee (compare Matthew 4:1–22 and Mark 1:16–20 with John 1:35–42)—Levi never hesitated. He responded to Jesus' unaccountable authority by abandoning his tax-collection booth forthwith and following Christ without a clue as to where that would take him, much less why.

As ever, Bonhoeffer is right on target: "If you believe, then answer the call. [Even] if you don't believe, then answer it all the same, because Christ bids you to do it." That's how we "learn" to believe. That's what a man born blind, whom Jesus had met near the pool of Siloam, was laboring in vain to tell those spiritually blind Pharisees.[3] "I don't know [anything about what you are saying]. One thing I *do* know. I was blind but now I see!" Just how that came to pass is as singular as the miracle itself. Nothing had been said to the man beforehand about his vision being restored, not to mention promises made. He had simply answered this call of sorts to go to the pool and wash out his eyes—as one who had been sent to perform a specific task so "the work of God might be displayed in his life."

Not that the blind man knew this to begin with. Nor had he any inkling he had been speaking to the Son of Man, much less the Son of God. Just as Matthew had done, he merely responded to the extraordinary appeal of an "ordinary" man he had never met. Yet by following His instructions to the letter, this erstwhile clueless servant (of all the protagonists involved) *learned* to believe when he wasn't even seeking to understand! Only later would Christ connect the mud-caked dots for His unwitting accomplice by asking him: "Do you [now] believe in the Son of Man?" To which he replied "Lord, I believe."

Nor should it pass unnoticed that this particular witnesses' *words* alone had little impact on either the skeptical Pharisees or his unbelieving parents, despite an otherwise inexplicable miracle staring them all in the face. It was solely by having *acted*—responding to Jesus' instructions explicitly—that a single pair of eyes were opened to the reality of grace. By virtue of having obeyed an innocuous command, he alone had a progressive epiphany of just who this enigmatic man really was: from someone he did not know; to a prophet whom others might follow; to one "from God" who deserved to be worshiped. And he did…Could there be a more eye-opening testimony of how one *learns* to believe?

This brings us to Jesus' last word on the matter. First, answering His call in faith the moment it comes; following Him thereafter to build trust; "learning" to *believe* in the Son of God—that's what the journey is for. This is how "faith" begets real faith, resulting in a total transformation of one's life's view such as propelled the blind man, Matthew, Isaac, myself, and countless other revolutionaries to destinations unknown, simply to dig new wells on His behalf where none existed before. That's our ultimate mandate—and His final verdict.

Mind you, the lifetime sentence that follows must be served "alone." For all of his false bravado (occasionally right, but never in doubt), that much at least even Peter understood—though characteristically he had to be reminded time and again. Speaking for the other disciples (as also befit his nature), Peter exclaimed early on: "*We* have left everything [behind] to follow you!" (Mark 10:28)—only to face Jesus' personal rebuke in the end: "If I want [John] to remain alive until I return, what is that to you? *You* must follow me" (John 21:22).

So, does forsaking all to follow Christ leave us alone as individuals? No, and here is why. The same Jesus who calls us to make a clean break with our past associations is also the Mediator of a new and eternal fellowship. Granted, we bring nothing to that relationship but ourselves—heart, mind, and soul. And though we must enter into it alone as disciples, we are never *left alone* as orphans. Our reward is the fellowship of His Church, where we share the Lord's heart, the Father's mind, and the very soul of the Spirit's presence.

Which brings to *my* heart and mind two soul-searching pieces of baggage borne as self-indictments that demand postscript verdicts. The first has to do with substance; the second with style. This matter of "substance" has convicted me on many an occasion, particularly as that relates to my proclivity to go it alone in the type of ministry I do. That's simply my nature—and insofar as God created this "character flaw," I can only pray it has somehow served Him well. Heaven knows, however, there are inherent shortcomings with such a Lone Ranger approach. For starters, every Christian acknowledges how important it is to be a part of a community of likeminded followers, whether that be a local congregation, a parachurch ministry, or merely a few close relationships in which we're held accountable to one another. Everyone benefits from having a so-called "reference group" as an anchor. This applies as much to nominal believers as spiritual revolutionaries.

Speaking from the latter's perspective with which I have only recently become familiar (and comfortable!), I began my Christian walk as a fiercely independent soul lacking the official approval of an established church. Rightly or wrongly, my sole allegiance was to Christ. Manmade substitutes neither satisfied nor reconciled what I perceived true discipleship to entail. I stand by that today. As a consequence, my own reference group vis-a-vis a "church of choice" has remained in a continual state of flux. That I regret—and, I don't mind admitting, miss.

Despite the sense of drift this lack of a denominational anchor has inculcated, I did derive some comfort early on in knowing that I was not alone in my dissatisfaction with simply "playing church." On the other hand, I've come to realize that my efforts alone can scarcely sustain the revolution of which I have become a part. At best, my influence on its extension has proved marginal—leaving one homebound commentator to point out the obvious: "A single voice in the desert has less impact than a united chorus in the marketplace."

On all these points I stand convicted. And yet…by the very nature of Jesus' emphasis on relationship building, in my defense I can't help but feel that such is the way His Kingdom is most effectively advanced—by, and for, *one person at a time*. Isn't that what Scripture affirms? Consider the following: Although John the Baptist sowed a veritable river-full of seed in preparing hearts for the Lord's coming, it was his baptism of Jesus that set the wheels of Christ's ministry in motion and gave it the legitimacy the Lord Himself desired. And what of His own encounters with a Samaritan woman at her well, the Gerasene demonic, or Saul on the road to Damascus—with all each implied for catalyzing ministries in their own right? Ponder too the experience of Philip the Evangelist, called from his successful ministry in Samaria to seek out a single Ethiopian eunuch—whose lone voice thereafter (it is confidently assumed) "launched a thousand ships" of faith toward distant shores far removed from the ongoing tempest in Judea and Galilee.

My point being, whatever (and wherever) your *own* calling, never underestimate the potential bounty of your solitary voyage—with or without the ballast of a reference group to steady the keel—while the Holy Spirit blows you where He chooses. As the trite cliché goes, "Who's to say the last person you brought to Christ might not turn out to be the next Billy Graham?" Never mind, then, the keel; Jesus controls the rudder and always steers you to ports of His calling—leaving the power of the Holy Spirit to secure the cargo once disembarking.

This, it seems to me, is the *substance* of discipleship—and for that approach I offer no apologies. It's simply a function of the limited sphere of influence a disciple is bequeathed. Did not Christ experience the same limitations as God in the flesh within an equally restricted domain—leaving His followers as messengers (and the Spirit's power) to consummate the Father's divine plan? Was that not what Jesus was intimating when He proclaimed: "I tell you truly, anyone who has faith in me will do what I have been doing. He will do even *greater* things than these…" (John 14:12)? "Trapped" within His own humanity, there was only so much time—and so limited a place—in which to disseminate the Good News, *one person at a time*. His indeed was a solitary consignment—as ours must also be.

So much, then, for substance. The issue of *style* is a more delicate conundrum for which I do feel I owe an apology. Not only do parts of this book risk coming across as "preachy;" many seekers may justifiably be put off by some of the "holier than thou" phrases that crop up within its pages. Having spent the first forty-seven years of my life steeped in skepticism as regards the evangelical culture, perhaps the greatest challenge I faced in revising this work for your sake was minimizing the use of such stock phrases as "God's plan for my life," "the Holy Spirit spoke to me," "by His grace," and, yes, "answering His call." All mass-marketed Christian books, by their very nature, are chockfull of what might seem trite, Pollyannaish (and down-right self-righteous!) buzz-words. Mine has been no exception.[4]

The fact of the matter is, how well this book sells is not as high on my wish list as you might think; what few royalties I accrue will add nothing to my "bottom line" as judged by my Lord and Savior. (There I go again!) Yet I do care about what impact these testimonials might have on the sacred byline appended to the life you've authored, which Jesus fervently desires to underline for all time in His Book of Life. And though I empathize with those of you who remain unconvinced as to the merits of such a life's view (more deeply than you might imagine, having been there myself!), in the end all I can fall back upon in my defense is a single, otherwise inexplicable, reality: *How else to account for the peace of mind and sense of purpose that have in-filled the last fourteen years of my life, as opposed to the incessant, reverberating angst that characterized it before?*

Speaking of bottom lines, bylines, and life's views, Lord knows how skeptical I was during my former life—and on a few occasions even now as a confirmed believer. Consider this televangelist's offering that literally turned my stomach as late as July 3, 2008, when I heard it: "If you want to be a part of what you've just seen [on our choreographed clip from the 'front lines while battling Satan'] and affirm Jesus' plan for your life, simply call on His name—and then *call this number*! Operators are standing by to pray with you." Implicit in this invitation to prayer is a donation somewhere down the road for his corporation's programming that we're being asked to pay for as "prayer partners." Apart from confirmed initiates who tune in nightly, could there be a more justifiably cynical response from the rest of those outside the loop?

Whether televangelist empires, mission boards, or, yes, even the local church, mark this well: They need *you* far more than you need them. Stated more diplomatically (for no one can dispute they all perform vital functions and do good works) but to the point: What *Jesus* needs more is your service for His Kingdom—not your money for theirs. Perhaps it's time to depend less on our pocketbooks as partners and spend more time nurturing the only partnership [read: relationship] that matters. He alone is Lord. The sole/soul corporate body in which to find temporal meaning and eternal life is His own. Everything else is simply tax-deductible "grace" of the cheapest sort.

Only by investing your spiritual resources to the full in His work will you learn to believe and reap the compound interest that your "life's saving" affords. Freely giving of oneself *on* mission—not just financial support *for* missions—has a huge and everlasting impact on your own bottom line, while accomplishing mighty things for God's Kingdom. In the end, nothing else counts on His ledger. Though it may seem counterintuitive to one day hear Jesus say you've "ended up in the red," that's how the bookkeeping is done there. You can take that one to the bank. It's redeemed in blood.

Post-Mortem

Sharing a personal relationship with the living God is, at once, His unmerited gift to us and our intended choice for Him. Perhaps there's no better place to plumb the depths of what that relationship can be than when and where it all started: on the sixth day of Creation in the Garden of Eden when God first "divined" us. By His own declaration, everything was good. The Potter and His clay were as one. We were family.

Then we sinned on the seventh day, breaking faith with God—and breaking His heart in the process. That's when He began to intervene in our lives as a concerned Father. Despite such unmerited grace, the remainder of Genesis tells a sordid tale of one failed relationship after another— failures that have been repeated through all generations to the present day.

A great beginning; intimations of a terrible end! Now if *you* were God, what should be done with these ungrateful reprobates originally created in the very likeness of yourself? Expunge them and wipe the slate clean? Probably. Yet God's ways are not man's ways. Instead of destroying His final creation, He called upon a man named Abram[1] to leave his home for some so-called "promised land" to give us all a new beginning.

Consider the repercussions of but one man's response to the Lord's call. From the seed of Abraham's obedience emerged a chosen people of God, the timeless truths of Scripture, and the Savior of mankind. Where would our own life journeys end without that solitary leap of faith? Dust to dung as the worm turns, to be frank. Far less often asked, what roadmap did God provide for Abraham to follow? In a word, *none*!

Things are different today. Unlike Abraham, we've been given many signposts to guide our way—yet still manage to miss the turnoff God intended us to take. "No matter," we rationalize. Our self-indulgent detours seem harmless enough in the early going, what with all those mesmerizing billboards littering the landscape that tell us what to covet, how to behave, or which siren beckons. At some point along the way, however, harsh reality sinks in: We're lost! We simply can't get to where God intends us to be by continuing down the wrong road. That means retracing our steps and returning to the Crossroad where we left the Lord (some more than once; others never having acknowledged Him to begin with) and went our own way. In that sense, the Christian walk is a chronicle of new beginnings— what Jesus termed "repentance," turning from self and toward God.

For most of us that promises to be a chastening experience. It's akin to returning down a dark "tunnel of brokenness" lit only by a smoking fire pot and a single torch—not unlike Abraham's fateful encounter in Genesis 15:7–21 when God first established His promissory covenant with the frightened patriarch. A "tunnel of brokenness" because *no one* enters it whole. The Potter must first break our cracked visages into pieces for remolding through the refining fires of this narrow aperture in order for His likeness to emerge. In that sense our tunnel becomes a tomb filled with crumbling icons scorched beyond recognition. The detritus of our past—a career setback, an unintended divorce—litters the passage behind us like so many roadblocks, as reminders we cannot pass that way again. There's no way to go but forward, hardly knowing what we will find (no, what we will *be*) at the other end. And what we ultimately discover is that there is more to repentance than "turning" from self and towards God. Genuine repentance means *dying* to self within the tunnel and embracing Jesus at the other end.

That's what the journey is for—*both* of them, in fact: Because we left is why He came. Taking repentant seekers by the hand, Jesus ushers us into the same sacred relationship that Abraham once acknowledged by faith as a covenant. This comes, however, with an obligation on our part to nurture the relationship thereafter. Let me give you a sense of what that entails.

Whereas God's intent for those outside the tunnel has always been to draw mankind to Himself through nature, the Word, and His Son, our intended response once within entails awe of the first, obedience to the second, and imitation of the third at the behest of the Holy Spirit. Only then will Jesus reveal His intent for our lives along the Way—as Master to servant from the beginning; Mentor to friend in time; yet Father to child always. During Moses' travails in the wilderness, the security of God's people was to be found in Yahweh's presence: a billowing cloud of smoke by day and a pillar of fire by night—the very same smoking pot and torch of Abraham's day now writ larger than life. Yet today, day or night, His invisible Spirit is present in each believer. Which is God's way of telling us that we have even less excuse now to ignore the tunnel and continue down the wrong road.

The problem from the beginning is that we've been given a special gift of free will as His children—created as we are in His image. For God knew that without choice there can be no such thing as love. To be sure, not everyone in the Father's Kingdom thought such a gift was a good idea at the time. Consider those skeptical angels standing aghast on the sixth day of Creation while God played in the dirt, molding His special piece of clay. One holy wag probably had the audacity to whisper in the Creator's ear, "Free will? Surely you jest! What if your special creation chooses *not* to enter into a relationship with you?" To which God wistfully replied: "Some will; most won't."[2]

Therein lies modern man's proverbial "thorn [of] the flesh"—what philosophers term "humanism"—born of the eighteenth century Enlightenment with the best of mortal intentions, yet bludgeoned to death by the "Be All You Can Be" generation of today. For most of our choices continue to be poor ones. That's the nature of the beast. From the lineage of Adam and Eve down through the centuries, sin has passed from one generation to the next. It's part of our *Genetic* makeup, shot through with self-destructive mutations far removed from God's holy genotype.

Now, insofar as we have been given minds to exercise free will and make choices, what we do with such gifts cannot help but follow a logical progression: "Sow a thought and you reap an action; sow an act and you reap a habit; sow a habit, reap a character; sow a character and you reap a destiny."[3]

Yet when we look into the mirror, what do we see? Probably an image that we vaingloriously seek to preserve by building our own Towers of Babel. We fancy ourselves to be *playing* God without *paying* Him the compliment of following the only blueprint He gave us in the flesh. For history (with a small "h") is replete with people like you and me who have labored in vain to build monuments to ourselves an eternity apart from what our very Creator had in mind. If that's *sad* history to read, it's also *bad* history to study—examining man's Towers of Babel as if they were worthy of scrutiny, if not imitation.

The truth of that matters is, *His* Story is all that matters! That's what God was intimating in no uncertain terms when He gave us an exemplary set of laws to live by—not only to protect us, but to display His omniscience and dispel any illusions we might harbor concerning our own. Having ignored the beneficent Father's counsel time and again, we remain recalcitrant children despite *absolute truth* staring us in the face. Should you question the premise, then consider what our secular conventions have done to His sacred Commandments:

COMMANDMENTS FOR GOD'S KINGDOM HERE ON EARTH	vs.	CONVENTIONS OF MAN'S POSTMODERN CULTURE
what to believe in and obey for all time		what to conform with and get by for now
an absolute code of conduct for righteous living		a relative mode of behavior for "political correctness"
timeless: applies to any age		temporal: defined *by* the age
a commitment through faith		a rationalization by nature

By virtue of being honored as *His* Commandments, the first four of the ten center on God. By virtue of being accepted as conventions, our respective contrapositions focus on self. That's why the first Commandments begin with "shall," as in "must;" the conventions with "should," as in "may."

HIS COMMANDMENTS	vs.	OUR CONVENTIONS
I. "You shall have no other gods before me"	vs.	"You should not impose your 'god' on others"
"I AM WHO I AM"		"I'm okay; you're okay"
God is Creator of His whole universe, determined to rest within it		Man is "maker of his own bed", destined to lay upon it
God created man *by* Himself, as a Father begets sons in His image		Man created "God" *for* himself, as a prop to support a psychological need
God in three Persons is the ultimate reality		Nature and its laws are the only reality
II. "You shall not make for yourselves idols...nor worship them"	vs.	"You should make your own works as idols and *worship* them"
For I am...a jealous God		For men are an envious lot
God has dominion over all creation, including man		Man has dominion over all nature, including his own
Everything we have is His to begin with		All that I possess I've rightfully earned
We are all one body in Christ, Who justifies us as His own		We are as one with the interest group that justifies who we are
III. "You shall not misuse the name of the LORD your God"	vs.	"You should not misconstrue the name of Jesus for 'God'"
Ask not what we can do for God, but what He does through us		Don't ask what God can "do," but what nature does by itself

His Commandments	vs.	Our Conventions
It's not what we say but how we *live* that speaks for God		It's not what "they" say but how they act that silences "God"
Only God is inerrantly good		All men are inherently good
Jesus is the answer!		So what's the question?
IV. "You Shall remember the Sabbath by keeping it holy"	vs.	"You should revere the sciences and accept their lordship"
Take God at His Word; only He is onmiscient		Take the philosopher at his word; his opinion is sufficient
Build altars to God that glorify His presence		Build monuments to yourself that justify your existence
Enter His rest to honor God		Engage respite to pamper self
Worship offers sacred community, bringing people to God, together		"Worship" belies secular convention, bringing people together, not to God

Which brings us back to those signposts God intends us to follow today, including an explanation of where they came from and how we can be assured they are a part of His divine plan. Look at it this way. With all due respect to God's Ten Commandments, before Abraham, man's old nature *knew* no law. After Christ, man's new nature *needed* no law, because it was written on our hearts by the Holy Spirit. The latter is synonymous with what C.S. Lewis terms the "Law of Human Nature," an inherent (and inerrant) sense of right and wrong. Here is a law man certainly didn't make, but one he knows he ought to obey because it was created by a *mind* infinitesimally greater than his own.

Look at it another way. As children we tried to please our parents—an enviable (if not infallible) standard of sorts—by floating our boats in their stream. As adults, we tack back and forth in uncharted seas of uncertainty, driven by the whimsical winds of society. So what happens when those standards change, as they always do, and we're left as ships without ballast? When do we allow the Lord to take the helm as we find ourselves tossed about in gales of competing value systems? Only when we accept a higher moral law exists, acknowledge Who created it, admit we are at odds with Him by having broken that law and have no way back to shore— then, and only then, will Christ calm the storm and Christianity finally speak to wayward man cast adrift in seas of relativism.

Given such unmerited grace, do you ever wonder why so many men in the Bible including kings such as Saul, David, and Solomon (not to mention pawns like myself) *failed* God in midlife? I suspect it has something to do with our makeup before we allow ourselves to be made over in His image. True, our Creator is always looking for clay to mold. Yet clay has no mind of its own (need we ask the terra-cotta warriors?), much less a divine plan. That's a lesson I had to relearn in Brazil when I found myself trimming sail in the clinic as a member of the crew, instead of doing brain operations as captain of the ship—something about God's plan, and not my own agenda…

Or yet another lesson, when I met the Lord face to face in El Salvador and finally tumbled to the realization of what Jesus meant by the term "Son of Man." Wading through a crush of bodies as we arrived at the clinic one morning, I was accosted by a wizened, toothless bag lady who grabbed my hand and stuck it into the side pocket of her tattered jacket. Extracting what looked like a wrapped piece of candy, she guided my hands as I fumbled to remove the wrapper. Deeply moved by her gift, I interpreted this as an act of kindness shown me in gratitude for what we were doing for her people. I nodded in appreciation and prepared to consume the tiny morsel—at which point she took my unwrapped treasure, belched loudly, and popped it into her mouth!

As it turned out, this was not my candy—but her *medicine*. Upon reflection, I realized that this humble soul was none other than Christ in disguise, bringing me down from atop my missionary pedestal. It was Jesus' way of reminding me I was there to serve Him through them. If that meant simply assisting an elderly woman whose hands were so gnarled by crippling arthritis that she could no longer unwrap her own medicine, then so be it—and the Lord be praised!

What made this encounter such an eye-opener, I learned thereafter, is that the Hebrew word for "son" equates with "servant."[4] A servant's function is to follow instructions; the master's role to give directions—regardless of whether the latter appears as God's begotten Son or mankind's forgotten bag lady. Understood. Yet, as Son of Man, Jesus also came to earth as Servant of Man. That service was paid in full on the cross. With complete justification Jesus could proclaim, "It is finished!" He had fulfilled His Father's command to the letter—and with his life.

Now is the time for each of use to do the same. As His disciples, the only justifiable standard of conduct worthy of God in whose image we were made is our best imitation of Christ. Once we have done all those things the Lord commanded by answering His call, only then can *we* proclaim (solely through His justification), "'We are unworthy servants; we have only done our duty" (Luke 17:10). 'Twas but a blessed solitary consignment…'Tis enough.'"

That's why He sent me to the mission field: to be refined by fire in Christ's service and remolded in His image. Yet my story is not important. His Story is. May you discover this timeless truth through your own. That's what the seventh day of Creation is all about—the time we have been allotted to *recreate* ourselves in the image we have lost.

EPILOGUE

My motivation for extensively revising *Trial By Fire: A Neurosurgeon's Conviction in Medical Missions* sprang from a bit of unfinished business and a ton of conflicting emotions. As for things left undone, it struck me *after the fact* that the title had not been developed in the original work to the degree warranted. What to have made of the word "trial" when juxtaposed with Scripture's use of "fire"? Surely more than some hackneyed metaphor with a dramatic flair; rather, a declaration of Jesus' intent for anyone who would call him or herself a "missionary." Adding potential insult to oversight, even the subtitle raised more questions than it professed to answer. Had His verdict on my behalf been *finding conviction* (as "a belief in") or *found convicted* (as in "coming up short")? Given such a flickering performance as a torchbearer for Christ, the reader probably had every reason to wonder.

On the positive of the ledger, I now had been consigned five further years of "war stories" from the front to tell. Should any one of those strike a responsive chord in but a single seeker, then this rewrite would have been worthwhile. Yet "taking care of business" with what might seem just another gratuitous personal testimonial may have proved redundant for everyone else, and justifiably so. God's final revelation, in flesh and blood, was *freely given* some two thousand years ago. Our intended response, long before now, was simply to have accepted (or, sadly, rejected) the Good News.

Lord knows, the world scarcely needs more books to embellish His Story. Words have always been cheap; most of those for sale nowadays, throwaways—faith based fluff in particular—with no more "redeeming" value than a veritable smorgasbord of in-filled "talking heads" numbing our senses. Even the digital age conspires against us, assaulting its proselytes with [cyber]waves of information overload. Search engines, blogs, online sermons.org (plus .com and .net), denominationally slanted Bible studies, self-absorbed faces and spaces—all to be accessed at the touch of a finger—threaten to relegate authors and sellers alike to endangered species. Not to mention iPhoned "notes to God" providing *direct access* to the Almighty! How, then, will Christian libraries in future generations compete, much less the weighty tomes they once contained and the stores that sold them? Why bother adding to the *refuse*?

As an old codger who still relishes the feel of bound print in hand, I grieve for the Christian bookstore in particular as a disappearing *refuge* in which to kick back and enjoy a good read, if not to satiate a spiritual craving. By the same token, no one who truly hungers for righteousness should require a steady diet of cleverly packaged variations on the same few themes to draw us back to God's Word. The Gospel message is simple. Jesus meant it to be.

We *do* have to be reminded, however, of what the Bread of Life cost Him to "produce"— and should cost each of us in return who claims to be stoking the proverbial oven as a breadwinner of souls for Christ. Hence, my impetus for kneading the dough with a question in one hand and an answer in the other before having presumed to feed the multitudes. Q: Who will do the reminding? A: Perhaps someone who's been on both sides of "Heaven's Kitchen" here on earth and had everything of temporal value to burn by entering. As for those lukewarm believers still straddling the threshold, wondering whether there really is a God who has a specific recipe for them to follow, that's another justification for rekindling sacred fires so others will not go hungry.

So much for unfinished business. What of the emotions that drove me to a "revise/copy/paste" of the original? First and foremost, was my prayerful decision some four years ago to return to private practice in Kansas City, Missouri, (while continuing to do short-term missions four to five times per year) little more than turning tail on what Jesus had intended me to become? As a born-again believer, had I been "delivered in the breech position" to assure that wherever I landed it would be on my own two feet—just in case things didn't work out and I could walk away? After all, what appeared to some a full-blown *retreat* in 2005 threatened to reprise my infancy as a half-breed missionary during the latter part of the 1990s in Springfield before I finally surrendered all to follow Christ abroad in 2001.

Such a sincere—perhaps even noble—commitment that had been! Yet, like all explanations (rationalizations?), there were two sides to the story. My former associates' calculated refusal to cover for me while away on mission in order to force my hand and secure a monopoly over neurosurgery in southwest Missouri for themselves was every bit as compelling (and sobering) as Jesus' call to join Him in the mission field.[1] So I had to make a choice. His indwelling Spirit made that for me by prompting a clean break with my past.

The end result was just what Christ had in mind: four in-filled years doing mission work overseas on His behalf, from 2001 to 2004.

Why, then, our return to the States in 2005 after such a redemptive redirection of my life and the affirmation that accompanied it? Never had my wife, Vicki, and I prayed over a decision more fervently. The implications were huge, considering where we had already been and the two alternatives that now seemed to best suit our spiritual gifts: Committing to Africa as career missionaries, or carrying the Gospel into another skeptical community back home.

So as to make the decision more difficult, Satan's voice would not be silenced. Was I re-entering the womb of my "first" life from which I had been so graciously delivered?[2] Now burdened by the possibility of having abandoned Christ's ultimate plan for which He had personally groomed me, I was haunted by my inner prosecutor's potentially incriminating question from the past: When I closed my practice in Springfield in 2001, had I been truly called by the Holy Spirit—or shamefully driven from the temple?

Shameful? No doubt. Never had I questioned my self-worth more. Being exiled from my erstwhile associates-turned-competitors' "kingdom [to] come," however, was hardly akin to being driven from the Lord's temple. First Corinthians 3:16 assured me of that: "Don't you know that you yourselves are God's temple and that God's Spirit lives in you?" To His way of thinking (or so I *think* He would think), there was ample historical precedent to comfort God's displaced disciples. That had been what the Ark of the Covenant represented for His desert wanderers and the synagogue later became for His chosen people after the fall of the temple. This culminated in His gift of the Holy Spirit to you and I (John 14:15–17)—as in "I am with you wherever you go."

Well enough; and praise be to God for having stood with me in the gap both when I found myself beleaguered in my own hometown and wherever He led me thereafter. Yet I also sensed from years of prayerful study that Jesus' promise of fellowship is given only to those who have *left all* to follow Him alone.[3] That's the very heart of what Christ was telling his first disciples in the Beatitudes and later personalized by comparative example in Luke 9:57–62.[4] With respect to those three latter would-be followers, no doubt I had a leg up on the first; for I painfully understood what "leaving all" to follow Jesus entails.

As for the second, I had already been freed (sadly) from any excuse for "staying put" in Springfield once my father passed away in 2001. Yet the Lord's reply to the third candidate's impudence in defining discipleship on his own terms now came back to mock me: "No one who puts his hand to the plow and looks back is fit for service in the kingdom of God."

Ouch! "Fit for service." That's precisely what I had been recreated to be—and what heretofore had defined me as His disciple. Was the "where," then, every bit as important to Jesus as the "how"? Was returning to private practice in the States a bit of "looking back" to a world I had once eschewed (perhaps in shameful exuberance!) at the expense of a higher calling the Lord had planned for me? Or was Kansas City to be a new venue in which to extend His Good News to the "lost sheep of Israel" [read: America]?

I can honestly say Vicki and I never looked back to Springfield; we closed that chapter of our lives (and ministry) with Psalm 31:21. But had Jesus seen our "about face" the same way—if not having orchestrated it? True, at least I finally had coverage for my patients from two new associates in Kansas City while away on mission. Although neither shares my calling as such, they are hardly threatened by it—as opposed to the blatant spiritual warfare I had encountered in Springfield. And what to infer in retrospect from our return to a new Midwestern home, where the reception of His Word has been so overwhelmingly (and unexpectedly) positive as a mainstay of my practice—not to mention the affirmation Vicki has received from teaching and nurturing those children in Bible Study Fellowship that she could never have biologically?

We also found comfort in recalling Martin Luther's choice as a "spiritual specialist" to leave the monastery and return to the real world as serviceable salt. The monastery was but a *part* of the world, Luther belatedly realized, where the religious elite isolated themselves to practice their calling while ignoring the rest of mankind—thus creating an artificial division between the few "doers" of the Word and the majority of "believers" left to their own devices outside its walls. And in one sense fulltime missions *is* a bit of a cloistered existence, what with working among peoples who expect you to be something special and, in fact, treat you as such. As a brotherhood of believers, moreover, mutual support exists 24/7 to provide affirmation in times of need. When that particular substrate is already so well seasoned, adding our two grains-worth to the mix arguably seemed superfluous.

This is not to decry the enormous sacrifices career missionaries make, who are literally giving their all in faith alone. Compared to their lifelong commitment, going on mission as a "short-termer" is not so much an exercise of walking *in* faith as taking a vacation *with* it. One always returns home to warm fires, appliances that work, entertainment at the touch of a remote, even a glass of wine on occasion—while the full-timer is already home, where none of the above (especially the last) apply.

If moving to Africa had become the only alternative apart from Kansas City, I must also confess to some troubling rationalizations as to why that option remained on the table until 2005. One compelling motivation for relocating to Kenya (as opposed to Vietnam, Nicaragua, or even Ukraine, where Vicki and I might just as easily have pitched our tent, dug a well, and built an altar) was the residency training program being established to serve the neurosurgical needs of all East Africa. Recognizing that no such sanctioned program exists, I fervently hoped to participate in that venture as a site director at Tenwek Hospital. Yet that calling, I now ruefully suspect, was very much an "of this world" mindset.

Why? Because nothing has proved quite so filled with pitfalls (one step forward; two steps back) than the infighting required to be a part of the program and convincing others that Tenwek, despite being a faith-based Christian hospital, is a viable training site. One month the issue is settled; the next, yet another obstacle has arisen, or new faces come on board that have to be "reconvinced." That's a sad reflection of the hospital governance's unfounded paranoia on the one hand (i.e. fear of its mission statement being subverted by the presence of trainees or instructors "outside the faith"),[5] and expectations of the program's secular leadership on the other (e.g. adhering to "political correctness" by avoiding proselytizing; suggesting that not moving permanently to Africa somehow signified a "lack of commitment;" and so on).

Such conflicting emotions in hindsight signified that I, as a modern-day Jacob, was wrestling with God and men simultaneously in an effort to secure both His *and* their blessing (Genesis 32:24–29). Yet the two can rarely be reconciled. To wit: if what one grapples over is of man, you will surely meet resistance and probably fail on that account; if from God, you may lose the skirmish but win the war with fruit that lasts. Could it be that my frustration was the Lord's way of warning me I might have followed the "right" path by moving to Africa for all the wrong reasons?

That, I think, was His answer—the call that Christ bid *me* answer by reentering private practice in the States while continuing to disciple at other venues (including Africa) where He had sent me over the past ten years. Were I to have set my foundation in Kenya, those relationships Jesus had nurtured elsewhere might well founder. As for the training program, it will do fine without me should circumstances beyond my control dictate. Not that the program director feels the same. In his own words: "Our candidates [of whatever faith] will benefit from a rotation at your Christian hospital because it's such a unique *in-filling* experience." The irony being, my esteemed director and good friend is a devout Muslim!

Nevertheless, until this revision was finished I continued to wrestle with the *Question*: Was my moving back to Kansas City the Lord's calling for the time being (that time being His!)—or a man's carping to use his professional skills 365 days a year instead of wilting on the vine between trips as a prematurely "retired" neurosurgeon? The latter arrangement, sad to admit, all too often afforded me a lame excuse to focus on the surgical cases to be done while on mission at the expense of the Good News I was sent to deliver. In that sense alone, then, this revision compelled me to cull such emotional chaff from Christ's *solitary consignment* that was to have guided my call to missions from the beginning. Had I been successfully engrafted onto Jesus' vine to be nurtured thereafter by His living waters? Or was I still clinging a decade later to the dead branches of my former life?

Unfinished business; unbridled emotions; unrequited verdicts—all had been left hanging in the balance of some twelve years of deliberations during my solitary trial by fire. Maranatha? At last, Blessed Assurance!

ENDNOTES

DYING TO SELF

1. Luke 14:25–35.
2. Matthew 12:34.
3. See Genesis 50:19–21. What was "it" specifically that God meant for good? To accomplish what is now being done, "the saving of many lives" (verse 20). As applied to Eric's family and close friends, the salvations that have resulted are for eternity.

DIVINE APPOINTMENTS

1. This is a prevailing theme in Romans 9, and a specific mandate in 1 Peter 2:9. Simply put, to be among the "chosen" is to have both received the call and answered it.
2. Philip Yancey refers to this as "the Great Reversal of God's Kingdom" in *The Jesus I Never Knew*, Grand Rapids: Zondervan, 1996.
3. Monica Hellweg, *Tracing the Spirit*, Mahwah, NJ: Paulist Press, 1983.
4. Matthew 7:14.
5. Judges 17:6.
6. Matthew 27:65.
7. Fear does funny things to despots. An emperor of a different place and time (Minh Mang, 1833) had ordered the arrest and murder of a French priest, one Francois Gagelin, for "preaching the religion of Jesus." Having read of Christ's resurrection, Minh had the corpse exhumed three days later to make certain Gagelin was still in his grave!
8. It is fitting that C.S. Lewis would title the chapter in which this citation appears "The Obstinate Tin Soldiers." *Mere Christianity*, New York: Touchstone, 1996 (original edition 1952).
9. Jeremiah 18:6; see also Isaiah 29:16.
10. Jeremiah 2:13.
11. Ezekiel 37:1.
12. Acts 17:22–24, 26–27.

THEIRS IS THE KINGDOM OF HEAVEN

1. Luke 14:25–33 (See Great is Your Reward in Heaven, p.183).
2. Matthew 4:23–24.
3. Deuteronomy 25:4.
4. Matthew 3:17.
5. 2 Corinthians 5:10.
6. Genesis 19:1–10.

THEY WILL BE COMFORTED

1. Acts 2:2–4.
2. Henri Nouwen, *The Return of the Prodigal Son*, New York: Image Books/Doubleday, 1994.
3. How often in medicine does an immediately preceding case color our management of the next! A year later, while in Iraq, I was faced with a similar tumor and clinical presentation and advised the woman *not* to undergo surgery. The only difference being, in the Muslim culture, it's the *husband's* decision to make for his wife. They both felt entirely comfortable with this choice—but only after I prevailed upon them to take the matter to prayer and, that, together.
4. Matthew 6:33 KJV.

THEY WILL INHERIT THE EARTH

1. Had I needed any further affirmation, that very evening while reading the Bible I was led to a virtually identical story in Mark 9:14–29. As God is my witnesses, I had never taken much notice of that particular healing before—much less Jesus' words to His disciples: "This kind can come out only by prayer."

THEY WILL BE FILLED

1. 1 Peter 3:15.
2. That would take two years of intensive study, laboring in vain to *disprove* the alleged inerrancy of the Bible, which culminated in my writing a Christian apologetic from the scientific, historical, and prophetic perspectives, entitled *Meeting Jesus on the Road*, Enumclaw: WinePress Publishers, 2003.
3. Ephesians 6:17.

They Will Be Shown Mercy

1. Acts 16:22–34

2. That's not as overstated as it might seem. A year after returning from Siberia, I was sent a newspaper clipping of a Russian cargo plane that had crashed—the very *same* plane we had taken on that flight, as identified by the number clearly visible on its tail jutting above the smoldering rubble.

3. Matthew 9:2–8; Mark 2:1–12; Luke 5:17–26.

4. Romans 10:14–15.

5. Acts 20:7–12.

6. Mark 9:14–29.

7. Mongolia, apart from Russia, was the first country to enter the Soviet Union in 1921.

Reality Check

1. Matthew 6:33.

2. Sadly enough, he was instrumental in the split. Someone very close to me had misinterpreted my changed demeanor as some form of "midlife crisis", and conveyed her concerns to my "brother" in Christ while I was away on mission. This information he thought my partners might like to know, despite it having been given in strict confidence. Their decision to terminate me was made within the very week of that disclosure. Once I was "out of the picture," that allowed them to form their own partnership— which had been their intent all along, as events subsequently proved.

3. Matthew 11:28.

4. Matthew 5:11–12.

5. This included four subsequent trips under such an arrangement over the next year, during which I never had one of my patients at home develop postoperative complications or problems that required my presence there. The Great Physician met their every need in my absence. There is, quite simply, no other way to explain it. Contrast that with the only two times Vicki and I tried to take a vacation, both of which required terminating the trip and returning home. Painful affirmation of a sort? Of course. Yet my wife's heart is so in tune with

God's plan for our lives together that we accepted this as a small price to pay for the privilege of sharing space and patients where He is working.

THEY WILL SEE GOD

1. Which is what brought me to the reality of Christ in the first place. See *Meeting Jesus on the Road* as regards the evidence supporting the infallibility of God's Word, including the irrefutable reality of Jesus' resurrection.

2. Genesis 32:22–32.

3. Ironically, his involvement with Hussein would temporarily thrust my unassuming friend into the international limelight once the body of Saddam's son was identified by the plate and screws Dr. Thamer had implanted to rebuild his leg following a second, and successful, assassination attempt.

4. President Bush's announcement to the world aboard an aircraft carrier in the Gulf, at once both preening and perversely comical, that our mission in Iraq "had been accomplished."

5. See Genesis 22:1–18.

6. Genesis 21:12.

7. Hebrews 12:1.

8. F. Scott Fitzgerald, *The Great Gatsby*, New York: Scribner's, 1925.

9. Acts 16:9.

THEY WILL BE CALLED SONS OF GOD

1. The phrase refers to Jesus rebuke of the Pharisees who were demanding that He silence those having the audacity to bless "this king" who came in the name of God. To which Jesus replied. "If they keep quiet, the stones will cry out [on behalf of peace]" Luke 19:39–40.

2. John 14:27.

3. The term is derived from the earliest missions' experience in China, where the people came to hear the Good News for the more practical reward of receiving a free meal in exchange.

THEIRS IS THE KINGDOM: REPRISED

1. Happily, this saint-of-a-sister was allowed to attend our team's farewell

banquet and reported, aside from being banned from the clinic, she had suffered no further consequences. Yet that was then; what thereafter? I had reason to wonder, if the account that follows is any indication of the communist party's elephantine memory for slights.

2.   Not that my communist friends admit this. "Oh, no! We've not embraced capitalism; we simply have a better understanding of market forces and the laws of supply and demand"(!) It should not pass unnoticed that at precisely the time party leaders were tumbling to the realization that Marxism had its limitations (1985), Paul Samuelson's classic economic text (with which every university student in America who has taken economics is familiar) was being translated into Vietnamese.

3.   Matthew 22:15–21; Mark 12:13–17; Luke 20:20–25.

4.   There is historical precedent for such subterfuge. During the French colonial era when Catholicism was first "accepted" among the emperors of the eighteenth century, a priest by the name of Pigneau de Béhaine was revered by the ruling hierarchy. Indeed, the funeral at the time of his death in 1799 extolled Pigneau as no foreigner in Vietnamese history, before or since, had been. A tomb commemorating his contributions was constructed on the spot, declaring on its stele that Pigneau's actions "deserve to be transmitted to posterity." Inexplicably, Pigneau's tomb and its stele have since disappeared. Perhaps the same fate has befallen the commemorative sculpture I had commissioned to be placed at the base of Marble Mountain for Dwight. If so, that would confirm my suspicions that a higher authority authorized the plaque's removal from the scope. Either way, a visit to Marble Mountain was *not* included in the itinerary during my visit to Vietnam in 2008.

5.   1 Peter 3:15.

6.   Some three years before, Le had resigned his role as both department chairman and government employee in the public hospital to enter private practice. There, physicians have no protection against the burgeoning number of malpractice claims currently plaguing their profession.

THEIRS IS THE KINGDOM: REAPPRAISED

1.   A force created by surface tension in liquids that are in contact with a solid surface. The surface (i.e. channel wall) tends to retract, enlarging

the conduit and allowing more water to rise.

2. Our so-called "common" well differs in one respect from an artesian well. True, the ultimate source of both comes from "above" (the first drawn from God; the second, from mountain runoff *forcing* the flow of water below upward). My point being, the Holy Spirit never *forces* His living water on the recipient. The Spirit must be drawn upon—*He does not push.*

3. John 4:10–14, 7:38; Revelation 7:17.

4. Hence the original intent *not* to revise the title, though my editor prevailed upon me to do otherwise.

5. I had in fact written a book on the subject based upon many such patients' families who imploded under the strain. Written long before becoming a Christian, I had no answers for the otherwise heart-rending experiences they related. What I can now conclude is that the broad majority of families who make it through are those bringing their faiths *with* them to the catastrophe. The interested reader is referred to Park, B.E. *Catastrophic Illness and the Family,* Boston: Christopher Publishing, 1992.

6. Through some thirty years in practice I have witnessed a disturbing trend among Americans: the notion that if they can't have their loved one back as he or she was before the onset of catastrophic illness, the overwhelming majority of surrogate decision-makers don't wish to be strapped with a chronic-care situation. As yet, I cannot speak for myself when confronted by the same; so I am not passing judgment, but merely making an observation.

CROSS-EXAMINATION

1. "Drives," as in both an "implicit motivation" for nominal Christians and an "instrumental wedge" between them, which bears no malice in pointing out the obvious: manmade denominations more often than not build walls between members of the body of Christ.

2. Where the television evangelists fit, who are forever seeking to "partner" with us (i.e. baldly defined as "funding *their* visions") is anyone's guess—though the man on the street is rarely short of negative opinions.

3. Is it any wonder that church scholars refer to this period as the "Middle

Ages," whereas skeptics today aptly describe that thousand-year interlude as the "Dark Ages"?

4. In all of ancient literature, whether secular or ecclesiastical, nothing is better and more frequently attested to than the Gospel accounts of the words Jesus spoke. Not only is there *less* variation in so-called "red-letter" Bible translations when it comes to what Jesus said; Matthew recorded Christ's sayings in something called the *logia* during the early A.D. 50s, as documented by Papias and cited by the first "official" church historian, Eusebius. Should the reader still not buy the infallibility of Jesus' words— or the Word itself—then at least believe in His miracles that legitimized His claim to be the Son of God (John 14:10–11).

5. "But the Counselor, the Holy Spirit, whom the Father will send in my name, will teach you all things and will remind you of everything I have said to you" (John 14:26). Whereas Scripture is God's unchanging Word, the Holy Spirit is its only interpreter. That's how the Holy Trinity works as One in the lives of true disciples.

6. See Romans 3:24–25, Ephesians 2:8, James 2:24, and similar passages.

REBUTTAL FOR THE DEFENSE

1. This list is not intended to be all inclusive. These were simply examples that spoke to me in my quest for scriptural affirmation. (Note: All emphases from quoted Scripture hereafter are mine).

2. Mind you, no promises of personal salvation for the messenger had been given as yet; just the duty. The pre-Christian era was a time in which God's *call* was received, whereas at the beginning of the Christian era His *promise* was given in Christ's Beatitudes. Hence Dietrich Bonhoeffer's succinct contribution to our understanding of both: "Only the *call* and the *promise* can justify the Beatitudes."

3. Parenthetically, that's a mandate for my own particular calling, taken from Scripture found in 1 Peter 3:15: "Always be prepared to give an answer to everyone who asks you to give the reason for the hope that you have"— which *Meeting Jesus on the Road* was intended to address.

4. I am indebted to Robert G. Tuttle, a fellow Duke alumnus, whose seminal book *Sanctity Without Starch: A Layperson's Guide to a Wesleyan Theology of Grace* (Anderson, Indiana: Bristol House, 1992) beautifully

synthesizes Wesley's doctrine in laypersons' terms.

5. To affirm that this was the divine intent for us all from the beginning, see Exodus 7:5, 17.

6. The quotes are taken from Mohandas K. Gandhi, *Gandhi: An Autobiography. The Story of My Experiments with Truth*, Boston: Beacon Press, 1993.

VERDICT

1. The invariably positive response I receive from my patients for having prayed with them before their operations is always gratifying—but should also be grounds for some critical self-examination. Jesus' warning (in Matthew 6:5) that those who "pray...to be seen by men...have received their reward in full," at least from the cynic's perspective, might justly apply to questioning my motivations!

In a similar vein, you may recall that Christ's Beatitudes from Matthew's Gospel were the first bits of Scripture I had memorized before embarking on the race He set before me. How telling, then, that halfway around the track, Jesus Himself thought it necessary to fall back alongside me and exchange Matthew's scroll I grasped as a baton for Luke's version of His Beatitudes (6:20–22)—appended to which were point-by-point repudiations of these very blessings accorded one whom He now perceived to have veered out of His relay team's lane. Despite what sacrifices I thought I had made to run the race to the end, those obviously had not been enough, to date, to justify my current standing in the pack. For I'd been given much—far too much—of a head start; accordingly, far more was expected of me as a "Mara[natha]thoner." The Lord made this abundantly clear: "But woe to you who are [still] rich,...well fed...and when mean speak well of you [as a follower]..."(Luke 6:24–26). Not that His intent was to expose me as some imposter lingering in the tunnel, waiting to sprint out of its entrance into the Kingdom's stadium ahead of nameless Frank Shorter wannabes, to the applause of angels in attendance at Christ's Olympiad. Rather, I risked my Mentor's disappointment alone in not having carried His cross fast and far enough to have left the excess baggage of my "real" life behind.

2. Risking persecution for righteousness' sake is one thing; sublimating pride for sake of forgiveness is quite another. That's always been my greatest struggle—of which Jesus is painfully aware. Yet here I sit at my computer, ostensibly "bringing the sacrifice of praise" to the Lord's altar, which is what this labor of love with my word processor has been all about. How much like Jesus, then, to soften my heart before leaving such a paltry "gift" at the publishing world's step (Matthew 5:24)! For I have one bit of unfinished business left unattended: owning up to the debt of forgiveness owed my former associates in Springfield. As such, this "public letter" will have to suffice until our own divine appointment face-to-face comes due.

    Dear John, Tom, and Mark:
    Thank you (and I mean that sincerely) for compelling me to make a clean break with my "first" life. Leaving one professional relationship has afforded me the opportunity to discover what being involved in a truly *personal* partnership entails. Whether here or abroad—be that in league with my new partners in Kansas City or my Divine Mentor worldwide—I've never experienced such fulfillment in my work. For, you see, without that crisis some twelve years ago, my call to service in Christ's name would have remained half-answered and His purpose for my life would never have been fulfilled. You may have meant it for bad at the time, but He ultimately meant it for good. When all is said (and has been done!), that's all that really matters. So there you have it. In truth, I never knew until now forgiveness could be so easy—but that's simply how grace works.
    In His name and service,
    Bert

    Yet another letter was written long ago to my three stepbrothers, as defined by the last eighteen years of my father's life with their mother, Mimi. Jesus certainly would not condone what I wrote at the time. Though I cannot help but stand by that as of this writing, all that can be postscripted as a second letter in my defense is this:

Dear Gary, Craig, and Brian:

It was your privilege by circumstance to have shared in Popo's life—and mine in Mimi's—as I'm sure we all appreciate in retrospect. Knowing Dad, I'd wager you've received a characteristic handwritten note of forgiveness from him by now, postmarked "Peter's Gate." That would have come easily for my father; it was simply his God-given nature to do so. Here on the other side of the Divide, thankfully, you and I remain works in progress. Which is why we still have so much to learn from him—and Him!—even now. Is it any wonder that Jesus' *quid pro quo* concerning forgiving others their sins (Matthew 6:14–15) follows immediately upon the heels of the Lord's Prayer, which ends with "deliver us from the evil one"? Praise the Lord that He's not done with us yet! As for my own forgiveness, I'm afraid it's far from complete. Yet so to, by His grace, is my sanctification…

Maranatha,

Bert

3.   John 9:1–38.

4.   That's why you won't find such books in Barnes and Noble (unless, of course, the author/pastor's church has enough financial clout to cut a deal beneficial to both parties)—or until Oprah tires of dabbling in New Age waters, returns to the source that once nurtured her, and endorses them.

POST-MORTEM

1.   Soon to be changed to "Abraham" once the Lord made a covenant with him.

2.   Attributed to Max Lucado, from his sermon "When You Can't Hide Your Mistakes."

3.   Ralph Waldo Emerson.

4.   Psalm 2:7. The Hebrew word translated "son" here can also mean "servant".

EPILOGUE

1.   I'd like to think God was directing both of us (just as He had used Pharaoh on behalf of Moses) with the same endpoint in mind: "I raised

you up for this very purpose" (Romans 9:17).

2. Or was this Jesus' way of "expanding my territory," a la the Prayer of Jabez, for the sake of His Kingdom?

3. That revelation I owe to the most compelling book I've ever read apart from the Bible, Dietrich Bonhoeffer's *The Cost of Discipleship,* without which no understanding of genuine discipleship would be complete. That too was a bit of "unfinished business," as addressed in the chapter "Cross Examination."

4. Luke chronicles three would-be disciples who *offer their services,* respectively, to Jesus with these words: (1) "I will follow you wherever you go;" (2) "first, let me go and bury my father;" and (3) "first, let me go back and say good-by to my family."

5. What a missed opportunity to witnesses for Christ! Should a candidate or instructor not be a believer, in such a nurturing environment as a mission hospital, he or she most likely *will* be by time the rotations end.